Criticism in the Wilderness

Criticism in the Wilderness

The Study of Literature Today

GEOFFREY H. HARTMAN

New Haven and London
Yale University Press

Published with assistance from
the Louis Effingham deForest Memorial Fund.

Designed by James J. Johnson
and set in Baskerville type by
United Printing Services, Inc., New Haven, Conn.
Printed in the United States of America by
The Murray Printing Co., Westford, Mass.

Library of Congress Cataloging in Publication Data

Hartman, Geoffrey H.
Criticism in the wilderness.

Bibliography: p.
Includes index.
1. Criticism–20th century. I. Title.
PN94.H34 801'.95'0904 80–13491
ISBN 0–300–02085–6
0–300–02839–3 (pbk.)

12 11 10 9 8 7 6 5 4

For my students

The epochs of Aeschylus and Shakespeare make us feel their pre-eminence. In an epoch like those is, no doubt, the true life of literature; there is the promised land, toward which criticism can only beckon. That promised land it will not be ours to enter, and we shall die in the wilderness: but to have saluted it from afar, is already, perhaps, the best distinction among contemporaries; it will certainly be the best title to esteem with posterity.

—Matthew Arnold, "The Function of Criticism at the Present Time"

Contents

Acknowledgments

There are many who have contributed to the writing of this book; above all, those to whom I dedicate it. In the preparation of the final manuscript I have been helped by Lise Davis and especially Jim di Loreto, whose expert typing and research assistance I came to rely on, and who suffered without murmur the revisions of a revisionist. The first seven chapters have not been published earlier in any form. Versions of other chapters have appeared in *Critical Inquiry* ("Past and Present" and "The Recognition Scene of Criticism"); *New Literary History* ("A Short History of Practical Criticism"); *Comparative Literature* ("Literary Commentary as Literature"); and *Salmagundi* ("Centaur: On the Psychology of the Critic").

"Leda and the Swan" is reprinted with the permission of the estate of W. B. Yeats, Macmillan London Limited, and Macmillan Publishing Co., Inc., from *The Collected Poems of W. B. Yeats.* Copyright 1928 by Macmillan Publishing Co., Inc., renewed 1956 by Georgie Yeats. "The Birds begun" and "At Half past Three" are reprinted with permission of the publishers and the Trustees of Amherst College from *The Poems of Emily Dickinson,* edited by Thomas H. Johnson, Cambridge, Mass.: The Belknap Press of Harvard University Press, copyright © 1951, 1955 by the President and Fellows of Harvard College. "The Red Wheel Barrow" is reprinted with permission of the publisher, from William Carlos Williams's *Collected Earlier Poems,* copyright 1938 by New Directions Publishing Corporation.

I wish to thank Gershom Scholem for permission to reproduce Paul Klee's "Angelus Novus," and Jacques Derrida and The Editions Galilée for permission to reproduce page 7 of *Glas,* copyright © 1974 by Editions Galilée.

Introduction

This is a book of experiences rather than a systematic defense of literary studies. The best apology for criticism (as for literature) is doing it; and, at present, reading it closely. Though we have perfected—some will say overperfected—the technique of close reading, it has been applied almost exclusively to creative writing rather than to criticism or nonfictional prose. What follows is an attempt to bring together my reading of criticism with my reading of literature: to view criticism, in fact, as within literature, not outside of it looking in.

The truth of art and the useful mediation of the critic are the argument, explicit or implicit, of all books of criticism, including mine. Every discipline tries to rationalize itself, its standing and its procedures. At the same time we distrust what is put under the name of reason as only, perhaps, a bureaucratic rationale. In the case of art, moreover, too many reasons have been given. Can one rationalize an institution as old as art? The excuses become an art in themselves. I prefer to *confess* what art has meant to me. It shapes my consciousness as if that were as material as language, and makes eyes and ears brood. It relieves the shift between work and leisure, or vacancy and the elation of intense thought. It gives words and takes them away. Through it I can feel in touch with myself, and sometimes with others. It is blind, as Kant said of imagination, close to a drive or instinct; yet often one feels a higher reason in it, which not only literary theory but the sciences of man, such as anthropology, psychology, and semiotics, try to grasp. In oppressive social systems it has always found a way to create a form of expression.

It is as much a staple as bread, even if it comes after bread and can't substitute for it. Without deciding ultimately about the value of art to society (I see no good in a battle over priorities, between science and the humanities, or vocationalism and more liberal curricula), we can insist that speaking with each other—and on a more than didactic level—has always been the distinguishing feature of life in society. Art, in conjunction with criticism, is not a luxury but is essential to communicating in a humane way. That I am incurably didactic may be as brute a fact as having a will or desire that life cannot satisfy; but what I do with that communication-compulsion, or what it does with me, is the issue. Life is not an academy, still less a military academy; instruction has to find a way to become art, a pleasurable and responsive activity, "the breath and finer spirit of all knowledge" (Wordsworth).

Each work of art, and each work of reading, is potentially a demonstration of freedom: of the capacity we have for making sense by a mode of expression that is our own, despite political, religious, or psychological interference. Because of the modern attitude that politics is fate, Malraux called art an "antifate"; and there is, at present, an adversary relation between civilized discourse and the political and technological drive for security—through thought-control or the subordination of the arts (and even the universities) to specified practical ends. But what is practical in the arts has always already moulded society. Without the arts, craft and workmanship deteriorate; without literature, there is no literacy except in the form of semi-articulate dialects, consumer jargon, orders of the day, technical memoranda. Even no sense of being here rather than there. "The classic is the local fully realized, words marked by a place" (William Carlos Williams).

Concerning literary study in particular, it is not sufficient to establish as a value that it too can be a science. The advances by Jakobson, Greimas, Barthes, Genette, and Todorov are generally acknowledged. Northrop Frye, in his *Anatomy of Criticism,* also sought to schematize literary study and make it more than case-law based on an indefinite accumulation of interpretive engagements. Yet the value of these studies is not proved by showing their scientific potential; for it remains doubtful whether advances in this area could or should rival those of the natural sciences. I. A. Richards's prognosis, near the conclusion of *Coleridge on Imagination* (1935), sounds ominous as well as ambitiously hopeful. "With Coleridge we step across the threshold of a general theoretical study of language capable of opening to us new powers over our minds comparable to those which systematic physical inquiries are giving us over our environment." Does this imply a managerial society full of technicians, operators, language therapists, a department of discourse control and emendation? Better the French Academy.

It is true that the relation of language to thought—scientific or social—has always been a crucial subject for literary and philosophical inquiry: Locke and Wittgenstein are as relevant here as Matthew Arnold, I. A. Richards, or Karl Kraus. We begin with a lack or an excess; with a confusion in thought or language; we brood over that chaos to purify it, or to produce order. Theory-making is part of this brooding and ordering. It cannot arrange things absolutely; it can only provide finer mental and verbal instruments. The act of reading, moreover, of specific and self-reflective interpretation, remains essential. We not only *apply* the instruments, we make them *play*. "Criticism is not content with applying them in a servile manner but transforms them through contact with new materials."[1] This creative sense of criticism is faltering: one faction, today, attacks the formidable stream of pedagogical exegeses issuing from the universities, the other attacks the abstruseness and dehumanized terminology of theoretical reflection. How did this divide between theory and prac-

1. I quote Tzvetan Todorov to indicate that, like Roland Barthes and Gerard Genette, he is more than a scientist of literature. In *The Poetics of Prose*, for example, he distinguishes between poetics as theory, and criticism as literary *praxis* or commentary that "dealing with 'structures' becomes structural itself. . . . the relationship between the author's and the critic's text is one of contagion, not analogy." But this distinction according to mode or genre undermines, of course, the idea of a purely scientific poetic theory, one untouched by literature's "contagious" materials. "The work of art (or of science)," he says elegantly, "always involves a transforming element, an innovation of the system."

See the Bibliography, below, for full reference to works cited in the footnotes.

tice come about? Is there hope for an unservile, an enlarged and mature, criticism, neither afraid of theory nor overestimating it?

Reading criticism closely, and seeing it as symbiotic rather than parasitic in relation to literature, led me back to its colorful past. Why was there, at present, so little exegetical daring? Why were historical and critical studies further apart than ever? Why the gulf between *philosophic* criticism and *practical* criticism, the former flourishing in Continental Europe, the latter insulating the writings of English and American teachers?

"Criticism is as inevitable as breathing," T. S. Eliot wrote in his first major essay. He did not want to emphasize it as an activity that should receive special attention: on the contrary, he saw it as a natural rather than specialized function. The growth of self-consciousness moved him to keep critical thinking in check. He raged finely against the dissociation of sensibility from thought, and declared it impossible to patch up a lost unity by eccentric —that is, independent—philosophizing. His attempt to subordinate the critical spirit is symptomatic; and my quarrel is mainly with the imperiousness of his view and the sidelining of a more intellectual "Continental" tradition.

May it not be that the condition diagnosed by Eliot is English rather than Modern and Universal; and that social and intellectual issues have gotten confused in a characteristic English way? Randolph Bourne, at least, after describing intellectual life in London during 1913 ("Significant discussion almost did not exist. A running fire of ideational badinage, 'good talk,' took its place. Every idea tended to go up in smoke. You found your tone either monstrously prophetic as of a young Jeremiah sitting at the board, or else unpleasantly cynical") concluded pointedly: "The national mind seemed to have made a sort of permanent derangement of intellect from emotion."[2]

2. "Impressions of Europe, 1913–14," in *History of a Literary Radical and Other Essays*. For the fun of it I add two remarks. The first is by Hermann Keyserling, in his *Europe* (trans. Maurice Samuel): "it really is a fact that a profound, clearly-formulated thought does not fit into the normal framework of English life. Already in the time of Queen Elizabeth, the German spirit (which, it is acknowledged, produced the Reformation with its demand for independent individual thought) was to the respectable Britisher a horrid spectre; even then intelligence

When we set Arnold beside Nietzsche, or set Eliot, Richards, and Leavis beside Lukács, Benjamin, and Valéry, the differences cannot be overlooked. I will try to understand how these critical traditions grew apart; to give a historical sketch of their increasing alienation from each other and Romantic origins; and to see whether mediation is possible. There may be other traditions too. We do not possess a careful study of theories of criticism in the light of their *text-milieu*: how theory depends on a canon, on a limited group of texts, often culture-specific or national. So the literary works analyzed and quoted by the New Critics are a special selection from literary history, as are those analyzed and quoted by Derrida or Barthes or Heidegger. It makes a difference whether philosophical texts are also considered as literary texts; whether one's notion of lyric purity comes from Emily Dickinson or from Mallarmé; whether Shakespeare, Racine, or Calderón is the ideal to be honored and combated; whether Goethe or Hölderlin or both are seen as epochal figures in the development of a literary heritage. These are conventional examples: the game complicates itself when the pre-Socratics, available only in gnomic fragments, are chosen over or against Plato's Socratic dialogues, or when an ignored constellation (Christopher Smart, Jakob Boehme) swims into view, or when the boundary between high art and popular art is transgressed.

Since the new work of art can be the older work recovered, and since this interpretive event cannot be predicted, literary studies are bound to remain in flux: disconcerting, disputatious, disorderly. New principles of order must be acquired by each major movement, each major change in the *text-milieu*; and because, so far, very little charting has been done of the interdependence of theory and text-milieu, I find myself following a personal and macaronic procedure in this book. I allow a formal idea within critical theory to elicit the analysis of a poem, and vice-versa; my shuttling between, on the one hand, two critical

---

was already regarded as an unhealthy product made in Germany." The second is by Basil de Selincourt, in *The English Secret* (originally *TLS* articles): "In framing a policy of education, above all, we must go warily; for a chief part of the educational process is the replacement of unconscious by conscious action of the mind, and, broadly speaking, [the] great English virtue is a virtue of unconsciousness."

traditions and, on the other, works of art and works of reading, should be deliberate enough to suggest that criticism is *within* literature. How criticism is a genre, or a primary text, I hope to make clear by suspending the a priori valuation of art over criticism, and reading even the critical work closely.

I suggest, most generally, that we have moved from the Arnoldian Concordat, which assigns to criticism a specific, delimited sphere distinct from the creative (which remains superior and the object of millennial hopes), to a New-Critical Reduction, with Eliot as its influential source. Criticism was valued *in* art and only tolerated *outside* art. The New Criticism emphasized those works in which critical and creative seemed to coexist but limited the critical essay by reducing its sphere of competence to specific, formal or evaluative, remarks on art. The analogy of literary-critical to philosophical or religious discourse was played down.

In one sense the reduction proved to be the opposite of a reduction. The critical spirit was acknowledged to be pervasive: it might be integrated into art but ultimately it could be absorbed, if at all, only by religious or cultural forces of a practical and powerful consistency. Yet precisely because of this sense of the rampant nature of mind, its runaway tendencies when not culturally invested, the New Criticism (in Allen Tate as in Eliot, in Cleanth Brooks as in F. R. Leavis) tended to inflate the artist's function. The New Critics demonstrated that art was indeed a "criticism of life," conducted in a vital, organic manner. Not only the novel but also poetry was tough-minded; its lyrical and thoughtful qualities—as in Dante, Donne, or Valéry—were not at odds. The pedagogical force of New-Critical essays, moreover, was remarkable: demonstration reinforced conversation, close reading and formal analysis sensitized the reader to complexities hardly noticed before, let alone tolerated. The scientific method was imported, perhaps to preempt it. So there was, even here, an intensification of the critical consciousness.

Yet this benefit was the byproduct of a theory that pointed, ideologically, in a different direction. For, as I have said, the critical spirit was honored principally when bound up with art. The Arnoldian Concordat became a Reduction because criticism no longer had a standing or creative potential of its own. Its focus was exclusively on the literary work, while its own autonomous or freelance qualities were denied.

The New Critical Reduction functioned, then, as an anti-self-consciousness doctrine, even if it avoided explicit recognition of that fact. Leavis's refusal to acknowledge that he was a theoretician *malgré lui*[3] showed how strongly fixed the aversion to theorizing had become. In Leavis there was something of that "Practical Devotional" strain, of that "grim inarticulate veracity" Carlyle had lauded in *Past and Present* as a dangerous hallmark of the English. But there was no aversion at all to censuring Teutonic philosophizing in the light of an English sensibility and a homespun ideology. The ideological factor, indeed, was often overbearing; and the claim made for literary criticism was far from modest, though made in the name of moral culture and a living language.

I don't want to underestimate Leavis. His honesty is trenchant and his judgments are cutting. Ruskin excepted, we have not had a stronger moral critic since Johnson: the very mistakes are principled and demanding. He refused to let technique or technology homogenize language. Nor was Leavis a tight little Islander. In an introduction to Marius Bewley's *The Complex Fate,* he calls for a "real cross-Atlantic interplay that will make the confident substitution of the unanimities of British 'social' civilization for the standards of criticism more difficult." He encouraged, nevertheless, a ferocious counter-etiquette, an inquisitorial and unflinching disdain for suspicious turns and terms of thought, perhaps for ideas as such. The "English School" is no fun; and to

3. See the Leavis-Wellek debate that took place in the pages of *Scrutiny* in 1937 and 1938; reprinted in *The Importance of Scrutiny,* ed. Eric Bentley. René Wellek greatly expanded the American horizon through founding comparative literature as a university department in the 1940s and through many important publications, including the *Theory of Literature* (with Austin Warren) and the *History of Modern Criticism.* Wellek's *Theory* supported the pedagogical and practical aims of New Critical formalism but made it more sophisticated by recalling Continental perspectives (Czech and Russian formalism in particular); his *History,* while delimiting literary criticism—as commentary that centered specifically on questions of literary art—mentioned such debts of criticism to philosophy as had already motivated his *Kant in England* and his attempt to place Coleridge in a German and philosophical, not only English, context.

break up one's sentences in the Leavisite, post-Jamesian manner does not of itself prove one is alive to language. Has the tradition of philosophic criticism dominant on the Continent nothing to offer Anglo-American practical criticism? Must every idea "go up in smoke," or be subject to the obverse snobbery of an unconventional edginess, an eloquently inarticulate scrutiny?

At the center of this book is a third phase of modern criticism: the Revisionist Reversal. It acknowledges the intellectual element in art but reinvests criticism with creative potential. It opposes those who abstract creative power from the critical essay. It is not afraid to see criticism as a contaminated creative thinking. I put the matter crudely: both "creative" and "power" are loaded words that would ordinarily be avoided, especially by the deconstructionist wing of the Revisionist movement. "Movement" may also be too sloganlike a word, as I argue at the end of my first chapter. But in an introduction one can't keep biting one's tongue. The emphasis shifts, in any case, to criticism or the critical essay, and within these to the issue of language: the language of criticism as well as the language of art, critical diction as well as poetic diction.

The concept of a specifically literary language, emphasized by formalist theories, becomes more rather than less of a problem. If literariness exists, what is the status of the critic's language? Can we standardize it, make it less ambiguous? What role does or should terminology play? Is the latter a necessary evil or an inventive nomenclature? Or, more generally, what role should theory play?

This latter issue is pursued more persistently in France. If theory presupposes a scientific language, there may be an untheorizable element in literature. One function of literature may even be, Todorov adds, the subversion of this scientific language, and "hence it is extremely rash to claim we can read [literature] with the help of the very language it calls into question." Hence also the working out of this perplexity, or of the problematics of reading, in a critic like Paul de Man. Is there, at all, a natural or proper diction in any of these areas?

In revisionist criticism, philosophical issues as old as Plato's *Cratylus* join up with the anthropological study of codes, semiotic theories concerning the arbitrary or conventional character of signs, and psychoanalytic visions of a psyche usurped or textured by immemorial words. The very status of commentary as a subordinate text is rethought: can we dichotomize the world of letters into creative literature and auxiliary commentary? Eliot had expanded our sense of the critical intelligence operative in art; what if commentary had its own creative or insubordinate quality?

Types of discourse may be types of power. The revisionists challenge the attitude that condemns the writer of criticism or commentary to nonliterary status and a service function. To that extent they are a political movement that attacks the isolation of the critic: isolation within the university and from broader, more public issues, but isolation also from inwardness and philosophical concerns. The relation of creative and critical must always be reenvisioned; and while the revisionists may overturn this or that orthodoxy, this or that fixed ideal, and while they specifically expose the falsification, even repression, of Romantic origins in Arnoldian and much New Critical thought, their reversal does not fix, once again, the relation of creative and critical. The variety and indeterminacy of that relation are disclosed in a radical way.

I have not been able to find an independent historical perspective on American criticism. I therefore talk of "Anglo-American" criticism. Perhaps this independent perspective must still be attained. The 1970s have seen an invasion of mind-snatchers from the Continent: an opening is created in American (more than in English) criticism by wholesale and relatively unhistorical importations from France, and to a lesser degree from Germany.

The 1980s, it would be my hope, might extend this opening to American philosophy. An emigration of ideas from within is needed. Emerson has been acknowledged, yet to center on him may be a premature enthronement. "I am not wise enough for a national criticism, and must use the old largeness a little longer," he himself averred. There is little of Emerson in Kenneth Burke, and more of Carlyle than of Emerson in Harold Bloom. Philosophic criticism, moreover, has many forms: can Edmund

Wilson's engagements with social and political history, as in *To the Finland Station* (1940), stand up to the Frankfurt School's study-in-depth of similar issues? Must we always return to Henry Adams for a more powerful "American" beginning to social criticism? Emerson, Thoreau, Royce, William James; the more specialized work of Peirce; the still unassimilated work of certain cultural thinkers like Veblen and Bourne; the overassimilated writings of Dewey; the speculative essays and books by Burke, Ransom, Blackmur, Waldo Frank, and Wilson; the American reception of Croce; the inspirational comments of Charles Olson and practicing poets; Trilling's wrestling with Freud; the curious episode of the Chicago Aristotelians; and now revisionist criticism —these require a more thorough mapping, a more dialectical consideration, than I can offer here.

My call for an independent American perspective should not be misunderstood. It is not motivated by a regressive or factitious nationalism. I know too well that a "national" and "emotional" solution was tried in the period that immediately preceded Eliot's attempt to purge cultural criticism of its softcore sociology and pseudoromantic aspirations. Eliot's "Tradition and the Individual Talent" of 1919 did not come out of the blue: its Neoclassical frame and concise, laconic style are best compared to Ludwig Lewisohn's *A Modern Book of Criticism,* which also appeared in 1919.

Lewisohn and Eliot agree that criticism is "no isolated thing" but "as present as the air." Yet how different that air, that atmosphere for each! In his slight yet oracular introduction, Lewisohn speaks for "the liberal critics of America" in tones vaguely reminiscent of Emerson's "American Scholar" and Shelley's "Defence of Poetry." He castigates the Philistines by holding up a vision of the professional critic who is "in contact with the infinitely varying moods that the World evokes in the soul, and with the flaming apparition of beauty in its myriad forms. And by virtue of his self-appointed office he is a guide, a universal guide, through the mazes of art and life." No wonder, Lewisohn continues, that "the average critic, who is either a teacher or a reviewer, shrinks from his true business, and devotes himself to formal studies in literary history, rhetorical trifling, or the expression of the average tribal reaction to new books and plays."

Lewisohn's selection begins with Anatole France's famous definition of the critic as one who relates the adventures of his soul among masterpieces, and it climaxes with Van Wyck Brooks's attack, in *Letters and Leadership* (1918), on Irving Babbitt's putdown of the younger generation as a "noisy revolt against all the forms of the past." In a final excerpt Brooks is supported by Randolph Bourne, who agrees that the academic critics have failed. They refused to discriminate between a vital and an outmoded past. But the World War has made it clear that the business of criticism cannot go on as usual. The younger generation, precisely the one condemned by Babbitt, has no choice but to "invent a usable past" (Brooks's phrase). Bourne concludes by offering *his* definition of the new classic.

> Finding little in the American tradition that is not tainted with sweetness and light and burdened with the terrible patronage of bourgeois society, the new classicist will yet rescue Thoreau and Whitman and Mark Twain and try to tap through them a certain eternal human tradition of abounding vitality and moral freedom, and so build out the future. If the classic means power with restraint, vitality with harmony, a fusion of intellect and feeling, and a keen sense of the artistic conscience, then the revolutionary world is coming out into the classic.[4]

My sympathies, sixty years later, are strongly with Lewisohn and Bourne. Bourne's conception of a new classicism rivals Eliot's; yet it is hard to respond over the long run to critical writing so impressionistic or programmatic, so devoid of formal analysis. Something is amiss with Lewisohn's tone in particular, close to propaganda, abstractly emotional or self-inspiring. It was Eliot who triumphed: a conservative modernist, backed by the authority of an audacious and difficult poetry.

Why Eliot triumphed is fairly obvious. It is unrealistic to invest the critic with religious aura. That flamboyant style, vatic and vapid, points to a perpetual adolescence bound to outmode itself, a wildish destiny that cannot be sustained in this manifest way. The burden on the individual, on the young or on the old

4. From "History of a Literary Radical," published in Lewisohn's collection before appearing in Van Wyck Brooks's edition. The best collection of Bourne is that edited by Olaf Hansen with a preface by Christopher Lasch, *The Radical Will: Selected Writings, 1911–1918*.

impressing the young, is too great. Paradoxically, the yoke of tradition is lighter in Eliot's view: one is acculturated or not, one carries the past in one's bones, one does not redeem or raid the tradition, one lets it come out and extinguish the personal. Though what is inherited must be renewed by great labor (as Goethe too had observed), it is really there, and not the chimerical creation of a backward-turned utopian hope.

Lewisohn's perception, moreover, that "Religion has lost its power; the social ideals have not yet achieved theirs," expressed a truth with disastrous consequences. The 1920s and 1930s see the rise of "political religions" (Eric Voegelin): the social ideals do finally gain power by usurping religious pathos and messianic hope, and establish themselves as theocracies with a secular face. For Eliot, in England, religious and social ideas could still cohere in Anglicanism; but not for Lewisohn in America. Pressured by slogans of Order from Right and Left, the critic could not fall back on a vaguely prophetic sense of democratic vistas. A harder intellectual tradition was needed. Bourne was capable of providing it: he attacked the superstructure of Anglophile conformities, pointing out that the "distinctively American spirit—pioneer, as distinguished from the reminiscently English—that appears in Whitman and Emerson and James, has had to exist on sufferance alongside of this other cult, unconsciously belittled by our cultural makers of opinion." His counter-ideal of a "trans-national America," that would no longer equate Americanization and assimilation, was echoed by Lewisohn in his remarkable autobiography *Up Stream* (1922).[5] Yet Bourne died young; and a philosophical Marxist criticism, comparable to that of Lukács or the Frankfurt School, did not emerge.

5. "The doctrine of assimilation, if driven home by public pressure and official mandate [as it was increasingly during the Great War], will create a race of unconscious spiritual helots. We shall become utterly barbarous and desolate. The friend of the Republic, the lover of those values which alone make life endurable, must bid the German and the Jew [Lewisohn was both], the Latin and the Slav preserve his cultural traditions and beware of the encroachments of Neo-Puritan barbarism—beware of becoming merely another dweller on an endless Main Street. . . ." *Up Stream*, chap. 10. As Irving Howe points out, we do not have a full-scale history of intellectuals in the United States, though he has made a sketch of the "New York intellectuals" of the 1930s to the present in *The Decline of the New*, Part 3. Alfred Kazin, in *On Native Grounds*, chap. 11, offers a just appreciation of Lewisohn and his milieu.

Van Wyck Brooks, though he diagnosed the situation as early as *America's Coming-of-Age* (1915), felt powerless. He denounced the split between theory and practice that forced art to become unreal. In America, he wrote, human nature "exists on two irreconcilable planes, the plane of stark theory and the plane of stark business; and in the back of its mind is heaven knows what world of poetry, hidden away, too inaccessible, too intangible, too unreal in fact ever to be brought into the open, or to serve, as the poetry of life rightly should serve, in harnessing thought and action together." He knew that a "resisting background" had to emerge from the "vast, vague movements of sentiment in the democracy." A critic seemed to stand on clouds, there was "no clinch in things, nothing to brace the feet against, no substance against which ideas can assume a bold relief."[6]

Brooks's critique was subverted by his own velleities, and did not survive partisan attacks on its unobjective and increasingly sentimental consequences. Like Lewisohn, he overestimated the influence of an artistic or intellectual guild, what Coleridge had called the clerisy. It is hard to imagine what "a troup of shivering young Davids—slim and frail but with a glint of morning sunshine on their foreheads" (Lewisohn's description of the young liberal intellectuals) could have done against an army composed not of professors but of politicized Goliaths.

Eliot had a better grasp on the fact that an unformulated individualism could not survive. He armed himself with the received past: established religion, classical art, conservative politics. Only, it did not include America. Almost by definition America had no usable past of its own. That was its weakness for Eliot, its strength for the American modernist. America was the future, the Newfoundland that still had not found itself spiritually but was des-

6. It is chastening to observe that Brooks's "resistant background" may have come first from an unexpected quarter: the conservative agrarianism of Southern writers who contributed to *I'll Take My Stand* in 1930. (They included figures later active in the New Criticism.) Portions of this manifesto sound strangely like the critical theory of the Frankfurt School that was also concerned with the industrialization of all values. John Crowe Ransom's contribution is an eloquent attack on a gospel of Progress that "never defines its ultimate objective, but thrusts its victims at once into an infinite series," and on an abstract or deracinated humanism unable to contain America's "vast industrial machine, with its laboratory centers of experimentation, and its far-flung organs of mass production . . . like a Prussianized state which is organized strictly for war and can never consent to peace."

tined to do so, being vast, capacious, and free of what William Carlos Williams called the "Plagiarism of the Traditionalists." This sense of an unlimited future—unlimited by a past still to be found—was the inspirational message of Lewisohn's *Modern Book*.

As I write this in 1980 the freedom attributed to American modernism, or to modernism generally, appears as a myth of potentiality that has revealed the emptiness generating all such myths. The contemporary American critic is aware of paradox and limitation: to find a beginning, to invent an origin, is to purchase one past by displacing another, which secretly oppresses us, or is already discredited. As the American past surfaces, only its abuses seem usable—for ideological attacks on the American way of life itself.

By now, however, American criticism has *its* complex fate. There is the immediate past, closely associated with intellectual journalism and social hope; there is another past that is more academic yet also intersects—especially in philosophy—with social thought. The expatriation of the 1970s, the swerve of literary criticism toward the Continent, provides a third deposit in this "tangled bank." Its difference from the earlier expatriate movement is that it turns Europe against England. Even American New Criticism, though it brought intellectual precision to literary and cultural studies, was still imbued with a predominantly English standard and canon of texts. Its formalism remained genteel, an evangelical pedagogy ("tainted with sweetness and light") rather than a technical philosophy or open cultural movement.

American criticism in the 1980s could flourish on a broad and flexible, a "transnational," base. It has no need to accept the last traces of the genteel tradition: any pseudoclassical reduction of the critical spirit (through a simplified theory of reference, for example), any assignment of criticism to a noncreative and dependent function with second-class status in the world of letters. For all criticism entails a rethinking, which is itself creative, of what others hold to be creative: a scrutiny of the presence of the fictive, and of the fiction of presence, in every aspect of learning and life.

The wilderness alluded to in my title is Arnold's, whose prediction at the end of "The Function of Criticism" stands as the epigraph to this book. Arnold identifies the critics, of whom he is one, with the generation that was destined to perish in the Sinai desert. But this wilderness is all we have. Arnold's fiction of presence was that our errand in the wilderness would end: that a new and vital literature would arise to redeem the work of the critic. What if this literature is not unlike criticism, and we are forerunners to ourselves? Perhaps it is better that the wilderness should be the Promised Land, than vice-versa.

Part I

A thing of beauty is a joy forever. But it is not improved because the student has had to tie his tongue before it. It is an artistic object, with a heroic human labor behind it, and on these terms it calls for public discussion. The dialectical possibilities are limitless, and when we begin to realize them we are engaged in criticism.

—John Crowe Ransom

To explain grace requires
a curious hand.

—Marianne Moore

CHAPTER ONE

Understanding Criticism

What difference does reading make? Is it perhaps, like traveling, a fool's paradise? "We owe to our first journeys," writes Emerson, "the discovery that place is nothing. At home I dream that at Naples, at Rome, I can be intoxicated with beauty, and lose my sadness. I pack my trunk, embrace my friends, embark on the sea, and at last wake up in Naples, and there beside me is the stern Fact, the sad Self, unrelenting, identical, that I fled from. I seek the Vatican, and the palaces. I affect to be intoxicated with sights and suggestions, but I am not intoxicated. My giant goes with me wherever I go."

Emerson is urging us to self-reliance; yet the more we read him, the more *he* is the giant, seductive or overwhelming, who stands in the way of a liberation he commends. There is no getting around him: we must think him through, allow him to invade our prose.

The difference that reading makes is, most generally, writing. The thinking through, the "working through" (the metaphor of work applied to psychic process being Freudian, yet appropriate in this context) is hard to imagine without writing. Certain poets, like Mallarmé, even seek a type of writing that would end reading as tourism or as merely a reflection on a prior and exotic fact.

The division of literary activity into writers and readers, though it may appear to be commonsensical, is neither fortunate nor absolute. It is crass to think of two specialties, one called *reading* and one *writing*; and then to view criticism as a particularly specialized type of reading which uses writing as an "incidental" aid. Lately, therefore, forms of critical commentary have emerged that challenge the dichotomy of reading and writing. Besides the involutions of Nabokov's *Pale Fire* (1962) and the essays of Borges, there are such experiments as Norman O. Brown's *Closing Time* (1973), Harold Bloom's *The Anxiety of Influence* (1973), Maurice Blanchot's *Le pas au-delà* (1973), Jacques Derrida's *Glas* (1974), and Roland Barthes's *A Lover's Discourse* (1977). They are literary texts in their own right as well as commentary. They belong to the realm of "letters" rather than to purely "critical" writing, and they make us realize that we have narrowed the concept of literature.

Even when its form is less spectacular, such criticism puts a demand on the reader that may cause perplexity and resentment. For it does not see itself as subordinated in any simple way to the books on which it comments. It can be pedagogic, of course, but it is free *not* to be so. It is aware that in philosophy there is less of a distinction between primary and secondary literature: ask a philosopher what he does and he will answer "philosophy." It could be argued, in the same spirit, that what a literary critic does is literature.

Yet the reader-critic's claim to parity is continually chastened by the fact that he remains addicted to reading, to traveling through those "realms of gold" in the hope of being instructed and surprised. His supposed self-reliance is undermined by a famous Miltonic axiom, Satan's boast to the angels in *Paradise Lost* (4.830): "Not to know mee argues yourselves unknown." That is the seductive boast of every book. We are tempted to enter an unknown or forbidden realm.

The spectacle of the critic's mind disoriented, bewildered, caught in some "wild surmise" about the text and struggling to adjust—is not that one of the interests critical writing has for us? In more casual acts of reading this bewilderment can be muted, for there is always the hint of a resolution further on, or an enticement to enter for its own sake the author's world. However, in *containing* this bewilderment, formal critical commentary is not very different from fiction itself. Fiction also carries within it a hermeneutic perplexity: there is a shifting of focus, or a changeable perspective, or a Jamesian effort to discern the "felt meaning." It is not Dr. Johnson alone who has his troubles with *King Lear*: on reading the exchange between Lear and a Gloucester whose eyes have been put out—

> *Lear.* Your eyes are in a heavy case, your purse in a light; yet you see how this world goes.
> *Gloucester.* I see it feelingly.

—we can only echo Gloucester's own words in accepting so appalling a mixture of pathos and pun.

The critic, then, is one who makes us formally aware of the bewildering character of fiction. Books are our second Fall, the reenactment of a seduction that is also a coming to knowledge. The innermost hope they inspire may be the one Heinrich von Kleist expressed: only by eating a second time of the tree of knowledge will we regain paradise.

Consider, in this light, Yeats's "Leda and the Swan."

> A sudden blow: the great wings beating still
> Above the staggering girl, her thighs caressed
> By the dark webs, her nape caught in his bill,
> He holds her helpless breast upon his breast.
>
> How can those terrified vague fingers push
> The feathered glory from her loosening thighs?
> And how can body, laid in that white rush,
> But feel the strange heart beating where it lies?
>
> A shudder in the loins engenders there
> The broken wall, the burning roof and tower
> And Agamemnon dead.
> Being so caught up,
> So mastered by the brute blood of the air,
> Did she put on his knowledge with his power
> Before the indifferent beak could let her drop?

It comes like a voice from nowhere, catching us too offguard. "A sudden blow: the great wings beating still . . . ." Where got Yeats that truth? Part of the magic to be resisted is the poet's imperious assumption of a visionary mode, as if it were self-justifying. His exotic and erotic subject matter displaces the question of authority. For Yeats may be a voyeur rather than a visionary: we do not know where he is standing, or how ancient his eyes are, or if they glitter. Though we grant him, provisionally, the authority of his poem, we note that his empathy runs parallel to Leda's and focuses on the unspoken promise of an initiatory or "strange" knowledge—in fact, on the first temptation Genesis spells out: "Ye shall be as gods, knowing good and evil." Leda, surprised by the swan-god, cannot but "feel the strange heart beating where it lies."

So fiction imposes on us, by a subtle or blatant seduction. We are always surprised or running to catch up or wishing to be more fully in its coils. This may explain why the detective novel, with its mock catharsis of false leads and inconclusive speculations, is a favorite of intellectual readers. Literary commentary is comparable to the detective novel: confronted by a bewildering text, it acts out a solution, trying various defenses, various interpretations, then pretending it has come to an authoritative stance—when, in truth, it has simply purged itself of complexities never fully mastered.

Seduction, then, in fiction or life, seems to contain the promise of mastery or, paradoxically, of joining oneself to an overwhelming intent even at the cost of being subdued. In more innocent language seduction is called *persuasion*; and rhetoric, or the art of persuasion, has always been criticized by competing arts, such as logic and dialectic, which assert a higher truth without being less vulnerable to the charge of seeking a powerful epiphany, or all-clarifying solution. Rhetoric, in any case, is to language what science is to the language of nature—a technique that can be mastered, perhaps for the purpose of further mastery. Yet it is also true that the verbal acuities of poetry or fiction challenge the rhetoric they use, as in the subtle, questioning progress of Yeats's poem. Rhetoric is the will doing the work of imagination, Yeats said.

At first we feel mainly the poet's rhetoric, his power in depicting an action that has power as its very subject. An episode that spans centuries is condensed in the representational space of a sonnet. The mimetic faculty is stirred by rhythmic effects (the additional beat in "great wings beating still," the caesural pause between "terrified" and "vague"), while inner bonding through repetition and alliteration ("beating . . . beating," "*H*e *h*olds *h*er *h*elpless . . .") tightens Yeats's verse as if to prevent *its* rupture. The energy of the event seems to produce its own enargeia, as rhetoricians call the picturing potential of words. The eyes are led along an axis that is sharper than ordinary sight: does "there" in "A shudder in the loins engenders there" refer to the place of vision as well as conception, to what is right *there* before the poet's eyes? He sees into the loins as into the heart. "Wisdom begins in images," Yeats remarked; rhetorical skill, the formal magic that recreates Leda, has made an image come alive.

Yet rhetoric in the service of mimesis, rhetoric as imaging power, is far from being *imitative* in the sense of reflecting a preexistent reality. Mimesis becomes poesis, imitation becomes making, by giving form and pressure to a presumed reality, to "Leda." The traditional theme, by being repeated, is endowed with a past that may never have been present. Leda is not even named within the poem; and the strongest images in the poem are not images at all but periphrases, like "feathered glory" and "brute blood of the air." These non-naming figures have the structure of riddles as well as of descriptions. Even the images in lines 10–12, stark metonymies, are a periphrastic riddle or charade for "The Destruction of Troy."

The last of these non-naming figures, "brute blood of the air," may be the most intriguing. Viewed in itself, detached from the representational frame of Yeats's lyric, it conveys a sense of internal generation, almost self-generation—something engendered from what is barely seen or grasped, that does not recall natural process so much as supernatural agency, not formation but transformation. It evokes the imminence of the visible in the invisible, an absence that can turn into a devastating presence. We are again projected beyond natural sight: air, as in omens, thickens, becomes concrete, theriomorphic, auguring; and to air there corresponds the airy womb of imagination, which also thickens here into an ominous historical projection, a catastrophe-creation of which "Leda" is but the legendary medium.

Less an image, then, than a phantasm is represented. More precisely: is it an image, or is it a phantasm? By phantasm I mean an image with hallucinatory effect: "out of nothing it came" (see

Yeats's "Fragments"). It cannot be explained or grounded by the coordinates of ordinary perception, by stable space-time categories. Does the poem revive a classic myth whose psychic truth is being honored ("to ground mythology in the earth" is one of Yeats's programmatic statements) or does it express a phantasm which that myth holds fast and stabilizes, so that mind can be mind and question it? Second quatrain and last tercet are questioning in form: one function of this form is to hold and elaborate what is happening.

I don't think I exaggerate the image/phantasm indeterminacy. Until we come to the one proper name, "Agamemnon," we are kept in the aura of an action whose reference is not fixed. Though a famous legend is presupposed, the poem effects a displacement from "Leda" and "Troy" to a non-proper, that is, unlocalized event that cannot be given a name or one name. The situating reference to "Agamemnon," the locking up of the action into the known if legendary context, is just that, a locking up; it does not resolve the indeterminacy; we continue to feel the imaginary within the reference myth, something that exceeds the latter like a riddle its solution, or periphrasis and metaphor the undisplaced word. As "Agamemnon" hovers between sonant matter and meaning, so the myth between phantasm and legend-laden image.

We cannot, in short, neglect the airy pretension of a poem that fills the vacancy of prehistory with a paradigmatic primal scene. What space or time are we in? Is the poet standing in his own mind? Or in the third heaven of a domestic séance? Is what he communicates a vision or the variant of a traditional theme or his recreation of a particular painting on that theme? Is he stationing a phantasm or framing something that even if it is an image is so nuclear in lines 10–12 that it could be detached from the poem and seen as Greek epigram or sybilline utterance?

These questions add up to a *hermeneutic perplexity*. Yeats's rhetorical skill has led us beyond or beneath firm knowledge, and we become unsure of the poem's real frame of reference. Who is (the) "Being so caught up"? Correlatively, we become unsure of the poet's authority: is he seer or subjective thinker or superstitious crank? It may be, of course, that it is we who think *against* the poem, who wonder why we were willing to suspend our disbelief and to accept this fiction. We could then follow our own suspensive or "negative" thinking, make it part of the subject matter. But in any significant act of reading, there must be (1) a text that steals our consent, and (2) a question about the text's value at a very basic level: are we in the presence of a forged or an authentic experience?

There is an alternative to this last question, but it leads to a further uncertainty. For to raise the question of authenticity could be to mistake the mode-of-being of poetry—to make a category mistake about it—by seeing poetry as potentially a revelation, a disclosure of previously unapprehended truth. Should not the very concept of fiction, and of the poet as image-maker, avert that perspective with the help precisely of a poet like Yeats, who is a maker of images and has no further claim? But what are images, then, and fictive images in particular?

Philosophy from Husserl to Bachelard and Merleau-Ponty, and theoretically oriented reflection on art from I. A. Richards and John Dewey to Wolfgang Iser and Murray Krieger, have worked closely with the assumption that aesthetic experience is related to perception (or perceptibility, *Anschauung,* the sighting of insight); further, that this relation is what is expressed by the centrality the word "image" has won. The "image" is the point where the received and the productive meet. Our ideational response to the work of art tends to analyze itself in terms that favor the "image." Even without seeking to explain this turn of events, we would find it hard to give up the by now historical liaison between image and formal values in art or between image and any model poetics—despite the counterthrust of semiotic theory and deconstructionist mediation. Perceptibility—that all things can be made as perceptible as the eye suggests—may itself be the great *classic* phantasm, the mediterranean fantasy, continued even by Romantic or Modernist artists who are aware that the image is also a resonance, a musical as well as visual phenomenon:

> Ces nymphes, je les veux perpétuer.
> Si clair
> Leur incarnat léger . . .[1]

1. Mallarmé, "L'Après-Midi d'un Faune." We have no word corresponding to "image" that would express the ideational surge of internal *sound* or *speech.* I sometimes use "soundshape" (Elizabeth Sewell) or "image of voice" (Horace's periphrasis for echo); and "resonance" can be called on to modify "reflection." Poetics

What images are, then, is a question that involves the make-up of our minds, or at least of our terms, our very language.

I have suggested that the image of Yeats's poem serves to stabilize a phantasm or to frame a fantasy. It is tempting to guess at an equation: the more image, the more fantasy. The phantasmic material is brought into a discourse it keeps motivating and unsettling. I have not identified, however, the phantasm or the fantasy; to do so would be to intrude a frame of reference of my own. I am not unwilling as critic or interpreter to do this: to suggest, for example, that the swan-god fantasy potentiates feelings of touch that at once stimulate and unrealize the eyes. A taboo may be breached that involves the relation we have to our own body-image, or the way we organize its capacities into a hierarchy of senses, higher and lower, animal, human, divine. Ordinarily I would have no choice but to develop the poem in this manner. All the more so if the taking-by-surprise so affectively rendered here is not simply a man's version of a woman's presumed desire for "divine rape" but goes behind that doubtful cliché to the question of how ideas of sight exceed sight and elicit monsters or masques. For the moment, however, I want to turn from a particular poem and explore critical thinking generally.

Critical thinking respects heterogeneity. Like good scholarship it keeps in mind the peculiarity or strangeness of what is studied. By "keeping in mind" I mean it does not make art stranger or less strange than it is. But what is strange about art? The word may point to the phantasm in the image. It may also point to historical otherness, to assumptions or conventions we have difficulty appreciating. Are we, however, talking about the strange

---

has barely begun to struggle with this issue, to take back its own from music, and to bring "clarity" into conjunction with "indeterminacy" via a more sensitive, more poetically centered, theory of meaning. George Steiner sees this challenge in historical terms: he has remarkable comments on the surfacing of inner speech between the seventeenth century and the present. Mallarmé's poetry, he suggests, or the subtle density of diction in his period, still managed to keep the "membrane between inner and outer speech" intact, while allowing the chiaroscuro of self-colloquy to filter through. That membrane is then pierced by psychoanalysis and other soundings. See "A Remark on Language and Psychoanalysis" and "The Distribution of Discourse" in *On Difficulty and Other Essays.*

or the other, or both? Strangeness involves a sense that the strange is really the familiar, estranged; otherness (alterity) precludes any assumption about this matter, or it demands of understanding an extraordinary, even self-altering, effort. Something more than empathy; something that carries empathy beyond itself to the point where, as Rimbaud declared, "I is an other."

In biblical hermeneutics there was often a conflict between regarding Scripture as *analogical,* or written in the language of men, accommodated to human understanding; and *anagogical,* or taking the mind out of itself, inspiring it until it appeared "beside itself." The question is whether we must insist on the one or the other: on the resolvable strangeness or the unresolvable otherness. Could we not say there must be a willingness to receive figurative language? To receive is not to accept; between these, as between active and passive, critical thinking takes place, makes its place. We cannot solve, a priori, the issue of strange *or* other; we can only deal with it in the mode of "resonance" that writing is. We rewrite the figure, in commentary or fiction, we elaborate it in a revisionary way.

That writing is a calculus that jealously broods on strange figures, on imaginative otherness, has been made clear by poets and artists rather than by the critics. The latter are scared to do anything except convert as quickly as possible the imaginative into a mode of the ordinary—where the ordinary can be the historically unfamiliar familiarized. But a poem like "Leda and the Swan" is not, or not only, a virtuoso staging of ancient myth, a re-presentation that gives it verisimilitude. Yeats sustains or fulfills a figure: myth is used to disclose the shape of history, and history (as we shall see) the truth of myth. Between Yeats's version and the received myth a *typological* relation forms itself. Even though the figures can be given their ancient names (Agamemnon, etc.) they stand in a complex *contemporaneity* to the poet.

This remains true even when the question of time is not raised as dramatically as in "Leda and the Swan." Where there is imaginative impact, and where that impact is worked out in art, a hermeneutic patience appears that can circumvent the desire for advent—or event—but cannot ignore it. In Yeats that patience is a contrary state of soul achieved despite the apocalyptic pressure of an era—his own time—with which he identifies. To abide or not abide one's time, that is the question. Wordsworth too is under pressure, but the way he broods on "a sudden blow" is quite different. However disparate the experiences depicted in "Leda and the Swan" and "I wandered lonely as a cloud," they deal with strong and sudden images. Wordsworth's poem is well known, but I quote it for convenience.

I wandered lonely as a cloud
That floats on high o'er vales and hills,
When all at once I saw a crowd,
A host, of golden daffodils;
Beside the lake, beneath the trees,
Fluttering and dancing in the breeze.

Continuous as the stars that shine
And twinkle on the milky way,
They stretched in never-ending line
Along the margin of a bay:
Ten thousand saw I at a glance,
Tossing their heads in sprightly dance.

The waves beside them danced; but they
Out-did the sparkling waves in glee:
A poet could not but be gay,
In such a jocund company:
I gazed—and gazed—but little thought
What wealth the show to me had brought:

For oft, when on my couch I lie
In vacant or in pensive mood,
They flash upon that inward eye
Which is the bliss of solitude;
And then my heart with pleasure fills,
And dances with the daffodils.

Why did Wordsworth refuse to classify "I wandered lonely as a cloud," with its picture of daffodils seen "all at once," as a "Poem of the Imagination"? Because, he said, the impact of the daffodils on his "ocular spectrum" had been too strong. His lyric moves in two directions, therefore: it respects the near-hallucinatory effect of daffodils that flash even on his inner eye long after they were seen (this reintroduces the coordinate of time), and it shows the receptive mind trying to regain the initiative, to be imaginative vis-à-vis a psychedelic image.

An instinctive phenomenologist, Wordsworth analyzed the insidious role of accident or surprise in stimulating the imagination. The problem, as he saw it, was one of separating essential from contingent in such incidents, and to arrive at a view of imagination that would deliver it from novelty or sensationalism—from the accusation that it depended on these quasiliterary drugs, on the need for an induced strangeness. Taken by surprise the mind might react with superstitious fantasies, or learn to forestall them by trivialized ideas of the supernatural, like the personified spirits in the inane and gaudy poetry around him, or the frantic marvels of the Gothic novel. The true strangeness of nature should be honored, as childhood had seeded it; images and sounds had their own life, their own agency, even if their impact on the mind derived also from the mind. For Wordsworth insisted that the "images" were not all on the side of nature; mind always blended with nature, even when imagination was involuntarily aroused; but this curious balance or harmony of image and idea—this "indeterminacy" in the act of imaginative perception—was precarious because the image tended to become a phantasm and so overbalance mind.

The pressure on mind or imagination, then, came from supernatural fantasies. Yet these did not work in a vacuum. Wordsworth was one of the first to talk of sensory shock in relation to the Industrial Revolution: the crowding into cities of people and experiences, the explosion of "news" in the Napoleonic era, that kind of daily assault on the senses. The natural rhythms, he felt, were faltering, eroding; life in rural nature was becoming a memory, and could not buffer consciousness as before. The health of the pressured mind depended, therefore, on preventing an alliance of supernatural fantasies with political fears and the siege of daily events. New images had to be liberated from within, or old ones cleansed and renewed; and we can watch this happening in another typical poem, "Resolution and Independence," where there is also a sudden appearance: an old leech gatherer (leeches were used for medicinal blood-letting) surprises the poet in a desolate region on the border between England and Scotland.

Though the scene is totally realistic, and there is ultimately no question that the old man is of flesh and blood (even if meagerly, almost skeletally so), the poet's mind under the pressure of the strange becomes strange to itself, and the line between imagination and reality begins to waver. The image is also the phantasm. To be surprised by daffodils or by the apparition of this Ancient of Days is curiously similar: behind the startlement lurks a potential phantasm. Strange fits of passion had he known.

These fits are not innocent, even if associated by Wordsworth with "wise passiveness." They are marks of the reception of otherness but they are equally signs of an exhausting mental struggle ending in a nearly vacant or inert state of being. Wordsworth's complacency is, at times, not far from Dr. Johnson's classicism: "Wonder is novelty impinging on ignorance." There is nothing new under the sun, and the principle of uniformity consolidates this disenchantment in the name of Nature or Reason. Or the struggle ends in too thorough an enchantment, an escape from the vacillation that enthusiasm brings. Sunk too deep or mounted too high, the soul finds its permanent support within, as in mysticism, psychosis, or the continuous allegory of gnostic fantasy. From so absent-minded a mode of being one can expect at most "a flash of mild surprise."

Let me return a moment to Wordsworth's "Resolution and Independence." It depicts as significant a temptation as "Leda and the Swan." Is this old leech-gatherer, met by chance, a decrepit vagabond, or is he an omen, a more-than-natural intimation of a more-than-natural way of sustaining one's life? May he be a kind of phantom: image and *image of voice* working so strangely on the poet that he loses his bearing and sees heaven in a leech-gatherer and infinity in a handful of leeches?

We are certainly close to something crazy in this poem, as Wordsworth's laughter, at the end, suggests: "I could have laughed myself to scorn to find / In that decrepit man so firm a mind." Wordsworth interprets his laughter morally and invents an exit—a Chaucerian "sentence"—to a perplexity which really has no end. The situation is intrinsically a hermeneutic one and focuses on Wordsworth's awareness of his quirky imagination, one that acts up with transformative zeal. The poet's choice lies, essentially, between a preemptive Gnosticism that sees not only a tale but an allegory in everything, and so must dull the sharpness of accidents, even of life in time itself; and a religious mania that exults in accidents and in the cathectic power of imagination to view them as magnalia rather than trivia. A third choice is the one actually made, but is coincident with *timing*: the poem's rhythm, a resonant writing-thinking, a revisionary elaboration that does not end or begin except formally.

The strangeness of fiction, then, does not issue from its objective character, so that when that object-quality is carefully honored by explication the fiction is understood. On the contrary, objectification may be a way of neutralizing the experience, by boxing it, labeling it "A Vision," and so forgetting the question of, for example, where Yeats is speaking from, and by what authority. It credits the rhetorical character of the enterprise too much or accepts the figurative language too readily. Hermeneutics is bypassed.

Hermeneutics has always inquired into the scandal of figurative language, when that was extraordinary or transgressive. Maimonides devotes an entire book to explaining the anthropomorphisms in the Hebrew Bible. Christ's language is often a stumbling block, and even today some of his parables appear harsh or obscure. The older hermeneutics, however, tended to be incorporative or reconciling, like Donne's "spider love that transsubstantiates all." The Bible and Greek culture, a faith and a philosophy, differing reports of a significant event (as in the case of the Gospels or contradictory traditions), even legends whose colorful features seemed to mask a basic structure: these might be brought into harmony with each other and become fables of identity. German idealism in its major phase, particularly the "identity philosophy" of Schelling, extended this reconciling perspective over the entire sphere of human knowledge, secular and sacred.

Criticism, however, a newer kind of hermeneutics, "affirms" the power of negative thinking.[2] How to define negative thinking,

2. For one influential view of negative thinking, see Herbert Marcuse, especially *Reason and Revolution* (1941) and a "Note on Dialectic" prefaced to the 1960 reissue. Also Theodor Adorno, equally dependent on but less appreciative of Hegel, whose *Negative Dialectic* (1966) rejects any thinking about history that results in

without converting it into a positivistic and dogmatic instrument, is of course very problematic. Not only a philosophy like that of Hegel, whose dialectic is a mode of negative thinking, struggles with this question: Keats's "negative capability" and Wallace Stevens's wish to ablute or withhold the name of the sun—to see it "in the difficulty of what it is to be"—are instances of a parallel concern.

Criticism as a kind of hermeneutics is disconcerting; like logic, but without the latter's motive of absolute internal consistency, it reveals contradictions and equivocations, and so makes fiction interpretable by making it less readable. The fluency of the reader is affected by a kind of stutter: the critic's response becomes deliberately hesitant. It is as if we could not tell in advance where a writer's rhetoric might undermine itself or where the reader might be trapped into perplexity. For the older hermeneutics the choice was clear: Yeats's supernaturalism would be blasphemous, competitive with a dominant faith, and so beneath interpretation; or it would be harmonized with that faith and absorbed. The heterogeneity of poem or original text by no means disappears in the older hermeneutics, but it appears only by way of the daring interpretation that is startling and even liberating in its very drive for harmony. Everyone knows the many marvelous acts of exegesis that try to launder the Song of Songs, that see it as a pious poem.

Modern critical exegesis faces a different situation. It must both suspend its disbelief in the scandalous figure and refuse to accept this figure as mere machinery, as only "poetic." It is not sufficient to resolve this dilemma by claiming that no one really takes Yeats's supernatural theme in a literal way. There it is, after

---

more than an "ever-new Mene Tekel, residing in the smallest things, in debris hewn by decay itself." Hegel's most famous statement on negative thinking is in the preface to the *Phenomenology of Spirit,* which speaks of "the seriousness, the suffering, the patience and the labor of the Negative." The presence of Sartre as writer and philosopher was, till recently, the dominant one in England and America: his dialectic too can be characterized as counteraffirmative and, while remaining deeply engaged with Hegel, is used to purge false totalizations from art and history. The Anglo-American tradition approaches "understanding" from the obverse side of "belief" or "provisional assent": see, for example, Eliot's essay on Dante (1929), or such recent statements as Wayne Booth's *Modern Dogma and the Rhetoric of Assent.*

all. How are we to think of it? Do we try to resolve "Leda and the Swan" into an "allegory" or a "symbol" or even a "philosophy of symbols"? But that would simply defer the entire question of how this visionary kind of writing can survive: perhaps *the* question when it comes to understanding poetry.

Some might say, at this point, that the survival of visionary or extravagant fictional modes—of nonrealism in fiction—is a matter for time to decide in conjunction with literature as an institution. But this is to forget how often the visionary strain is kindled by scholarship itself: by revivals that include the more learned critics. These "extraliterary" forces are part of the institution of literature. The recovery of pagan forms of rhetoric and myth in the Renaissance, the revival of Celtic and Northern mythology in the eighteenth and nineteenth centuries, the more recent explosion of interest in the matter of Araby and Polynesia, even the continuing presence of Classical themes and figures—these are unthinkable without the devoted, worried, ingenious researches and reconstructions of a host of scholars and critics.

The commentary has entered the text, Sainte-Beuve remarked of Ballanche, whose *Orphée,* a prose epic, was an imaginative rehearsal of Vico's philological speculations on Roman law and literature. Philology is made flesh and provides a new art form as well as a new science. It is hard to conceive of Joyce's later work without Vico. It is hard, also, to consider twentieth-century Modernism without recognizing the importance of the Cambridge Anthropologists (Frazer, Harrison, Murray, etc.), who inaugurated a new revival of the Classics on a broader—an Orientalist and anthropological—base. Nietzsche too started as classicist and philologist. Picasso tells us that the old Musée de l'Homme in Paris (Trocadéro), its collection of masks and fetishes, played a crucial role in his own development and so in that of modern painting and sculpture. As if reading were inevitably a journeying East—and often a resistance to that drift—the Leda phantasm or similar "dark italics" (Wallace Stevens) have underwritten all significant movements of our time, both in art and philology. Leda—or Sheba, Edda, Roma, Gradiva, Orienda—is also part of the hoard of scholarship.

Understanding Art and Understanding Criticism are, even historically considered, cognate activities. Yet while poets and novelists often borrow from each other and seem to communicate across national lines, critics and scholars find it much harder to do the same. The Yeats scholar may skirmish with the Wordsworth scholar, but only the rankest amateur will venture a triangulation of these major writers with Hölderlin. The survival of "supernatural song"—or the difficulty of interpreting visionary trends and their modern persistence—has been central to German hermeneutic scholarship, yet in the Anglo-American domain it all continues to be explained by the term *secularization,* which is not reflected on (as in Max Weber) but accepted as an explanatory concept. Nothing is involved save an admirable technical achievement, a calm transfer of properties from one area (the supernatural) to another (the natural).

There is, of course, some truth to this honoring of technique. Technique is a modern and demystified form of magic. In Yeats, as in Goethe, art itself is the magic: it naturalizes mystery by creating so clear an image of it. Yeats's poem grounds an exotic mythology in common psychic experience: the seduction of strangeness and our childish yet persistent interest in the instant of conception. Both types of experience, of course, haunt us because they master or determine us. An active imagination must strike back, repeatedly, at this passivity. The swan-god's supernatural nature encourages in us thoughts of *our* natural supernature.

Yet only the former, supernatural nature, is evident in "Leda and the Swan." While the god is both swan and god, Leda remains Leda. Her humanity is problematized, not redeemed or exalted. Though the assault of the divine on human consciousness is less disturbing here than in other lyrics by Yeats—the bewilderment is Leda's rather than explicitly the poet's—the scene Yeats now projects, now meditates on, builds up masterfully a contrast between mastery and mystery, divine power and human knowledge. "Did she [Leda] put on his knowledge with his power . . . ?"

Through this question Yeats tries to imagine Leda as a person rather than as a medium (persona) through which the god acts. The question implies a further question: if Leda, knowing what the god knows, seeing what the god sees, still has a face, how do we envisage it? Is it gay, mad, or transfigured: does it "see" in the ordinary sense of the word? The idea insinuated is the insufferable one of a human being having to foresee all that consequence. The sudden blow entails an "elision of the richly human middle term" (Thomas Whitaker), a divine disregard cruelly apparent in the first tercet:

> A shudder in the loins engenders there
> The broken wall, the burning roof and tower
> And Agamemnon dead.

The ultimate indeterminacy, then, centers on this face that cannot be imagined. Face or mask, human or inhuman stare: the indistinctness cannot be resolved, and is roused by no more than an intonation, a questioning and quasimusical statement. "Agamemnon," similarly, is more and less than a name. It is a sound-shape with a curious hum and a recursive inner structure. The m's and n's bunch together, so that "Agamemnon dead" is the climactic "And" writ large. The consequence leaves the cause behind, for who could bear that visionary knowledge, that AND? Only a nonperson, a god, or a woman metamorphosed into divine impassibility. Or . . . the poet, who has here, in this very poem, become impersonal and painted himself out of the picture.

Is the poet, then, the last of Leda's brood, the last of these births that are also vastations? The depersonalization of Leda is brought into contact with a poetics of impersonality. The poet *is* present, but as part of this myth, even as an unnamed, unacknowledged deity. Yeats's final question, to which no answer can be given, is undecidable only as it brings us close to the unthinkable. If Leda did put on the god's knowledge, what then? We begin to understand the reserve of that question, and that Yeats wants us to intuit the psychic reality of crazies like Cassandra, or mythic figures vastated by seeing too much and who are mad, divine, or both. A myth of origins is made to yield a clue to the origins of myth.

I have used "Leda and the Swan" as a fable for the hermeneutic situation. Yeats's lyric is, in genre, a prophecy after the event (*ex eventu*) and recreates the psychic milieu from which such myths of annunciation come. This psychic grounding is interesting, but intensifies rather than resolves the problem. A discontinuity remains between natural and supernatural, between the mortal psyche and elated states of mind. In a famous notebook passage (13 June 1852), Emerson talks of "Miss B—, a mantua-maker in Concord, [who] became a 'Medium,' and gave up her old trade for this new one; and is to charge a pistareen a spasm, and nine dollars for a fit. This is the Rat-revelation, the gospel that comes by taps in the wall, and thumps in the table-drawer." In *A Vision,* Yeats inserts "Leda and the Swan" into a section given the byline of "Capri"; but "Capri" could also have been "Naples" or "Cuma" or other sibylline places. The impersonality theory that T. S. Eliot and the New Critics furthered (it has links also to Henry James), though less magical or mystical, is no less a form of mystery management.

A critic aware of the survival in art of the *language* of mystery and myth is in a case exactly parallel to Yeats's. What offends cultural standards may still attract us because of its imaginative daring and peculiar organization. Like an observer of alien rites, the critic is often caught between acknowledging the consistency or attractive horror of what he sees and rejecting it in the name of his own enlightened customs. The split may tear him apart, even at a distance.[3] And if, like Kurtz in Conrad's *Heart of Darkness,* or the spy at Bacchic orgies, the critic then immerses himself in the destructive element, he still creates, as it were, the writer who has gone in search of him. The critic is always a survivor or someone who comes late. So the *character* or *role* of being a critic is implicated in this conflict between mastery and mystery, or rhetoric and hermeneutic hesitation.

The theological writings of the young Hegel are instructive in this regard. Hegel wishes to understand the triumph of Christianity over paganism without vulgar apologetics, without denying the integrity of previous life forms and even their present

3. Cf. Clifford Geertz, "Found in Translation: On the Social History of the Moral Imagination," *Georgia Review* 31; and Ludwig Wittgenstein, "Remarks on Frazer's 'Golden Bough,'" *The Human World* 3. See also Richard H. Bell, "Understanding the Fire-Festivals: Wittgenstein and Theories of Religion," *Religious Studies* 14 (1978): 113–24.

intelligibility. He shows "critical" respect for that which once was and which cannot be entirely superseded. To understand Christianity in its concrete historical life, alien or archaic religious forms must be recalled by the dialectical consciousness of the critic who sees them as stages in the march of reason toward an absolute form. "The heathen too had intellects," Hegel writes. "In everything great, beautiful, noble and free they are so far our superiors that we can hardly make them our examples but must rather look up to them as a different species at whose achievements we can only marvel." A religion, he continues, "particularly an imaginative religion, cannot be torn from the heart, especially from the whole life and heart of a people, by cold syllogisms constructed in the study." The supersession of paganism by Christianity, therefore, can only be explained by a process far more inward, specific, and dialectical than the model of Providence offered by Christian apologists.

For Hegel the very mobility of human consciousness at once uncovers and resolves contradictions in the forms of life it continues to institute. If there is Providence it must be understood as the totalizing process we call history, and which the philosopher reads as he runes. The pattern of the Gothic novel of Hegel's time, which introduced a strange or uncanny event gradually resolved into the familiar and rational (Kleist's *Marquise of O—* endows this *surnaturel expliqué* with its finest psychological shading), is modified in the direction of modern social anthropology. The strange is construed rather than explained; hermeneutic hesitation leads to a more positive awareness of otherness; and if a teleological rationalism wins the day, that day is as long as history itself and includes mysteries denser and more detailed than are found in the Nine Nights of Blake's *Vala*.

It would be foolish not to claim Hegel as a hermeneutic thinker just because the patience of the negative moment in his system is structural, and the ruins of time are always transcended by an eagle-eyed dialectic. Though Hegel remains a master builder he recalls a capacity we feared was lost: the power of the mind to keep interpreting despite evidences of death, to build on and by means of negation. As this "questionable shape" he confronts Jacques Derrida: "What remains today, for us, here and now, of a Hegel?" Composed of explicit or inner quotations, of verbal debris, *Glas* (whose opening sentence I have just quoted) labors in Hegel's shadow to remove his absoluteness and create a negative or deeply critical work of *philosophic* art.

This philosophic work of art was, of course, an aspiration of German Romantic thinkers. Friedrich Schlegel's *Athenaeum* fragments foresee a synthesizing criticism that would combine art and philosophy. Whether the desired work would be more like art or more like philosophy was an intriguing question never quite answered. Nor is it answered at the present time. Even should Plato's curse be lifted, and poetry be admitted once more into the Republic, ". . . can philosophy become literature and still know itself?"[4]

What is required is a work of power in which philosophy recognizes poetry. Yet a happy ending, as in a comedy of reconciliations, cannot be assured. The recognition scene may lead to tragic or uncertain vistas. After so long a separation, there may not be a shared language anymore. Heidegger fears that, yet he tries to recover a simulacrum of the original, unified language. And literary studies that compare, for instance, Hegel's *Phenomenology* to a Bildungsroman or to the elaborate passage work of a Gothic tale, one that never quite purges from its enlightened scheme a dark and daemonic idea, are important not because they colonize philosophy or subject it to the claims of literature but because they raise the question of whether that philosophical work of art is possible even as a heuristic idea.

But the philosophic work of art can also be understood from the side of art. In that spirit I want to conclude: to show how effectively Kleist's *Marquise of O—* rouses the reader from the dogmatic dream that everything can be resolved. Kleist makes us into charmed and bewildered readers who feel that hermeneutic hesitation is the essential quality of philosophical art.

Despite its formal resolution (closure) Kleist's novella unsettles, and keeps unsettled, the relation of the human imagination to the sphere in which it moves. The story begins with a startling

4. I quote the ending of Stanley Cavell's *The Claim of Reason.*

solecism. A highborn widow announces in the local newspapers that she is with child and asks the father to come forward that she may marry him. The story then gives the background to this scandalous act and tells how a father is found. Yet we cannot be sure that this "foundling" is the father. Not to accept him as that would mean, however, to abandon the search for "natural" truth and entertain one of two positions: that there is a supernatural cause for the marquise's "unconscious conception," or that a positive identification of the father is less important than his acceptance of that role, demanded by the institution of marriage. A natural relation may prove to be fictional or self-covenanted.

Kleist's story leaves us in this bind, which is perhaps the only thing that ties it, and us, together. He suggests that natural bonding in human life is so fragile that even when it is strengthened by an etiquette he so beautifully renders, only the violence (war, rape, haste, scandal) breaking that bond is memorable, or else the bind—perplexity of mind—itself.

Now in Hegel also the riddle of historical existence involves a rift between man and nature. Man leaves the path of natural being, betrays his bond, and continually projects his own self-alienation. This riddle is intensified rather than explained by the Hegelian dialectic, which binds all the violent repetitions we call history together. What is strange in Hegel's story is not so much the "dark" past in relation to the "enlightened" present, but the repeated—if dialectically repeated—link between self-alienation and self-realization. "Man's life is thought," Yeats wrote in "Meru"; he cannot cease "Ravening, raging, and uprooting that he may come / Into the desolation of reality." The violence of the spirit vis-à-vis the natural world (Yeats's philosophy of history is explicitly centered on it, as in *A Vision*'s "Dove or Swan" which is preceded by "Leda and the Swan") is modified only by a laborious and patient mode of negativity—something like philosophical analysis, or a hermeneutic hesitation that construes rather than explains spirituality.

There is a rift, then, between the human imagination and the natural or social sphere, one which no supernatural thought, no violence of spirit, can repair. Spirituality, in fact, in its very violence—even the violence of its drive for harmony and reconciliation—is simply a supreme form of the negative. *The Marquise of O—* is full of this violence of spirit, but it meets us initially as a form of writing: as the scandal of advertising, a magnificent, subversive act of womanly abasement with (in that society) the force of graffiti. When she advertises for a husband, the marquise is no less spiritual, no less *protestant,* than when she insisted on her immaculate state. But now she calls for the demon lover to appear, to take on human form, and so to deny the possibility of an immaculate or purely ideal conception. What is negated by the story is also sublated, to use Hegel's terms: the force of a woman's voice, or of the child's voice in the woman, the voice of someone who gives up without giving up a deeply imagined possibility.

The critical spirit, to conclude, does not automatically place itself on the side of reason, enlightenment, or demystification. Since the Enlightenment, in fact, it has sought to develop a style of discourse of its own which could respect the difference, perhaps discontinuity, between "ordinary" and "extraordinary" language. In England, the problem of "poetic diction" which arose after Milton—whether that kind of diction contains, residually, an archaic but still important understanding of religious mystery, or is a mystery only in the sense of "craft"—is a symptom of the general problem of diction, in criticism as well as in poetry. The temptation for criticism to become a type of science, with its own axioms and formal principles, would have been even stronger if this division in language (often simplified into one that opposes prose to poetry) had not continued to challenge the systematizers in several ways. (1) Can literature heal the division in language; or is it as divisive as it is reconciling? (2) Is a comprehensive theory of verbal artifacts, comprising prose and poetry, ordinary and extraordinary language, possible? (3) What should the verbal style of the critic be: how "ordinary," how "prosaic"?

One thing we have learned: whatever style of critical inquiry may be evolving today, criticism cannot be identified as a branch of science or as a branch of fiction. Science is strongest when it pursues a fixed paradigm or point of reference, however subtly modified, however self-transformed. Fiction is strongest as para-prophetic discourse, as prophecy after the event—an event constituted or reconstituted by it, and haunted by the idea of traumatic causation ("A sudden blow," "A shudder in the loins"). But contemporary criticism aims at a hermeneutics of indeterminacy.[5] It proposes a type of analysis that has renounced the ambition to master or demystify its subject (text, psyche) by technocratic, predictive, or authoritarian formulas.

This criticism without a name cannot be called a movement. It is too widespread, miscellaneous, and without a program. Its only program is a revaluation of criticism itself: holding open the possibility that philosophy and the study of art can join forces once more, that a "philosophical criticism" might evolve leading to the mutual recognition of these separated institutions. A corpus of works with some commonality of purpose is already in evidence and will be discussed in what follows, but it would be a mistake to identify what is happening with tendencies surfacing in the last ten or twenty years. These tendencies and the polemic swirling around them are described in chapter 10 ("Past and Present"). My examples from Yeats, Wordsworth, Hegel, and Kleist are meant to point to a longer-range view in which the problem of how to understand visionary or archaic figuration—perhaps figuration as such—draws criticism constantly back into the sphere of hermeneutics through the persistence of the Ancient Classics and Scripture: a language of myth and mystery that has not grown old and continues to be explosive, in art as in politics.

5. See below, "Criticism, Indeterminacy, Irony."

CHAPTER TWO

The Sacred Jungle 1: Carlyle, Eliot, Bloom

In the conclusion to his comprehensive work *The Symbolism of Evil,* Paul Ricoeur calls us "the children of criticism," who "seek to go beyond criticism by means of a criticism that is no longer reductive but restorative." The intellectual scheme revealed by those words goes back to the German Romantics. It presupposes that as moderns we aim at a second naiveté in and through critical reflection. It also presupposes that the concepts of immediacy and of the sacred ("the immediacy of the symbol") are identical and that it is the aim of restorative criticism to disclose that identity. Criticism, as a form of *romantic* irony, rediscovers hermeneutics, for in its very negativity it becomes a mode of discovery. True irony, Friedrich Schlegel writes in his notebooks, is not merely a striving for something without end (*Unendlichkeit*); it is the attempt to possess it by a "micrological" thoroughness in both poetical and philosophical matters. This education toward living in the Universal (*Bildung zum Unendlichen*) Schlegel also characterized as "applied mysticism." Ricoeur is a late if effective proponent of insights into the way that the negative converts itself and allows our penchant for interminable analysis to understand and even appreciate its apparent opposite: religious or enthusiastic forms of closure. "I can still today communicate with the sacred," affirms Ricoeur, "by making explicit the prior understanding that gives life to the interpretation. Thus hermeneutics, an acquisition of 'modernity,' is one of the modes by which that 'modernity' transcends itself, insofar as it included forgetfulness of the sacred." Alluding to Heidegger by way of Bultmann, Jung, and others, Ricoeur continues: "I believe that Being can still speak to me—no longer, of course, under the precritical form of immediate belief, but as the second immediacy aimed at by hermeneutics."

Words like these remain in touch with Romantic philosophies of history which predicted that we would emerge from the dark passage of an age of doubt and criticism into a new, more organic or total belief.[1] A similar "principle of hope," though shadowed about by the image of gyres or the cyclical and eternal wheel of time, continues to shape Yeats's *A Vision.* A beautiful machine converting old myth into fresh credence, Yeats's prose poem is a construction looking toward the same change as these speculative histories, which he turns into a unanimous philosophy of symbols. But there exist, in our own century, countless if less vigorous testaments for the rebirth of the supernatural through intellectual and even technological means. When we read in 1935 that the true potentiality of film lies "in its unique faculty to express by natural means and with incomparable persuasiveness all that is fairylike, marvelous, supernatural" (Franz Werfel), we find ourselves back in the Romantic period, in the days of *Lyrical Ballads* (1798), when Wordsworth's new realism aimed to "excite a feeling analogous to the supernatural," while Coleridge would take supernatural events and procure for them a provisional belief.

To connect the issue of achieving a second immediacy ("to reestablish response in depth through conceptual mediation")[2] with that of the reanimation of symbols from art or religion clari-

1. This positive nihilism had already reached a high point in Novalis's "Genuine anarchy is the generative element of religion" ("Wahrhafte Anarchie is das Zeugungselement der Religion"), which comes from his essay "Christianity or Europe" (1799), written with the experience of the French Revolution in mind. Heine, looking back on those romantic, all-embracing nihilists, remarked nastily that Friedrich Schlegel was so inclusive in his perspective because his vantage point was really a church tower.

2. See Terence Des Pres, "Prophecies of Grace and Doom: The Function of Criticism at the Present Time," *Partisan Review* 42 (1975): 277. Cf. my "Romanticism and Anti-Self-Consciousness" in *Beyond Formalism.* A powerful defense of Hegelian conceptual mediation ("denkende Vermittlung") comes when Hans-Georg Gadamer criticizes historicist or objectivist reconstruction as a mode of self-forgetfulness. See *Truth and Method,* p. 150.

fies the importance of the Romantic movement as well as its subsumption by Hegel. "The principle of restoration," he wrote, "is found in thought, and thought only: the hand that inflicts the wound is also the hand that heals it." That hand, that *main-tenant,* haunts modern artists and intellectuals alike. Though merely a figure of speech, it points to the literal hand that writes the figure being reanimated.

That I move so quickly, using quotations, should not obscure the great divide that opened between Continental and Anglo-American thought in the nineteenth century. The distrust in England and America of Hegelian or "conceptual" mediation was never entirely allayed by French intermediaries, of whom Ricoeur is only one of the latest. Nor could a poet succeed, even when as strong and influential as Yeats. At the confluence of French and British traditions, Yeats's system, expounded most fully in *A Vision,* tried to revive the ancient, moribund symbols for a hyperconscious readership. Only by ancient symbols, he said, can a "highly subjective art escape from the barrenness of a too conscious arrangement into the abundance and depth of nature."

Yeats proved to be too mannered-magical; or it became obvious that his beautiful machine was driven by a Gothic motor. The situation in England and America between the wars was, in any case, so complex that I can only guess at causes that lay behind an evident result. Anglo-American critics did not see *through* French culture to German lines of thought with which the Symbolist precursors of Yeats and Eliot were still in touch. They continued to follow an anti-self-consciousness tradition of their own, which placed the "dissociation of sensibility," or the unfortunate and purely hypothetical separation of thinking and feeling, or saying and being, somewhere in the seventeenth century. It seemed to be post Donne or post Shakespeare or—in one polemical version—the work of Milton, his inhibiting and antivernacular effect on the living language.

The revaluation of Romanticism is a special feature of post–New Critical or revisionist criticism in America. The term *revisionist,* in fact, is perhaps most appropriately applied to the rethinking of literary history now going on, which questions a periodization that has given "modernity" a polemical and prestigious life separated from Romantic origins. But the revision that is occurring is not a matter of redressing the balance, or adjusting claims, or seeing continuities rather than discontinuities: it thrusts us back into an awareness of the problematic persistence of enthusiastic, poetic, and even archaic forms in contemporary life.

This chapter cannot summarize what so many scholar-critics have worked at faithfully over the past thirty years. Nor can it put together the jigsaw-puzzle relationship of European and Anglo-American thought in the area of literary understanding. But I can describe as a foreshortened historical sequence the forgetting of Romantic, and especially German Romantic, thinking. To recover from the "forgetfulness of the sacred" we have first to remember that other attempt to deal with an apparently archaic or daemonic subject matter in a "modern" way. It is not, of course, the German element that is crucial, and it would need, in any case, a more specialized study to show why German Romanticism was seminal. We would also need a consideration of the role of French thinkers, both artists and critics, in mediating radical German thought; and other European figures, like Croce and Ortega, might be considered. Even in England the turn away from German Romantic thought was not absolute; an expansive and focal mind like Walter Pater's, able to refine so much strange knowledge, from pagan times to Hegel, throws a prose bridge over those severed traditions and allows a resonance of their accommodation to persist in subsequent thinkers. Not only Yeats but also Stevens echo Pater's mode of philosophical criticism: unschematic, refracted, mobile, though more persistently profiled than Emerson's.[3] I hope that the ensuing historical sketch can suggest the intricate relation

3. Pater's *The Renaissance* (1873), his remarkable Bildungsroman *Marius the Epicurean* (1885), and even *Plato and Platonism* (1893) transcend apology, tract, and familiar essay: they may provide, after Coleridge, the first English (rather than German) instances of "philosophical literature." It is no accident that the inaugural quotation in *Plato and Platonism* is from the *Cratylus* dialogue that discusses "in what proportion names, fleeting names, contribute to our knowledge of things." Like Shelley, Pater understands the cohabitation of skeptical and visionary thought in Plato. The complex arc that joins Shelley (especially his *Defence of Poetry*, composed in 1821 but not published till 1840) to Emerson and Pater and curves back to Heideggerian philosophy as well as to French "Travels in Cratylia" is suggested by a comment on Socratic irony in chapter 7 of *Plato and Platonism*. Noting how often "it may chance to be" is used in Plato, Pater comments: "The Philosopher of Being, or, of the verb 'To be,' is after all afraid of saying 'It is'."

of critical and creative, and sometimes critical and religious, elements in post-Enlightenment society. To that end, also, I devote a further chapter to Walter Benjamin, who among modern critics understood Romantic origins best.

> What is lacking in England, and has always been lacking, that half-actor and rhetorician knew well enough, the absurd muddle-head Carlyle, who sought to conceal under passionate grimaces what he knew about himself: namely, what was *lacking* in Carlyle —real *power* of intellect, real *depth* of intellectual perception, in short, philosophy.
>
> —Nietzsche, *Beyond Good and Evil*

In England, the most sophisticated anti-Romanticism came from Matthew Arnold. He claimed that while the English Romantics were writers with great energy and creative force, they did not "know" enough, and so missed the chance of becoming universal figures, like Goethe. They could not transcend their national and parochial base.[4] T. S. Eliot, in an introduction to his first collection of essays, *The Sacred Wood* (1920), quotes Arnold on the Romantics and adds: "This judgment . . . has not, so far as I know, ever been successfully controverted." In *The Use of Poetry and the Use of Criticism* a dozen years later, he expands Arnold's list. "We should be right too, I think, if we added that Carlyle, Ruskin, Tennyson, Browning, with plenty of energy, plenty of creative force, had not enough wisdom. Their culture was not always well-rounded; their knowledge of the human soul was often partial and often shallow." Who, then, will escape whipping? If there is one criterion that distinguishes the present movement in criticism from that prevailing, more or less, since Eliot, it is a better understanding and higher evaluation of the Romantic and nineteenth-century writers.

4. See "The Function of Criticism at the Present Time" in *Essays in Criticism* (1865): "It has long seemed to me that the burst of creative activity in our literature, through the first quarter of this century, had about it, in fact, something premature. . . . the English poetry of the first quarter of this century, with plenty of energy, plenty of creative force, did not know enough. This makes Byron so empty of matter, Shelley so incoherent, Wordsworth even, profound as he is, yet so wanting in completeness and variety."

In Arnold's estimate of the Romantics, there is more irony than truth. For revisionist studies have shown that these same Romantics were clairvoyant rather than blind precursors of later movements that tended to disown them while simplifying the radical character of their art. The irony deepens when we recall that philosophical criticism in the German style was *almost* introduced to England via Coleridge's *Biographia Literaria.* But Coleridge broke off the attempt with the excuse that he wished to reserve such "Constructive Philosophy" for his never-written *Logosophia.* Chapter 13 of the *Biographia* is interrupted by what might be called a *letter* from Porlock (Locke? Poor Luck?); that is, from a very prudent, practical-minded friend advising Coleridge not to proceed further in his kind of hypostatic discourse. Philosophical criticism, therefore, which had attained a first flowering in the work of Schiller, Fichte, Schelling, and the Schlegels, was to develop chiefly within a German matrix. It became increasingly alien to the English mind.[5] While the two countries remained, for a while, eager to learn from each other in matters of art, in matters of criticism a serious split—a real "two cultures" situation —soon emerged.

It manifests itself as early as Carlyle's *Sartor Resartus,* composed in 1830–31, only fifteen years after Coleridge's *Biographia.* Here, indeed, English is a "Babylonish dialect" made of Germanisms, Swiftian gusto, and a baroque simulacrum of the earthy, archaizing diction of northern England. The book's crazy, mockingbird style is meant to be a nauseous cure or asafetida for British empiricism. "Teufelsdröckh," the name of its hero-author, means devil-dirt, or possibly devil-print. "Diogenes," his first name, means divinely born.

Matthew Arnold, recognizing the un-English character of the style, issued the warning: "Flee Carlylese as you would the devil." The rough, Germanizing wit of *Sartor* shows not only that, as in medieval times, wit and mystery go together, but it inserts an English work into a tradition which remains almost exclusively

5. "I have read some of Hegel and Fichte, as well as Hartley . . . and forgotten it; of Schelling I am extremely ignorant at first hand, and he is one of the numerous authors whom, the longer you leave unread, the less desire you have to read" (Eliot, *The Use of Poetry and the Use of Criticism*).

Teutonic, and leads from Luther through Jean Paul Richter to Nietzsche and Thomas Mann (compare *Dr. Faustus*). Nietzsche, though always keeping his distance from Carlyle, may have owed to him part of his awareness that no previous age was as prepared "for a Carnival in the grand style, for laughter and a high-spirited revelry, for transcendental flights of sublime nonsense" (*Beyond Good and Evil*). In "The Function of Criticism" of 1923, Eliot quotes from the editorial columns of an unspecified newspaper which not only associates "humorous" with "nonconformist" qualities, but attributes this combination to "the unreclaimed Teutonic element" in the English character.

Carlyle's remarkable style is, I am suggesting, an aspect of his covert transfusion of Northern religious enthusiasm (directly described by Walter Scott when dealing with the Covenanters in *Old Mortality*) into German nature-enthusiasm and its transcendental symbolics. Carlyle maintains, of course, a defensively humorous distance from Teufelsdröckh's exotica by pretending to be his editor. But the problem of distance is a complex one: it involves defining the genre of a book that is at once commentary and fiction.

The "Clothes Philosophy" of *Sartor* stresses mediation: it distances humanity from nakedness, nature, even from the textual source (Teufelsdröckh's German manuscript, supposedly discovered by the "editor"), which is presented in *Sartor* only in an excerpted or retailored ("resartus") form. "We never get Teufelsdröckh unmediated," says G. B. Tennyson. But no writer who goes through the detour of a text gets himself unmediated.

Carlyle's disgust, moreover, at this potentially infinite regress of mediation—even though it provides a saving distance from absolute inwardness or solipsism—is quite obvious. His solution is to foreground the mediatory process, to make the writer's distance from any source so palpable that the retailored text is endowed with a factitious presence of its own. The very feel of *Sartor* depends on the "fragments, the titles, the passages taken from here and there, the works unfinished or stopped in mid-passage . . . double and single quotation marks for passages cited, and editorial interpolation in the midst of quotations" (G. B. Tennyson). It is as if something groundless were being foregrounded—which, taken out of metaphysics or German *Naturphilosophie* and articulated as a theory of language, could evoke Heidegger and Derrida.

The formal effect, in any case, is a fading of the distinction between original and commentary. Quotation is king, yet everything is quotation. In *Sartor* criticism has found its carnival colors. Carlylese, instead of being a metalanguage, merges with the idiom of its source: its originality is its impurity, the contamination of gloss and original. But since the source is invented, Carlylese is actually a self-educing prose, maintained by the fiction not of a source alone, but of a source that needs an editor-translator-interpreter. Here is feigning indeed, though in the service of criticism.

Yet equally—this is the Puritan joker—in the service of religion. For Carlyle's attitude toward Teufelsdröckhian metaphysics is exploitative as well as empathic. German metaphysics, he wrote, is "a disease expelling a disease." He thought of it as literally the *crisis* and providentially appointed cure in the long illness of unbelief or excessive self-consciousness. It would eventually consume itself. He too may have the disease, since it is contagious, part of the "Spirit of the Age"; but the fever of his style has its creative as well as suffering aspect.

Sartor, then, is the Age of Criticism producing—out of itself as it were—a fiction. The Negative is converted into Being, to echo Hegel; and this holds for the verbal style and genre of the book as clearly as for its famous journey from "The Everlasting No" to "The Everlasting Yea." We are dealing not with a historical curiosity but with a creative historiographical act—a revision of the English language which succeeded more in America (if we think of Melville's prose) than in England. Carlylese is a richer and rougher English, one that pretends to be contaminated by German; yet the German source is simply a device that motivates a different critical idiom. An enthusiastic type of criticism replaces an English type which was, and continues to be despite Carlyle, a critique of enthusiasm.

The issue of enthusiasm is not separable from that of religion, and could draw us into a complex analysis of the relation of literary style to religion and politics. The relation of enthusiasm to political fanaticism is a fearful reality that hovers over English history and the establishment of *via media* institutions from the reign of Elizabeth on. Literary criticism like everything else became a *via media* institution. Though the fear of enthusiasm gradually receded into the *angustiae* of the Gothic novel it was given a temporary renewal by the French Revolution with its regicide, its Reign of Terror, and its atheistic religion of reason.

It seems hardly credible, therefore, that the future author of *The French Revolution* (1837), who began *Sartor* in the year of the July revolution (1830), and failed to place his book with a publisher, perhaps because of the Reform Bill agitation, should so neglect the French scene. But the Northern (Anglo-*Saxon*) and Calvinist axis was the essential one for him, in terms of the difficult relation of literature, religion, and enthusiasm. Eighteenth-century Paris had been a mere *hortus siccus,* the "most parched spot in Europe," and even French revolutionary turmoil served only to reveal the poetry in history, to heave up huge symbols of repressed religiosity that pointed to the real creative ferment of mankind —religious rather than secular, religion struggling with the secular, and criticism with belief.

That *Sartor* uses one culture to criticize or complete another is not the important thing, however daringly performed. Its recovery of the relation of criticism to enthusiasm—to the religious question—and its understanding of what is common to criticism and fiction are more crucial. In these matters Carlyle is a genuine precursor of the philosophical critics of today.

Criticism differs from fiction by making the experience of reading explicit: by intruding and maintaining the persona of editor, reviewer, reader, foreign reporter, and so forth. Our struggle to identify—or not to—with imaginative experience, usually in the form of a story, is what is worked through. Both paradigmatically and personally the critic shows how a reader's instincts, sympathies, defenses are now solicited and now compelled. The psychological drama of reading centers on that aroused merging: a possible loss of boundaries, a fear of absorption, the stimulation of a sympathetic faculty that may take over and produce self-alienation.

This is felt to be too threatening even now whenever a critic fudges the line between commentary and fiction—this *merging,* which most criticism methodically *prevents,* but which Carlyle *represents.* After Carlyle, the "explicit reader" enters certain American authors (Poe and Melville, for example) in the fictional guise of a narrator who has barely escaped a visionary merger, or else as a too palpable authorial presence. In a countertradition, that of Flaubert and James, the author disappears, or evokes what has been called an "implicit author." But the emphasis remains on the sympathetic imagination, or on an enthusiast always about to merge, out of idealism, with the destructive element.

Should we discount the psychic danger of merging—the anxiety it evokes even in such formal activities as reading—an obverse difficulty may appear. This is the tendency to distance oneself too much, to make of distance a defense by claiming that origins are fake or contaminated or (at best) motivating fictions. It can lead to something that parallels Gnosticism's separation of the pure origin or pure good from a world created by the usurpatory demiurge; so "Teufelsdröckh" and his "editor" find themselves in unexpected theological company. The issue such an analysis raises is, again, the relation of fiction, criticism, and theology.

How much is implied by Emerson's famous statement in "Self-Reliance" (1841) that in reading others our rejected thoughts return with a certain alienated majesty? Could it imply identity with the pure origin, and a falling away from it when we lack self-reliance? "By our own spirits are we deified," Wordsworth wrote of poets in their strength: it is an extreme form of Gnosticism from its optimistic, even manic side.

"But thereof come in the end despondency and madness," Wordsworth adds. There is a dark obverse to the quest for autonomy and originality. What Emerson says of our reading can also be said of our dreams. We eventually recognize them as our rejected thoughts coming back with a fearful or majestic luster. The question is whether we *can* acknowledge them as ours. To do so is to take responsibility for them; to take on, for good or bad, a certain sublimity. In his optimistic moments Emerson sees no problem in this. Yet the distortions of the dream-work itself, and the many anti-self-consciousness theories that spring up in the nineteenth century, indicate there is a problem. So Carlyle talks in *Characteristics* of the "ideal unconscious," a strange notion when we think of how Freud viewed the unconscious at the end of the century.

A revisionist like Harold Bloom approaches Gnosticism from that darker, Freudian side. He calls his special theory of reading one of "misreading" because he stands close to a negative Emersonianism. We know the possible sublimity in us, but knowing it implies we have purchased knowledge by its loss. Bloom regards each writer as a demiurge who falsifies or "misreads" his source, which is always more sublime—namely, the canonized text of another writer-demiurge. Initially, Bloom honored William Blake as the great revisionist who was not cowed by the Bible, who used the Gnostic argument to deny ultimate authority to the biblical writings. The Bible was Urizenic, the book of the demiurge, a misreading to be corrected. Blake went even beyond Milton in claiming to reenvision the "Eternals" who existed before the demiurgic god of this world—and his bible and religion—were created. An essential turn in Bloom's perspective came when he saw that Blake was as self-deceived as every writer who made this claim: Blake is, if anything, less original than the Milton who figures as the Teufelsdröckh of his poetry. According to *The Anxiety of Influence* and its sequels, no return to a point before creation, or Milton's recreation of it, is possible; there is, likewise, no one true reading but only a series of misreadings that compete in the world against each other and for the text.

Misreading is a wrong-headed term, more spirited than helpful. It alerts us to the fact that reading is not purely disinterested, or contemplative, or theoretical. It is as practical as the English tradition has always claimed. Yet this tradition, by adapting and simplifying a scientific ideal, reduced practical to utilitarian, or to whatever might be communicated without error.

I would like to convert Bloom's insights into the following reflections. Are not intense readings, like Cartesian doubt, a complex defense against a *dieu trompeur*—that is, against the author-demiurge of that strange, wonderful, seductive reality we call a fiction? Fictions, in this light, are fabrications that make us aware, by a kind of contagion, of the artificial or magical force of all constructions, including those of science. The nightmare of being deceived is now roused in broad daylight; we move, like Descartes (see his *First Meditation*) or like Carlyle's Teufelsdröckh, among garmented ghosts.

Bloom tries to codify the defense mechanisms that characterize the creative writer—or, for that matter, the creative reader. Reading at its closest leads to the counterfabrication of writing, just as writing involves a "misreading" of prior writers. We cannot gain real insight into an artist or ourselves by pure contemplation, only by the contemplation that making (*poesis*) enables.

The analogy that Bloom draws between critical and fictional thought is reinforced by an analogy between critical and religious thought, despite the fact that criticism as a distinct activity with scientific hopes was often in conflict with religious systems. Bloom brings in parallels from heterodox religious movements, or uncovers the heterodox—especially Gnostic—impulse in orthodox ones. In his psychotheology the sourcy demiurge has to be at once incorporated and repressed by the new poet-demiurge. When Wordsworth claims to "pass unalarmed" Milton's apocalyptic visions, "Jehovah—with his thunder, and the choir of shouting Angels, and the empyreal thrones," Bloom sees it as a self-curtailment or sacrifice: it allows Wordsworth to pass *Milton* unalarmed, in order to take possession of his own subject: "The Mind of Man, / My haunt, and the main region of my song." Literary autonomy is conceived as a freeing of oneself from an influential master by a curtailment or sacrifice of this kind.

According to Bloom, then, poetic history, at least since Milton, unfolds as a series of sacrifices. Each poet advances into Modernity "more . . . Flying from something that he dreads, than [like] one / Who sought the thing he loved." A catastrophic theory of creation is suggested that resembles Nietzsche's demystification of ascetic ideals in *The Genealogy of Morals* (1887), the calculus of progression and regression in Ferenczi's *Thalassa* (1924), and the counterevangelical picture of progress that Walter Benjamin personified in his well-known "Theses on the Philosophy of History" (1940):

> One would have to picture the angel of history like this. His face is turned toward the past. Where *we* perceive a chain of events, *he* sees one single catastrophe which keeps piling wreckage upon wreckage, and hurls it in front of his feet. The angel

> would like to stay, awaken the dead, and make whole what has been wrecked. But a storm is blowing from Paradise; it has got caught in his wings with such violence that the angel can no longer close them. This storm irresistibly propels him into the future to which his back is turned, while the pile of debris before him grows skyward. This storm is what we call progress.[6]

That criticism is a contemporary form of theology will seem sadly obvious to those who object to its inflation. That criticism should resemble fiction in its passionate or enthusiastic qualities is also accepted only by way of pejorative comment. Yet when Eliot calls his earliest collection *The Sacred Wood* he hints at a problem that concerns him throughout his career: the relation of both criticism and poetry to the religious sphere. In *The Use of Poetry and the Use of Criticism* of 1933 he quotes Jacques Rivière: "It is only with the advent of Romanticism that the literary act came to be conceived as a sort of raid on the absolute and its result a revelation." This time, however, Eliot's purpose is not to attack the Romantics but to point out that this kind of Romanticism includes "nearly everything that distinguishes the last two hundred and fifty years or so from their predecessors." Left unclear is whether we preserve the sacred wood by staying outside or by raiding it. Eliot at least acknowledges that the great writers of the modern period have considered trespass or profanation inevitable.

Such books as Bloom's *Kabbalah and Criticism* do not seem to inhabit the same world of discourse as Eliot's. The language, the materials, the mode of self-presentation—it is all very different. Yet *kabbalah* (literally, "reception") is one of the Hebrew words for tradition, and the sacred wood in this instance is the Bible as "received" by medieval interpreters calling themselves Kabbalists, who claim that their understanding of the sacred text is a literal and orthodox one. It is clear, however, that they have penetrated the wood—now more like a jungle—and are wildly, sublimely conscious of the danger of profanation.

It is the *relation* between poet, critic, and pre-text which fascinates Bloom; and the model of reception he takes from the

6. I have slightly modified the translation by Harry Zohn in *Illuminations*. For an extended discussion of this passage, see chapter 3.

Kabbalists is at once more systematic (theological) than anything in Eliot, and more personal. Profanation, as in Kafka's famous parable, is structured into the critical ritual, into the model as contemplated or applied. "Leopards break into the temple and drink the sacrificial chalices dry; this occurs repeatedly, again and again: finally it can be reckoned on beforehand and becomes part of the ceremony."

What this means when we consider a canon of secular authors rather than the Bible is that the "spiritual form" (Blake) of the dead writers returns upon the living, like those leopards. It has to be incorporated or appeased by tricks that resemble Freudian defense mechanisms. And in this there can be no progress, only repetition and elaboration—more ceremonies, sacrifices, lies, defenses. That we esteem these is the woe and wonder Bloom constantly commemorates. The literature of the past is an "unquiet grave."

For Eliot, however, this return of the dead is limited by a trust in the established religious ritual and an urbane thesis of impersonal integration. The thesis is not naïvely progressivist, yet it flatters our capacity to bear or recreate the past without the distortion or the sparagmos that Bloom insists is necessary. "The Poet has," Eliot declares, "not a 'personality' to express, but a particular medium, which is only a medium and not a personality, in which impressions and experiences combine in peculiar and unexpected ways."

The turn of this sentence makes it impossible to give "medium" a mystical or Yeatsian sense: it buries the dead and orders all things well. So does Eliot's most celebrated statement, which hovers at the edge of an unexpressed theology of communion or psychology of incorporation. "Someone said: 'The dead writers are remote from us because we *know* so much more than they did.' Precisely, and they are that which we know" ("Tradition and the Individual Talent," 1919).

Thus, the corpses that sprout and speak in *The Waste Land* are carefully reduced to voices moving symphonically through a poem that acts as their requiem. "They are that which we know"; Eliot's muted evocations make us realize it. A remarkable achievement, quite close to the madness of hearing inner voices, of being "impersonalized" that way, but the voices, or ghosts, are kept within the locus of the poem, shut up there as in a daemonic wood. In their asylum is our peace.

It is not a wood, of course, but an "Unreal City," and Eliot's vision of it is as urbane as the modern religious sensibility permits. I feel tempted to put beside it the surreality of Teufelsdröckh's Mad Hatter in the "O'Clo' " district of London:

> Friends! trust not the heart of that man for whom Old Clothes are not venerable. Watch, too, with reverence, that bearded Jewish High-priest, who with hoarse voice, like some Angel of Doom, summons them from the four winds! On his head, like the Pope, he has three Hats,—a real triple tiara; on either hand are the similitude of wings, whereon the summoned Garments come to alight; and ever, as he slowly cleaves the air, sounds forth his deep fateful note, as if through a trumpet he were proclaiming: "Ghosts of Life, come to Judgement!"

It is a difficult and impressive transmogrification, almost a return of the Wandering Jew. The baseless fabric of the vision, however, soon appears. "To most men," Carlyle adds, "as it does to ourselves all this will seem overcharged. We too have walked through Monmouth Street; but with little feeling of 'Devotion': probably in part because the contemplative process is so fatally broken in upon by the brood of money-changers who nestle in that Church, and importune the worshipper with merely secular proposals." The episode is simply a cadenza to Carlyle's or Teufelsdröckh's transcendentalist argument. The ghostliness of things appears when the body is stripped from the clothes rather than vice versa, when the *nakedness* of the clothes is exhibited. A moment of "natural supernaturalism" is created. Carlyle jokes that it may have been in Monmouth Street "at the bottom of our English 'ink-sea,' that [Teufelsdröckh's] remarkable Volume first took being."

To find anything comparable to Carlyle's visionariness we must go not to the pale Orientalism Addison tries out in his parable of Mirzah's Hill ("Then is Monmouth Street a Mirzah's Hill, where, in motley vision, the whole Pageant of Existence passes awfully before us," Carlyle writes of the same episode) but to Blake, De Quincey, and spectral moments in Jean Paul—or to

France. There are found the true hustlers of the East. Victor Hugo formulates his theory of the *grotesque,* and Balzac creates supermimetic figures, characters from low or bourgeois life bathed in a visionary atmosphere. Somewhat later Baudelaire, one of Eliot's sources, will understand the traumatic rather than urbane aspects of allegory. Reduced by Neoclassicism to a genteel notation —yet preserving a hidden life which kept it authentic even in abbreviated form—allegory now turns monstrous in its very urbanity. It transforms the playful ghostliness of Gothic artists and discloses the real unreality, the quotidian shocks of the city.[7]

Eliot is not concerned with intellectual revolution or a mediumistic profaning of the dead, but with purifying the language, with enabling it to digest—if it must—a "heavy fund of historical and scientific knowledge." One result of this conservatism is a distrust of "ideas," that is, excess baggage of a spiritual or intellectual kind. Allegory that tends to overload language either by pictorializing the newest science (e.g., Newtonianism in the eighteenth century) or reconciling an archaic with a more refined form of belief (Christian typology, Spenser's "dark conceit")—allegory as free-form science or free-form theology—is subdued to a poetics of the image. Eliot's conservative Modernism identifies the poet's critical or intellectual ability mainly with that of purification, the filtering out of "mere ideas" or technical terms not yet polished into poetic diction.

Therefore his anger at Gilbert Murray's archaic translation of Euripides and his backhanded compliments to those "delightful writers" who "burrow in the origins of Greek myths and rites; M. Durkheim, with his social consciousness, and M. Levy-Bruhl, with his Bororo Indians who convince themselves that they are parro-

7. In his studies of Baudelaire and in *The Origin of German Tragic Drama* (a meditation, first published in 1927, on the emblematic and Baroque *Trauerspiel* of seventeenth-century Germany), Walter Benjamin recovers a powerful theory of allegory. Paul de Man and others have demonstrated that Benjamin obliges us to revise (1) the distinction between symbol and allegory, which valued the former over the latter, and (2) a view of literary history that placed the French *Symbolistes* and such English poets as Yeats and Eliot under the poetics of the symbol. The revisionists argue either that the symbol is not a *symbole* (which remains close to allegory) or that a theory of symbols, often drawing on Coleridge's understanding of Goethe and Schelling, but neglecting Coleridge's own art, distorted the study of poetics during the "Modernist" period.

quets." Therefore too his dismissal of "a curious Freudian-social-mystical-rationalistic-higher-critical interpretation of the Classics and what used to be called the Scriptures." Eliot does not deny our intellectual or spiritual burdens, but he would like critics and poets to meet them as problems of craft, translation, and verbal digestion.

"We need a digestion," he writes in 1920, "which can assimilate both Homer and Flaubert. We need a careful study of Renaissance Humanists and Translators, such as Mr. Pound has begun. We need an eye which can see the past in its place with its definite differences from the present, and yet so lively that it shall be as present to us as the present." By the time of his famous essay "From Poe to Valéry" (1948) that Renaissance optimism has faded into a mood strangely close to Freud's *Civilization and Its Discontents.* The burdens of language may be too great.

> This advance of self-consciousness, the extreme awareness of and concern for language which we find in Valéry, is something which must ultimately break down, owing to an increasing strain against which the human mind and nerves rebel; just as, it may be maintained, the indefinite elaboration of scientific discovery and invention, and of political and social machinery, may reach a point at which there will be an irresistible revulsion of humanity and readiness to accept the most primitive hardships rather than carry any longer the burden of modern civilization.

Seen against the background of Eliot—and acknowledging the integrity of a career that tried to save neoclassical standards of decorum from being swamped by "the burden of modern civilization"—the appearance of Bloom is a Teufelsdröckhian event. A ghostly and tricky dimension enters which plays havoc with the established rituals of criticism. It is not merely that a critic like Bloom is impure, that he makes no attempt to fend off the vocabulary or conceptual novelties of the "Sciences of Man." But the entire enterprise of criticism becomes unreal: no longer a distinct, well-fenced activity, delimiting mine and thine. The critic does not pretend to forget himself in the work of art, as the artist had presumably done in creating it: the consciousness of tradition produces something quite different from the "extinction" of personality Eliot sought as his ideal. It makes every strong literary personality of the past into Hamlet's father's ghost, a revenant and a "questionable shape."

The interpreter now evokes the writers of the past in such an engaged and personal way that it is *more* difficult for us to "digest" or "assimilate" them. There is a dyspeptic quality about Carlyle's prose: the dead do not rest lightly on the cultural stomach:

> In the way of replenishing thy purse, or otherwise aiding thy digestive faculty, O British Reader, [Teufelsdröckh's book] leads to nothing, and there is no use in it; but rather the reverse, for it costs thee somewhat. Nevertheless, if through this unpromising Horn-gate, Teufelsdröckh, and we by means of him, have led thee into the true land of Dreams; and through the Clothes-Screen, as through a magical *Pierre-Pertuis,* thou lookest, even for moments, into the region of the Wonderful, and seest and feelest that thy daily life is girt with Wonder, and based on Wonder, and thy very blankets and breeches are Miracles. . . .

(For "blankets" and "breeches" read "defense mechanisms" or figures acting as such.)

Yet Carlyle saves poetry by allying it with transcendental feelings. These are dark even more than happy, of course: Wordsworthian "tremblings of the heart . . . to think that our immortal being / No more shall need such garments." We see through a clothes-screen darkly, because without that screen the specter of solipsism and the mystery of isolation—of being naked in the sight of God or segregated within the human community—would be too hard to bear. Carlyle's extreme Protestantism (which touches here a Hebraic denial of mediations) is relieved by this vision of a miraculous fabric of "organic filaments" that weave us together; yet the fabric seems to be literary rather than natural, or made principally of books, letters, writings. A fascinating sequence of thoughts leads Teufelsdröckh from the whimsical yet terrifying thought of solipsistic isolation—basically a discontinuity in the clothes-screen—to the more ghostly concept of Tradition which Bloom allows us to set against Eliot's:

> Wondrous truly are the bonds that unite us one and all; whether by the soft binding of Love, or the iron chaining of Necessity,

> as we like to choose it. More than once have I said to myself, of some perhaps whimsically strutting Figure, such as provokes whimsical thoughts: "Wert thou, my little Brotherkin, suddenly covered-up within the largest imaginable Glass-bell—what a thing it were, not for thyself only, but for the world! Post Letters, more or fewer, from all the four winds, impinge against thy Glass walls, but have to drop unread: neither from within comes there question or response into any Postbag; thy Thoughts fall into no friendly ear or heart, thy Manufacture into no purchasing hand: thou art no longer a circulating venous-arterial Heart, that, taking and giving circulatest through all Space and all Time: there has a Hole fallen out in the immeasurable, universal World-tissue, which must be darned-up again!"
>
> Such venous-arterial circulation, of Letters, verbal Messages, paper and other Packages, going out from him and coming in, are a blood-circulation, visible to the eye: but the finer nervous circulation, by which all things, the minutest that he does, minutely influence all men, and the very look of his face blesses or curses whomso it lights on, and so generates ever new blessing or new cursing: all this you cannot see, but only imagine.
>
> If now an existing generation of men stand so woven together, not less indissolubly does generation with generation. Hast thou ever meditated on that word, Tradition: how we inherit not Life only, but all the garniture and form of Life; and work, and speak, and even think and feel, as our Fathers, and primeval grandfathers, from the beginning, have given it us?—Who printed thee, for example, this unpretending Volume on the Philosophy of Clothes? Not the Herren Stillschweigen and Company: but Cadmus of Thebes, Faust of Mentz, and innumerable others whom thou knowest not. Had there been no Moesogothic Ulfila, there had been no English Shakespeare, or a different one. Simpleton! it was Tubalcain that made thy very Tailor's needle, and sewed that court-suit of thine.

Eliot could not have objected to the thought, but his names, Homer and Flaubert, are very different from Cadmus, Faust, Moesogothic Ulfila, and Tubalcain.

It will not do, though, to see a substantial identity of Bloom and Carlyle, with Bloom adding a different kind of strangeness to art: Hebrew-Gothic instead of Saxon-Gothic. For Bloom's role is more Satanic than Teufelsdröckh's, in the sense that he *ac-*

cuses poetry in order to save it. Or, to use a related figure, he engages on a Faustian wager against poetry, one that seeks to break the illusions of art by subjecting them to the extremest, the most reductive aspects of Freudian or Nietzschean analysis. He will not believe that art is consolation, or that poetry can endure as an abiding force unless it survives a greater degree of probing than the New Critics, even with their criterion of toughness, applied. Perhaps that is why he puts poems up against interpretations so different in their verbal decorum that the disjunction becomes alarming. A suspicion arises that the relation of the interpreter to his object is ambivalent. The poetry means too much, and that is the trouble with poetry: its presence, even as an object on the page, is so clear, and its claim on our voice so clear. Poetry makes a ghost of our own voice, though we ourselves do not always know that. There is always a "concealed offense" of this kind which is more important than any overt or "avant-garde" scandal.[8]

To uncover the offensiveness of poetry is to acknowledge that its greatness has not been integrated into our lives. The dead are that which we don't wish to know. When Eliot writes, "We need an eye which can see the past in its place with its definitive difference from the present, and yet so lively that it shall be as present to us as the present," he is giving life to a lie. A very attractive lie; but a great poem can only be "purified" of its greatness, not into greatness. Criticism betrays it to our sight.

In Shakespeare's *As You Like It,* Rosalind, disguised as Ganymede, asks her unsuspecting lover, Orlando, to woo her as Rosalind so that she might cure him of his love. This wooing has the kind of complexity Bloom restores to the interpretive relation. A disguised text asks us to woo it in the name of what it is, yet appears not to be. The reward is a marriage of true minds, though a delayed marriage that brings out a duplicity that helps to break

8. "Concealed offense" is Kenneth Burke's term, in his *Philosophy of Literary Form*. For Bloom that offense comes through the poet, because the latter writes inevitably in the shadow of the Hebrew Bible, and the poet can almost be defined as a concealed prophet, one who has "repressed the voice that is great within us." If we allow Eliot his revisionist quest for an authentically English (i.e. non-Roman) Catholicism, we should understand Bloom's quest for an English Hebraism.

desire into more sophisticated versions of its gratuitousness. Bloom is more Shakespearean than he knows, yet he sacrifices the mock labors or trials, so skillfully motivated by Shakespeare, to a tragic curtailment which language as language libido—as wit—bravely denies. His version of gnosis shows at best the valedictory fullness of the melancholy Jaques, whose language is always at odds with his wish to say "good-bye."

Gratuitousness of desire, fullness of language, and wit of interpretation surely go together. They make an "as you like it" that is free to feign yet not free not to feign. Neither Gnostic nor Gothic paradigms, however, do more than convert the unknown into the known, the unacknowledged influence of the *maiores* into a tragic trap. Art undoubtedly exhibits, like the tyranny of covenants and laws, "the vanity and presumption of governing beyond the grave" (Thomas Paine), but it also allows a response as free, imaginative, and self-tasking as its own must have been.

CHAPTER THREE

The Sacred Jungle 2: Walter Benjamin

It is but twenty-five years since Walter Benjamin's writings began to be published in full. Whatever the merit of this extraordinary man of letters, whom it has now become fashionable to invoke, his interest in both Marxist thought and Jewish mysticism has made him a war zone subject to incursions by competing factions. Is he a religious thinker, or is he a social thinker inspired primarily by Marxism? Though the terms of the debate seem naive, they suggest that religious and political modes of thought are enemy brothers disputing the same territory. After Marx and Freud, there is a tendency to make religion part of the problem rather than of the solution, and to expel it from the enlightened analysis of human experience. It is as if certain kinds of interpretation were exclusive, or as if the only way a new mode of understanding could legitimate itself was by dispossessing the old—according to the model of revolutionary action.

There are clearer thinkers than Benjamin in the Frankfurt School. Horkheimer indicts the social system with a moral fervor that is unashamed and cogent. "The blind sentence passed by the economy, that mightier social power which condemns the greater part of mankind to senseless wretchedness and crushes countless human talents, is accepted as inevitable and recognized in practice in the conduct of men." Or, "Individuality, the true factor in artistic creation and judgment, consists not in idiosyncracies and crotchets, but in the power to withstand the plastic surgery of the prevailing economic system which carves all men to one pattern." Quite possibly, there are also better literary sociologists than Benjamin. Adorno's early analysis of Kierkegaard, of his penchant for describing "Interiors," anticipates and rivals Sartre's capacity for detailed generalization. Yet Benjamin, who cannot let go of any ideas, whose prose thickens involuntarily, is often more interesting, not only because, as Horkheimer acerbly remarks about difficult writing in a one-dimensional age, "it may not be entirely senseless to continue speaking a language that is not easily understood" but also because that crowded language, in Benjamin, is, for reasons to be explored, curiously unprogressive or exitless.

In his major project on nineteenth-century life in Paris, Benjamin interprets Baudelaire as a historical sensor who recorded a shock at the epicenter of his work. The analysis is too fine and sustained to be summarized, but it tries to connect this shock with the experience of living in a giant city of the capitalist era. We are told that the mass of people, but also of sensations—of urban reality as constant sensory assault that isolates both worker and idler—is deeply imprinted on Baudelaire, even when it does not serve as an explicit theme. His lyric poetry is based on an "experience for which the shock experience has become the norm"; this shock is parried or absorbed by poems that are a fantastic combat, or more precisely a fantastic fencing match: "ma fantasque escrime."

The importance of Benjamin's analysis is not its truth, which may be trivial (because the experience of shock is so comprehensively conceived that he has no trouble in conjoining theories and remarks by Freud, Valéry, Marx, etc.) or unverifiable (because shock can only be studied by the hollow it leaves, by defenses presumed to be formed in its wake). The importance of his analysis resides first in the vigor with which it is carried, by analogy and metaphor, into all sectors of daily life, as into the subtlest aspects of literature; then in the unspoken rigor with which it excludes a rival perspective, the religious, that continues to haunt the features exposed by a socioeconomic interpretation.

Let me illustrate the first and energetic aspect of Benjamin's analysis by a quotation that seeks to establish how what is true of Baudelaire's lyric is true of life generally in the era of large-scale industrialization. "The shock experience has become the norm." This means that, like the medium of poetry, other media "process" shock or the constant impinging of "news":

> Man's inner concerns do not have their issueless private character by nature. They do so only when he has less of a chance to assimilate external concerns into his experience. Newspapers constitute one of many evidences that his chances have indeed lessened. If it were the intention of the press to have the reader assimilate the information it supplies as part of his own experience, it would not achieve its purpose. But its intention is just the opposite, and is achieved: to isolate what happens from the realm in which it could affect the experience of the reader. The principles of journalistic information (freshness of the news, brevity, comprehensibility, and, above all, lack of connection between the individual news items) contribute as much to this as does the make-up of the pages and the paper's style.[1]

The privatized individual, in short, is not a creation of Nature or God but a by-product of socioeconomic developments. Benjamin deplores that fact, but even more that we are losing the sense of isolatedness. For the alienating pressure of working conditions on the worker, or of the urban masses on the observer, becomes muted by the omnipotent technics of capitalist and totalitarian politics. They hold out the hope that the solitary can be made as adjustable as a machine that accomplishes many steps smoothly, actuated by a single touch. (The Nazi concepts of *Gleichschaltung* and *Anpassung,* which demanded the coordination under a unified command of all professions and activities,

1. This quotation, as well as the following one and the study on Baudelaire's sonnet, comes from "On Some Motifs in Baudelaire" (1939), found in *Illuminations,* ed. Hannah Arendt. I occasionally modify Harry Zohn's translation. The other major texts for Benjamin's work on Baudelaire from approximately the same period are "Paris, Capital of the 19th Century," translated by Edmund Jephcott for *Reflections,* a companion volume of selections, ed. Peter Demetz; and "Central Park," a series of aphorisms first published in vol. 1 of T. W. Adorno's edition of the *Schriften.* For an earlier discussion of the Baudelaire sonnet, see *Gesammelte Schriften,* vol. 1:22, pp. 547 ff. On Benjamin, cf. Fredric Jameson, *Marxism and Form,* pp. 60–83; Jürgen Habermas, "Consciousness-Raising or Redemptive Criticism" (1972), translated in *New German Critique,* no. 17 (1979); and T. W. Adorno, *Über Walter Benjamin.*

are ominously relevant here.) A push-button mentality emerges to alleviate the isolation it fosters. Servomechanisms that diminish our dependency on others, on organic types of social cohesion, eventually force us to become servomechanisms ourselves, within some rigid political machine; or else "strays" (comparable still to nineteenth-century *flâneurs*) who do not want to know their loneliness, and whose life is governed by tactile and optic experiences that function as mimetic shock absorbers.

> Of the countless movements of switching, inserting, pressing, and the like, the "snapping" of the photographer has had the greatest consequences. A touch of the finger now sufficed to fix an event for an unlimited period of time. The camera gave the moment a posthumous shock, as it were. Tactile experiences of this kind were joined by optic ones, such as are supplied by the advertising pages of a newspaper or the traffic of a big city. Moving through this traffic involves the individual in a series of shocks and collisions. At dangerous intersections, nervous impulses flow through him in rapid succession, like the energy from a battery. Baudelaire speaks of a man who plunges into the crowd as into a reservoir of electric energy. Using a periphrasis for the experience of shock, he calls this man "a *kaleidoscope* equipped with consciousness." . . . There came a day when a new and urgent need for stimuli was met by the film. In a film, perception in the form of shocks was established as a formal principle. That which determines the rhythm of production on the assembly line is the basis of the rhythm of reception in the film.

The second aspect of Benjamin's analysis—the exclusion, but really only the occlusion, of the religious perspective—is already apparent when we reflect that the word *shock* denotes an experience which used to fall into the category of ecstatic, mystical, or daemonic. Freud transferred the seed-time of that experience to the earliest years of development. Even if Benjamin should be right in evoking so strongly the normativeness of shock in contemporary society, the prematurity of the human organism that makes it trauma-prone is a biological fact independent of and relatively unaffected by the technological or industrial character of society. We all come crying into the light, ripped untimely from the womb. The human baby's long period of dependence means that overexposure, together with overprotection, is the very condition of infancy. Only the actualization in later psychic development of this trauma-prone stage may have a social determinant or be expressed in symbols taken from that area of experience. What Benjamin shows, then, is not the way shock is linked to a particular set of socioeconomic conditions, but *shock itself* in or under multitudinous forms of representation. The mystery of culture is how various, complex, and apparently limitless are these expressions of the supposedly fixating experience of shock.

Benjamin's analysis is buttressed by a reading of "A une passante," a Baudelaire sonnet in which, as Benjamin admits, the crowd is not named, though everything is said to hinge on it:

La rue assourdissante autour de moi hurlait.
Longue, mince, en grand deuil, douleur majestueuse,
Une femme passa, d'une main fastueuse
Soulevant, balançant le feston et l'ourlet;

Agile et noble, avec sa jambe de statue.
Moi, je buvais, crispé comme un extravagant,
Dans son oeil, ciel livide où germe l'ouragan,
La douceur qui fascine et le plaisir qui tue.

Un éclair . . . puis la nuit!—Fugitive beauté
Dont le regard m'a fait soudainement renaître,
Ne te verrai-je plus que dans l'éternité?

Ailleurs, bien loin d'ici! Trop tard! *Jamais* peut-être!
Car j'ignore où tu fuis, tu ne sais où je vais,
O toi que j'eusse aimée, ô toi qui le savais![2]

The poet's reaction to a fleeting glance is certainly marked by extravagance and shock ("Un éclair . . . puis la nuit"). But can we interpret what happens as the effect of city life on sexuality?

2. In the deafening street that howled all around me, / Tall, slender, in mourning dress, her grief majestic, / A woman passed by, her elegant hand / Raising and balancing the ceremonial hem; // Agile and noble, and her legs statuesque. / And I there drank, clenched like a man in a fit, / From her eyes, livid sky where storm is born, / Drank the softness that charms and the pleasure that kills. // A flash . . . then night! Beautiful fugitive, / Whose look has suddenly made me feel reborn, / Will I never see you again till eternity dawns? // Elsewhere, far from here! Too late! *Never* perhaps! / For I don't know your course, and you don't know mine, / O you I would have loved, o you who must have known it!

These verses, Benjamin writes, "reveal the stigmata which life in a metropolis inflicts on love." And, "What is unique in Baudelaire's poetry is that the images of women and death are permeated by a third, that of Paris." Baudelaire is said to suffer the kind of sexual shock that besets a person forced back on himself by the very crowd that brings the fascinating figure to him. Would we say the same thing about Dante, of his fugitive first and second meetings with Beatrice, described in *La Vita Nuova*? Florence too was a city, although not in the era of capitalism. Is not the literary or religious analogy stronger than the ideologically induced social interpretation?

It is, conventionally, religion that parries such numinous or libidinous images. "Fugitive beauté / Dont le regard m'a fait soudainement renaître" is indistinguishably gallant and religious in its diction, just as "je buvais . . . / Dans son oeil, ciel livide" is a perversion of such diction that evokes the poet's desire to liquidate distance, to incorporate by a vampirelike act the source of the image, or the very organ that allows it to be caught at a distance.

The rage for intimacy, for transgressing all distance, is the more striking in that the woman wears mourning. The poet's precipitation, though purely imaginary, consorts strangely with her dignified bearing. It is tempting, therefore, to view what happens as a hunt, and the sonnet's rhetoric as a "howling" that mingles tones of grief and rage, lust and loss (the French *hurler* in line 1 is related to the Latin *ululare*). Whether the poet is part of the pack or its victim remains unclear, but the woman appears on the scene as a noble animal, a deer in some fabulous rout, who would certainly have been the victim had not her allure returned that fate to the poet.

If this primitive, epiphanic resonance exists, the woman embodies in a modern or city context what Benjamin elsewhere defines as *aura*: "the unique phenomenon of appearing distant, however close a thing may be." She stands out, near yet far, in a physically or psychically crowded situation; and the poet's drive toward intimacy, his precipitation of spirit, seems to go toward death as much as rebirth. The ideal attracts him only in that splenetic, darkly haloed form.

How strange, then, that Benjamin did not use this sonnet to illustrate the decay of the aura at a time when the masses desire "to bring things 'closer' spatially and humanly."[3] He does, of course, later in the essay, appropriate and demystify Baudelaire's notion of "correspondences," and to that extent he secularizes the aura. The aura is something like an intimation of immortality, but with a contradictory aspect: it flashes up from within ordinary life, like epiphanic gleam or cathected desire, and it also defends against this shock by evoking a "pays natal" or *déjà vécu* that is deeply if abstractly fulfilling. (Wordsworth's "Ode: Intimations of Immortality from Recollections of Early Childhood" also apposes the darker or disruptive and the sustaining qualities of such visionary gleams.) But the connection between the transcendent and the secular or decayed function of the aura remains unclear. The aura is a kind of *news* that immediately disqualifies itself as such. It could even be regarded as a principle of psychic economy necessitated by the pressures of a real, capitalistic economy: a defense mechanism, that is, against shock, labor, and pure secularism.

Benjamin could have pointed out that the aura, in Baudelaire's sonnet, is indeed present as a sense of "correspondence" between *passant* and *passante,* that the fugitiveness of the glance exchanged (the glancing moment or "Augenblick") is of the essence. The *flâneur,* Benjamin once wrote, is the priest of the *genius loci* when that genius has lost its sacred and unique place, when it has become a wandering spirit or homeless voice. It is in the air as a startling image: the poem, then, or Baudelaire's quasi-priestly activity is to recover and inscribe those exilic images, to restore spirit to place, if only in a poem. The unreduced notion

3. For Benjamin's fullest discussion of the aura, see "The Work of Art in the Age of Mechanical Reproduction" (1936), in *Illuminations.* A review, written in 1929, of Franz Hessel's *Walking in Berlin,* already links aura and *genius loci* through the sensibility of the *flâneur.* Cf. Emerson in "The Poet" (1844) for a more pastoral-musical—and Swedenborgian—conception of the aura. "Over everything stands its daemon or soul. . . . The sea, the mountain-ridge, Niagara, and every flower-bed, pre-exist, or super-exist, in pre-incantations, which sail like odors in the air, and when any man goes by with an ear sufficiently fine, he overhears them and endeavors to write down the notes without diluting or depraving them. . . . The condition of true naming, on the poet's part, is his resigning himself to the divine *aura* which breathes through forms."

of the aura, applied directly to this sonnet, would have reintroduced the question of religious or cultic residues. Yet Benjamin was tempted to give his analysis its socioeconomic turn at the price of occluding a radically religious perspective.

The socioeconomic interpretation is not so much wrong as incomplete. Though powerful in its capacity to embrace interior and exterior, private and public, trivial and magnalian phenomena, it can become as facile in its insights as it is productive in the display of historical facts. There is no need to make the desire for intimacy, depicted by this sonnet, depend so closely on a supposed pressure of the masses and their deformation of the erotic life. Even if Benjamin's insight has virtual truth, the prior focus for interpretation is not sexuality in the context of city pressures but sexuality as it leads to guilty knowledge, to the knowledge of mutual nakedness (Genesis 3:7) in the primal scene of conscience as Western religion conceives it. That is not, perhaps, an exciting way to look at things—except that Baudelaire transforms the primal scene.

Something modern, a Parisian street, is made old again. The poet *infects* us with the thought that the mourner is hypocritical or that she is, as the sonnet's pointed ending implies, his "semblable." This imputation, a precious poison, acts as an imaginary bonding stronger than love. That he would have loved her is placed on a level with that she *knew* it, as if there were two things to be balanced: loss, or the missed opportunity of love, and the curious gain of guilty knowledge.

"O toi qui le savais!" The knowing glance, the complicity established by it, joins poet and woman more than sexual possession itself; the pleasure of the sin is less than knowing it is a sin. Pleasure kills (line 8), but what is desired is rebirth (line 10). Hence the reflections that turn the passerby into an accomplice are part of a moment of self-transcendence not of incrimination only. Baudelaire is religious rather than moralistic in evoking a quasi-sublime figure whose darkness might purify, or whose bearing is not affected by the imputed knowledge. She wears that knowledge as appropriately as mourning. Her mind, like her flesh, is statuesque: it suggests a realm—an *ailleurs*—beyond good and evil, even beyond corruptibility. She is indeed a "fleur" who holds out, fugitively, figuratively, the promise of new birth, a second innocence or "chair spirituelle" growing out of the suffering, the "mal" of the human condition.

The poet's despair of social existence, of bonding his life with another person's, is too radical to be given a social interpretation. That is why conventions such as mourning in grand style suggest to him unconscious hypocrisy; here the décor of mourning merely strengthens sexuality. The woman's visual impact is further aggrandized by the background of stunning noise; we feel her silence though no such attribute is mentioned; sight takes over, as "en grand deuil" tacitly becomes "en grand oeil." But sexuality itself is also degraded as a lasting means to intimacy. The possibility of union, of being one with another, is postponed to "eternity" (line 11) or utterly doubted. "Somewhere else, far from here! Too late! *Never* perhaps!"

Baudelaire's woman in black is in contradiction with time. She completes time because she arouses the sense of secret "correspondence." "O you who knew it" verges on "O you who always already knew it." The passing stranger seems to possess an eternal knowledge. The barest contact—a stolen glance—discloses that she is the poet's soul sister, independent of further proof or fulfilment. By that same token, however, she does not complete time but rather defers or ruins it. Fulfilment is projected onto a plane that is infinite or empty, perhaps both. She is originally, from eternity, elsewhere: *allegorical.*

In the beginning was mourning? We are not told what loss the *passante* has suffered, what she is mourning for; and from the poem's perspective Baudelaire himself is the mourner. The cause of mourning cannot be localized, and "Allegory exits empty-handed." In fact, since what the mourner knows can only be the very knowledge the poet is left with, she may be wearing the "grand deuil" for him: for a loss she must inflict, or a knowledge of loss which is his only fulfilment. By that anticipation she disorients all temporal perspectives. Time seems to mourn itself in this mother, madonna, mortal victim.

"Everything becomes Allegory for me," Baudelaire wrote in his poem "The Swan," and Benjamin agrees that "Baudelaire's genius, which is fed on melancholy, is an allegorical genius." The link between melancholy and allegory is also part of Benjamin's book on the German tragic drama (*Trauerspiel*). In the Baudelaire sonnet we seem to have a *Trauerspiel* in small; the poem discloses a discontinuity between existence and meaning, existence and values that come from existence. The same discontinuity led the German Baroque drama to its enlarged use of emblematic and allegorical writing. "Allegory dwells most permanently where transience and eternity clash most intimately." In his study on Baudelaire, such radically religious insight is transposed into a socioeconomic interpretation by a provocative though unprogressive *coup*. The two modes of interpretation, in fact, are so alike in Benjamin's hands that one must either reject his understanding of Marxist analysis or puzzle about a compatibility he has revealed.

> [To leave the sphere of pure theory] is, humanly speaking, only possible in two ways, either through religious or political observance. I cannot admit that there is a difference between them from a quintessential point of view. Nor yet any mediation. I am speaking of an identity that manifests itself only in the paradoxical transformation [*Umschlagen*] of the one into the other (whatever the direction), and only under the indispensable condition that every reflection on action is without reserve and conducted in a sufficiently radical manner.
>
> —Benjamin, Letter to Gershom Scholem, 29 May 1926

If the scandal of Benjamin's development as a critic lies in its apparently progressive yet radically unprogressive character, it may be that the very notion of progress—even of dialectical resolution—has become problematic, as in the allegorical Angelus Novus passage of "Theses on the Philosophy of History" (quoted above, in chapter 2). Benjamin locates his sense of an impasse between the claims of religion and politics in the very era of Baudelaire: Baudelaire and Marx are near-contemporaries, and both deal with the fact that "modernity . . . is always quoting primeval history." Take the modern city or metropolis: it reveals a subterranean life, as when a Parisian street in "La Passante" evokes a primitive scene. Perhaps following the lead of Marx's *The Eighteenth Brumaire* (1852), Benjamin interprets this regression as indicating a historical impasse. The ambiguity produced by the "submerged city" as it rises up in these poems means that the "law of dialectics" is at a standstill. The ambiguity is a contradiction that remains unproductive and converts everything into "cultural history," into picturable aesthetic commodities and a generalized fetishism that still fascinates the belated *flâneur* as he moves dreamily through those nineteenth-century Parisian arcades, sampling great things and small, *nouveautés* and *spécialités*.

"This standstill is utopia, and the dialectic image therefore a dream image." Many of Baudelaire's apparitions, including the *passante,* seem dreamlike or surrealistic: they arrest the poet, keep him confined within a world he knows too well. Benjamin criticizes Baudelaire for this *luxe,* for succumbing to novelty ("As in the seventeenth century the canon of dialectical imagery came to be allegory, in the nineteenth it is novelty") and to a version of *l'art pour l'art.* Sartre will come to a similar critique of Baudelaire; the observation cannot be taken lightly.

But if one looks not to the law of dialectics as it affects history; if one stays with the poem as a repetition of a *temporal* dilemma that has no clear issue, then that standstill could be valued by Benjamin, because it deepens the problematic relation of time and progress. Baudelaire renews allegory, though there is indeed a strain between allegory and modernity; but he also shows it to repeat the oldest wisdom we have. The "illusion of perpetual sameness" in Baudelaire does not reflect, as Benjamin asserts, "the illusion of novelty . . . like one mirror in another." It reflects the unredemptive, repetitive character of time, for which the only news would be the end of time, or as Benjamin said in an early "Theologico-Political Fragment": "Nature is Messianic by reason of its eternal and total passing away." This is the ultimate passage-work (*Passagenwerk*).

The relation of these different orders—the temporal (profane), the sacred, the political—might lead through Baudelaire back to Pascal, through Ernst Bloch to Spinoza, and through Gershom

Scholem to the tension between theocratic and mystical thought in Judaism. Yet Benjamin's work on Baudelaire, his most sustained project, tries to cut through the Sacred Jungle and build a One-Way Street (at the risk of its being a dead end)—just as Asja Lacis must have cut through him.[4]

Benjamin's first phase of Baudelaire studies concluded in 1924, when he published a translation of some of the *Fleurs du Mal* prefaced by his most explicitly theological essay, "On the Task of the Translator." His dissertation on the German tragic drama was completed shortly after this, in 1925, though not published till 1928; it was also during this time, after meeting Asja Lacis, and reading Lukács's *History and Class Consciousness,* that he began to experiment deliberately with the Marxist interpretation of literature.

The Baudelaire project thus divides clearly into a religious and a secular phase; but this fact does not provide its own interpretation. One phase displaces without replacing the other; the later phase involuntarily "quotes" the earlier and brings the interpretive activity into the winged yet unprogressive orbit of the Angelus Novus. What remains of this foundering motion is, nevertheless, powerful and symptomatic: the project, even in its dejected form, illustrates the relation between language and life. Though Benjamin eventually expands the interpretive focus beyond verbal kinds to all social artifacts, his exegetical powers were trained by biblical commentary; and it could be argued that the kind of analysis performed on a few extracts of the Talmud by the famous modern Hebrew poet Bialik (in his essay "Hallacha and Aggada," translated into German by Gershom Scholem, and

4. "This street is named Asja Lacis Street after her who as an engineer cut it through the author." Benjamin's epigraph to *One-Way Street* (aphoristic reflections first published in 1955) refers to a Latvian woman and radical thinker he met in 1924, with whom he fell in love, and who helped to sustain his interest in Marxist thought. A letter of 1931 from Gershom Scholem to Benjamin warns him that he might be "not the last but perhaps the most incomprehensible victim sacrificed to the confusion between religion and politics, the working-out of which in their genuine relation can be awaited from no one more confidently than from you." See the letter printed at the end of Gershom Scholem's *Walter Benjamin: Die Geschichte einer Freundschaft* (1975). The rhetorical complexity in Benjamin's writing is such that the One-Way Street never comes about.

known to Benjamin through that source) provided a model for him during both phases.[5]

In "Theses on the Philosophy of History," the question of the relation of religious to revolutionary forms of thought is renewed by way of paragraph-parables with some of the density of talmudic shorthand. The urgent prose of these fragments has a countdown character: it may express a fear of dispersion, with the exile and refugee fashioning his testamentary style, and it certainly expresses Benjamin's impasse concerning the idea of progress, together with an attempt to mobilize the more radical aspects of religious tradition for political purposes. Though historical materialism has as blind a belief in progress as any other secularism, it offers, according to Benjamin, the basis of a philosophy of action.

Aestheticism was never the answer. There must be action; yet the field of action, for the writer at least, includes the past: its relation to the crisis at hand. The force and complexity of biblical commentary helped to convince Benjamin that there was no simple location of historical meaning. The one-dimensional, progressive claims of conqueror or would-be conqueror are disabled by hermeneutic reflection. The past remains a dialectical field of forces and cannot be foreclosed by the pseudoappropriations of a totalitarian propaganda. "Only that historian," Benjamin writes, "will have the gift of fanning the spark of hope in the past who is firmly convinced that *even the dead* will not be safe from the enemy if he wins" (Thesis 6).

It is clear that Thesis 9, on the angel of history, subverts the very idea of winning. *In hoc signo vinces*? Any authentic reflection on history is a vision of ruins; and against philosophies of progress that discount the dead or vanquished Benjamin erects

5. C. N. Bialik, *Essays*. To show the mutual importance of the fluid, free-style commentary called "Aggada" and the dry legalism of the "Hallacha," Bialik reveals the latter's expressive potential, particularly how in its very density it reflected the existence of the Jews at that time, their struggle for survival through the preservation of the Bible and its language, their war against spiritual as well as physical dispersion. The relation of Hebrew to Aramaic, as of a sacred to a more profane tongue, was being worked out; and this battle, though taking place in the academies, was far from being academic. It involved—and still involved in Bialik's era, which saw the renewal of Hebrew—the destiny of the Jews, even if expressed by means of paradigmatic or legalistic issues.

this *Vexierbild* of the Bad News Angel. It is he who keeps the dead alive, that is deadly, who envisions for us their defeated force rather than their easy transumption by the latest political rhetoric. I want to look more closely at Benjamin's picture of this angel, because it raises formally the question of the function of images in his life.

An angel is a messenger, but the image is the message here. Stasis and stare predominate: the mouth itself stares. There is shock, as in Baudelaire. An "Augenblick" or an equivalent "Aufhören" propels the angel involuntarily into the future, from a threshold identified as the past, and which prevents his return by piling debris before him. The angel would like to stay rather than go into the future, not because he is happy, but because his vision of the dead is unresolved: catastrophe and hope remain intolerably mixed. Ruin is not speculated away as in certain dialectical-progressive philosophies of history. Here nobody wins. Ruin is part of the very force that overcomes it; even the "storm blowing from paradise" is assimilated to that "single catastrophe" as it combines in one figure the disparate themes of exile and eschatological hope.

How could this baffling and baffled image underwrite a theory of action? On one level it does the opposite: it explains Benjamin's inaction, his failure to join Gerhard (Gershom) Scholem in Jerusalem. His friend, whose verses introduce this heraldic picture, had left Berlin for Israel in 1923. Since that time Benjamin had been poised to go, like Scholem's angel that spreads its wing in order to return ("Mein Flügel is zum Schwung bereit / ich kehrte gern zurück . . ."). Yet Benjamin did not go. Something always intervened; some erotic or fatal diversion; he turned back from turning back to Jerusalem; he glimpsed a deeper happiness, if it was happiness, and he described it in two hermetic fragments on Klee's "Angel." In these, as Scholem the scholar of Jewish mysticism has pointed out,[6] the idea of a natal genius or guardian spirit is conflated with that of "new" angels created by God for the sole purpose of raising their voices. Having sung,

6. See "Walter Benjamin and His Angel," originally in *Zur Aktualität Walter Benjamins*, ed. Siegfried Unseld (Frankfurt am Main: Suhrkamp, 1972); now in translation by W. J. Dannhauser in *Denver Quarterly* 9 (1974): 1–45.

they die: origin, voice, and death coincide in the *nu,* the timeless moment, granted these ephemerids. Additionally, Benjamin sees Klee's picture as a transportable *genius loci,* as an icon that has not lost all the aura attached to its origin; indeed, Klee's picture, or its conglomerated web of mystical ideas (natal genius, *genius loci,* new angel, journalistic talent or the gift of catching correspondence, of being a "correspondent" in both secular and occult senses of the word) draws him into time, conceived as a contradiction of two kinds of happiness. One is the ecstasy of the unique or the new, the unlived event as pure promise; the other is the bliss of feeling the return of the same, of recovering a sense of fate, of repeating what has been—from the beginning.

Thesis 9, then, is but the written space of a contradiction, one which subsumes yet is not reducible to a political either/or: Moscow or Jerusalem, Zionism or Communism, Messianism or Journalism. Benjamin's style, to which one always returns, is like Jacob's struggle with the angel for a definitive name or blessing. But Benjamin makes no progress. His necessary angel is an image of the image-in-exile: of aura (presence) displaced from its religious origin, and as such more dangerously free, more likely to be misused. As when imagination is politicized. Benjamin strives to be a journalist rather than a literalist of the imagination.

Even from its strictly literary side the angel-image is a displacement. It recalls allegorical Progresses and Triumphs associated with Renaissance and Baroque art. It represents, however, the obverse of a Triumph and discloses the latter's impotence. The result is admonitory: the parodistic resurgence of the Angelus figure in this context suggests that philosophies of history, even when demystifying and progressive, remain indebted to archaic and allegorical figuration.

Benjamin's own allegory does possess one striking feature that survives its critical or deconstructionist impact. Catastrophe, instead of remaining fixed in the past, and hope, instead of being an eschatological or future-directed principle, reverse places. Catastrophe becomes proleptic, as in Baudelaire's "Passante": it ruins time and blocks, even as it propels, the angel. As for hope, that is located mysteriously *in* the past, a defeated potentiality or "retroactive force" which turns the true historian (identified by

Benjamin with the historical materialist) toward those who are vanquished; not simply to represent or recuperate them by a gratuitous act of sympathy but because the vanquished are the volcanic pavement on which the victors march. It is they who give history its materiality, its uneven, unquiet subsistence. "The gods who are defeated, think that defeat no refutation," as W. Ker remarked in his book on the Dark Ages.

This chiasmus of hope and catastrophe is what saves hope from being unmasked as only catastrophe: as an illusion or unsatisfied movement of desire that wrecks everything. The foundation of hope becomes remembrance; which confirms the function, even the duty of historian and critic. To recall the past is a political act: a "recherche" that involves us with images of peculiar power, images that may constrain us to identify with them, that claim the "*weak* Messianic power" in us (Thesis 2). These images, split off from their fixed location in history, undo concepts of homogeneous time, flash up into or reconstitute the present. "To Robespierre," Benjamin writes, continuing Marx's reflections in *The Eighteenth Brumaire,* "ancient Rome was a past charged with the time of now [*Jetztzeit*] which he blasted out of the continuum of history. The French revolution viewed itself as Rome incarnate" (Thesis 14).

Benjamin's relation to images, especially in the "Theses," remains complex and unresolved. The picturesque moment, or its Hellenic prototype—an ideal blend of physical charm and spiritual intensity, or of greatness reconciled with repose, which dominated the European mind after Winckelmann—is not a problem. The Bad News Angel, as the imaginary portrait of a statue, as an inverse Nike, destroys that repose only incidentally. Benjamin's problem is with images as such. The pathos we find is Hebraic, not Hellenic. Though remembrance is enjoined, the images from the past are theurgic, even necromantic. What is "memory as it flashes up at a moment of danger" (Thesis 6) except voice or image as it might have appeared to Saul in the cave of the Witch of Endor? The pathos, then, is that of the Jew who is not allowed voice or image except in the form of commentary and quotation, who is denied the image as a place of repose or as an icon blasted out of the past.

Angelus Novus, watercolor by Paul Klee, 1920.
Reproduced with the kind permission of Gershom Scholem.

A renascence through images is sacrilegious; but what of the *written image*? Paul Klee's picture of the New Angel, which Benjamin owned, and which inspired Thesis 9, has very little image to it. The signifying limbs of that angel are scrolls, didactic yet impotent. Indeed, the angel's shape is like Torah scrolls unraveling, and they avert dissolution only by forming a minimal image or emblem: something between childish scribble and mystic gematria. Perhaps the angel itself is becoming the scroll that must be read. Such self-heraldry is touchingly awkward, because touch is removed by those grotesque multiple hands or fingers that take the place of wings. Can this angel hand anything on? We feel the passion of the signifier. It cannot attain, touch, transmit.

One of the saddest sentences Benjamin wrote concerns Kafka in relation to Jewish tradition: "He sacrificed truth for the sake of clinging to its transmissibility, its haggadic element." The distinction being made relies on the difference in talmudic writings between *haggada* (story, troping, free elaboration) and *hallaka* (law, the truth of the letter, the unmodifiable character of ritual). Truth and tradition ("transmissibility") are now in opposition. We are reminded not only of Bloom's analysis of this bind in the relation of later to earlier poet but of all contemporary criticism that presents itself as commentary on a received text yet cannot be called submissive to it. "Kafka's writings," Benjamin continues, "are by their nature parables. They do not lie modestly at the feet of the doctrine, as the haggada lies at the feet of the hallaka. Though apparently reduced to submission, they unexpectedly raise a mighty paw against it."

"Eine gewichtige Pranke," the text reads in German. In Kafka that paw-prank is often a startling—frightening and comic at the same time—resurrection of a casual metaphor or figure. Something apparently without guile rises up to impede the "progress" of the story and becomes a life-and-death matter. So in *The Judgment* the son tries to put his senile father to bed.

> "Don't worry, you are well covered up." "No," cried his father, cutting short the answer, threw the blanket off with such strength that it unfolded fully as it flew, and stood up in bed. Only one hand lightly touched the ceiling to steady him. "You wanted to cover me up, I know, my little scamp, but I'm not all covered up yet. And even if this is all the strength I have left, it's enough for you, too much for you. . . . But thank goodness a father does not need to be taught how to see through his son." . . . And he stood up quite unsupported and kicked his legs out. He beamed with insight. . . ."So now you know what else there was in the world besides yourself; until now you have known only about yourself! It is true, you were an innocent child, but it is even more true that you have been a devilish person!" [As quoted in *Illuminations,* trans. Harry Zohn]

Here the prankish paw is given to the father, and Benjamin comments on this very passage in his Kafka essay: "As the father throws off the burden of the blanket, he also throws off a cosmic burden. He has to set cosmic ages in motion in order to turn the age-old father-son relationship into a living and consequential thing. And what consequences!" Nothing is more ordinary than a blanket, nothing apparently more without guile than the son's gentle act. Yet we are suddenly confronted by a parable in which, as in the Talmud or certain dreams, the argument is from light to heavy, and the whole reversible relation of fathers and sons, founders and usurpers, originators and imitators is involved.

What is transmitted, then, is the difficulty of dying, and the superficiality of all progressive schemes that cover up the old order, that try to lay it to rest. Eliot had the same trouble with thc dead who could not be buried. He tries to honor them, by equating truth and tradition, but the psychic problem of incorporating the dead startles the economy of his prose.

An artist like Kafka exhibits the agony or macabre comedy of succession. He too refuses to die as storyteller and mythopoeic artist. The split between truth (immediate, apodictic, iconic) and tradition (mediated, didactic, figurative) inspires parable novels that are in revolt against all proof-texts. Every image of progression, every suggestion of touchstone efficacy, is contaminated and disabled by a "haggadic" element, or an ironic pathos that is linked, like Benjamin's angel, to fable and religious symbol.

Nietzsche supported Goethe's suggestion that the "deepest pathos is still aesthetic play." This convertibility, perhaps a legacy of "romantic irony," haunts the contemporary mind. In the realm of story or history convertible pathos may appear as an unusual *turn*. A prankish paw manifests itself. "Here only one thing is absolutely necessary: a hand, a free, a very free and unrestrained hand" (Nietzsche, *Genealogy of Morals* 3:20). The frolic of that hand dooms intention: we cannot be sure to whom the hand belongs, who is writing, who is disturbing the homogeneous medium. "Where got I that truth?" Yeats asks about a gnomic truth indistinguishable from an image. "Out of nothing it came."

The writer's hand becomes the writing hand, a *penna duplex* (Coleridge) which outmaneuvers the prohibition against images through the blind touch that is writing. This winged hand, winged pen, cannot be appropriated to a single person. A "main-tenant" appears that untenants the writer, that is directed but also phantomized by a corporate or, as in tradition, incorporated entity. The idea of inspiration or spectral guidance originates here; and we imagine a "feathered glory" like the god in "Leda and the Swan." Or like Milton's Raphael, maieutic and hermeneutic, a creature of multiple wings waking Adam and Eve to their manifest destiny.

> Like *Maia's* son he stood,
> And shook his plumes, that Heavenly fragrance fill'd
> The circuit wide. [*Paradise Lost* 5. 285–87]

How different Benjamin's angel is! How different, too, his understanding of the relation of truth and transmissibility, even if *Hebrew* evangelism, that is, the desire to have writing and meaning coincide, remains the background! Criticism approaches the form of fragment, pensée, or parable: it both soars and stutters as it creates the new text that rises up, prankishly, against a prior text that will surely repossess it.

Let me turn, in conclusion, to another image tainted by religious or supernatural fancy, but far less glorious. Its provenance is folklore, or the Romantic revival of folklore; it is daemonic and tricky through and through, and has its roots in Benjamin's childhood reading.

The image is that of a little man, a hunchback. The first of Benjamin's theses or reflections on history tells of an automaton in the form of a puppet who could play chess and win against all opponents. Inside the puppet, says Benjamin, was a hunchback, "ein buckliger Zwerg," who directed the puppet. The philosophical counterpart of this machine ("Apparatur") Benjamin calls historical materialism, and he identifies the hidden hunchback with theology. Historical materialism, he explains, is a match for anyone as long as it enlists the services of theology, a theology that today is small and ugly and has to keep out of sight.

That theology may be the secret passion within modern politics is an insight found in many contemporary thinkers. Benjamin's emphasis is, like that of the Frankfurt School, on "Apparatur," or on the way a machine mentality penetrates contemporary existence. It suggests that investing technology, and perhaps inventing it, is the old desire for mastery and dominance. Yet the hunchback-puppeteer keeps out of sight not only because theology has been discredited, but also because the machine is beautiful, and the human form questionable in its light. Our fascination with technique, with neat solutions and totalitarian harmonies, inflicts on the psyche and body of man a new, quasi-religious shame that turns them into hunchbacks, unless they are coordinated and programmed like the machine.

What Benjamin gives us, then, is an emblem of society as a machine-theater. Technology is theology modernized and made aesthetic. There is a ghost in the machine; and it is still the old cultic desire for control of self and others. Fear of this ghost leads us back to Gothic presentiments, but it is a complex, a thrilling fear. For though the ghost in the machine be nothing but the masquerade of presence—*aura* converted into *Schein*, or religious mystery expressing itself as the aesthetic magic of theater, film, or any politico-theological contrivance—it is still our way of grieving for the "glory" (synonymous with "aura") whose loss Wordsworth deplored in the Intimations Ode: "Turn wheresoe'er I may / By night or day, / The things which I have seen I now can see no more." Yet we fear the restoration of wonder as much as its loss: the danger of being suckered by charismatic persons and their miracles of rare device.

Schiller exploited this fear in *Der Geisterseher* of 1793, perhaps the most powerful Gothic novella ever written. In it the invisible controlling dwarf is the Church of Rome attempting to ensnare the soul—and with it the state power—of a German Protestant prince. His conversion to Catholicism is to be brought about by a renascence of wonder achieved through an escalating series of tricky apparitions. The strength of Schiller's story does not lie, however, in the shock of its denouement, in which the supernatural is explained or unmasked as machinery (that of the Catholic Church), but rather in our difficult feeling that Schiller himself is merely motivating a device, that the construction of the story-machine is what is important and that, similarly, life may be a condition in which we cannot tell the puppet from the puppeteer. As in the successor of the Gothic tale, the formulaic detective story, *Apparatur* is all there is, and the idea of self is a pawn or illusion in its ongoing game.

Can we spot a wonder-working dwarf or a daemonic language game or simply a "will to power" in the machine of discourse we call criticism? The very currency of the word *criticism* seems to deny it. It points to an advised, reflective, and self-exposing scrutiny. Criticism, moreover, unlike historical materialism, is not lucky. It does not win its game with anyone: not with the artists who resent it; nor with social thinkers who look down on its headgame of words, sounds, and minute particulars; nor with activists who believe in proving arguments and converting minds by intellectual or other means. Even when the academic sort of criticism tries to become scientific and put on an effective *Apparatur*—when it assumes the armor of dialectics or semiotics or psychoanalysis—the dwarf secreted within proves to be more of a *Schlemazel,* or figure of bad luck, than *Mazel,* or good luck.

The critic is inextricably a figure of pathos *and* aesthetic play. He is a latter-day clown, close cousin to the little hunchback. The romantic or religious passion, in all its calculating if displaced strength, may be the hump he cannot shake off. Wizened, shrunken, crippled though it may be, we know there is power there, if only because we show it instinctive fear and keep it out of sight. A "bucklicht Männlein," or little hunchback, is also the subject of a reminiscence from Benjamin's Berlin childhood and plays a role in the essay on Kafka. Benjamin remembers a spooky little parasite from Scherer's book of poetry for children. This little man hinders or anticipates our every step, and sups on our substance without our being able to prevent it:

Will ich in mein Stüblein gehn,
Will mein Müslein essen;
Steht ein bucklicht Männlein da,
Hat's schon halber 'gessen.[7]

This *kakadaimon* or Fiedler Freak is what literary criticism should acknowledge once more. Otherwise it may be drawn unawares into the demon's service.

But is the secret "hump" daemonic or religious in character, and repressed by modern progressive thinking? Or is it language, a diction that still engages such thoughts and images? What al-

7. "When I want to go into my little room, to eat my porridge, there's the little hunchback who has already eaten half of it." Moving use of the same ballad is made by Thomas Mann when he describes Hanno's nightmare in *Buddenbrooks.*

lows us to read and teach such poems as Yeats's "Leda and the Swan" or Blake's *Vala* without disgust—indeed, with a fascinated understanding? Or why is Benjamin attracted to a superstitious lyric about a hunchback, claiming that it stands to the core of German folk tradition as Kafka's Odradek to Jewish legend?

To characterize this region as daemonic matters less than to recognize its verbal power. It seems to promise a renewal of the word through a new literature drawn from its source. That may be the demon's lure, of course. For the redemption of the folkish (in the form of heterodox mystical or repressed vernacular currents) has always been fraught with ideological implications. Herder praised Shakespeare for maintaining the continuity of learned and popular traditions, something German literature, imitative of the French, had failed to do. Wordsworth's and Coleridge's *Lyrical Ballads* try no less to redeem a naive form by a sophisticated regression. Whether the popular ballad is really of popular origin can be doubted, but not that it embodied a force of language that was felt to be in decline. The tricky native pathos of "Liebes Kindlein, ach, ich bitt, / Bet fürs bucklicht Männlein mit"[8] still moves us, as it did Arnim and Brentano, who rescued the ballad by putting it in their hornbook for adults: *Des Knaben Wunderhorn* (1806–08).

The issue of language has now reached criticism itself, which becomes aware how much it has given up or repressed. Criticism is haunted by an archaic debt, by the eccentric riches of allegorical exegesis in all its curiously learned, or enthusiastic and insubordinate, modes. We have no *Wunderhorn* for critics. Yet the digressive essays of Coleridge, the freakish style of Carlyle and Nietzsche, Benjamin's packed prose, Bloom's and Burke's conquering chariot of tropical splendors, the outrageous verbalism of Derrida, or the "ridiculous terminology" (Artaud) of psychoanalysis, even the temperate taxonomic inventiveness of Northrop Frye—these amount to an *extraordinary language* movement within modern criticism. We cannot distinguish in this movement the vernacular energies from an artificial rage, but perhaps that has always been a defining condition of literariness. Criticism is freed from a neoclassical decorum that, over the space of three centuries, created an enlightened but also over-accommodated prose.

8. "O dear little child, I beg of you, pray also for the little hunchback."

CHAPTER FOUR

The Sacred Jungle 3: Frye, Burke, and Some Conclusions

The Arnoldian tradition received the English Romantics in a defensive and limited way. What was considered valuable was their "creative power"; what was lacking was "knowledge," or the integration of intellectual with creative power. Such integration made Dante exemplary, while Shakespeare and Donne showed it could be achieved, with strain, in the modern period. Perhaps there would be a second Renaissance, a literature of imaginative reason as Arnold called it, growing out of a more intensely self-conscious and critical age, one which could not rely on the unified world-view theology had once provided.

That poetry thinks does not seem to be a startling proposition; but that Romantic poetry thinks, that its visionariness is a form of conceptual mediation, has been a hard-won discovery of recent years. In England, at least; yet academic circles elsewhere have not been wiser. *The Prelude* did not receive a full German translation till 1975, and Wordsworth is still treated as a provincial poet without "philosophic" interest in comparison to Hölderlin. Byron alone was popular from the beginning, while Blake and Shelley gained some acceptance abroad because of their revolutionary flair. But the relation of politics and poetry is precisely what was simplified on the Continent: and it was discounted (because of a distaste for French ideologizing, or rushing from ideas into action) in England. When Arnold mentions the simple, childlike ideas of the Romantics, one can suppose he means, chiefly, their attitude toward the French Revolution, among other adolescent fervors.

Northrop Frye in *Fearful Symmetry* (1947) corrected rather than challenged the post-Arnoldian point of view. He inserted Blake in the line of Homer, Dante, and Shakespeare as a poet from whom a "total form of vision" could be derived. Blake was made the forerunner of a great new mythmaking age. "The age that has produced the hell of Rimbaud and the angels of Rilke, Kafka's castle and James's ivory tower, the spirals of Yeats and the hermaphrodites of Proust, the intricate dying-god symbolism attached to Christ in Eliot and the exhaustive treatment of Old Testament myths in Mann's study of Joseph, is once again a great mythopoeic age." Frye adds *Finnegans Wake* as an analogue to Blake. What Arnold was waiting for, and what Eliot had pronounced as flawed in Blake, is already upon us. The critics are behind. They have largely forgotten their language. "The allegorical approach to literature is often . . . spoken of as a fantastic freak of pedantry, though it lasted for centuries, and probably millennia, whereas our modern neglect of it is an ignorant parvenu of two centuries and a half." Frye says he merely completes the "humanist revolution" inaugurated by the English poets and commentators with his insistence that, since Chapman, "the conception of the Classical in art and the conception of the scriptural or canonical in religion have always tended to approximate one another; that the closer the approximation, the healthier it is for both religion and art; that on this approximation the authority of humane letters has always rested."

I admire this but have problems with it. What Frye calls "approximation" is surely "accommodation": the work of the critic or commentator rather than of the poet, whose mind is by no means as unified as Frye pretends. Was Blake wrong in finding an antithesis between Christian and Classical culture, with one fostering the arts of war, the other the arts of peace—through *mental* fight? Was Milton mistaken in his scruples about using Classical materials, however strongly they spoke to his imagination? Frye admits zestfully that "anagogy" may be needed to supplement analogy or allegorical commentary, to establish Blake as a "typical poet" and unify the "large number of theories which seem to demand some kind of fitting together" in the light of Blake's system. What would Blake have said about such "fitting"?

The principle of reader reception, of accommodation—*of restoring public ability to respond to mythopoeic art*—is the real aim of a book that not only puts Blake into the Eliot galaxy but insists in a radical Protestant way on the capacity of the non-elite reader, on his ability to be instructed and lifted into the heaven of visionary verse.

Yet how much unifying is to be tolerated in a good cause? Frye passes on the last page from words to the Word itself, "which signifies the unit of meaning, the Scripture, and the Son of God and Man." In Blake, he continues, "there are no puns or ambiguities or accidents in the range of the meaning of 'word,' but a single and comprehensible form. . . ." Thus Blake's imaginative grammar or iconography is pursued to the point where words themselves fade out. The textual surface always in movement, always betraying or exceeding synthesis, as if language had a life of its own, is subdued to "one language," however generous, one "great drama of death and redemption," however magnanimous.

Frye is clearly under the sway of Eliot's ideal of order, which he tries to broaden and extend. "It is with criticism as with so many other aspects of contemporary life: for better or worse the reign of *laissez faire* is over, and the problem of achieving order without regimentation is before us." It is no accident that in the 1930s Kenneth Burke was studying "sinister unifying" in art and politics. Neither Eliot nor Frye would appreciate my Burking *order* as *ordure* to bring out the anxiety for purity that arises in a mass culture, whether we accept or reject it as a culture. Yet English poetry was from the beginning a vulgar if illustrious thing, a promiscuous intermingling of various linguistic inheritances, a jostling of high and low styles without the benefit of a Dante. Erich Auerbach's analysis in *Mimesis* of Poins's bantering with Harry (*Henry IV,* Part 2) demonstrates something about English, as well as about Shakespeare, in the context of the other national literatures. Auerbach has a firmer hold on the antithesis between Neoclassical purity and the Christian exaltation of low and humble life, which as a *materna lingua* is always breaking through the *sermo patrius.*[1] It is surely at the level of words as

1. For the distinction, see Leo Spitzer, "Muttersprache und Muttererziehung," in *Essays in Historical Semantics.*

well as the Word—wrongly reduced, in any case, to a grammar of archetypes however imaginative, a Yeatsian Philosophy of Symbols—that Blake and Joyce and, let us add, David Jones are effective. Frye knows this, even if he cannot give the language of Blake a sufficient theoretical frame, and so pronounces him to have relatively little "surface." For it is Falstaff, or his hostess, who has the last word in *Fearful Symmetry*. "There is still much to be seen by the light of the vision Blake saw—perhaps the same light that broke in on the dying Falstaff when he babbled of green fields and played with flowers, and on his hostess, when she told how he had gone into 'Arthur's bosom', and how he had talked of the Whore of Babylon." Though Arthur and Abraham can be joined by a redemptive iconography that unifies a Hebrew with a Celtic or British archetype, in Shakespeare the visionary babble remains vision *and* babble. The mistake, the lapse, is part of the essence: the word takes its revenge on the Word.

Though Frye, then, goes beyond the Arnold-Eliot axis when he proposes a concept of creative criticism, of the creative element in reading (behind which we glimpse a radical Protestant perspective), the result is strangely Catholic. "Creative" turns out to mean the courage to produce an allegorical interpretation. Frye's reading of Blake is a form of allegoresis, allegory extended by anagogy: no longer, of course, in the service of an institutionalized belief, but one that takes the privilege of allegorical expression to itself. Frye continues Blake, as Blake Bunyan; Blake and Frye are still typological artists working out of the "inner light" tradition of Protestant thought. They are archaizing rather than typical modernists. A critical reading of Blake is still wanting, therefore; or a way to distinguish critical from allegorical commentary.

At some point, however, the question of what is Protestant and what is Catholic—the relevance of *historical* religion to the study of art—becomes too fine or disputable. And this is where Frye's insistence on archetypes as the organizing principles of all imaginative activity, culminating in the *Anatomy of Criticism* (1957), has a clarifying and disburdening effect. Blake himself claimed that his poetry was visionary rather than allegorical; it is indeed the *immediacy* of that mediated form called allegory which Blake tries to capture. Is it possible that allegory had, once upon a time, an unmediated, primary existence? As in the days of Vico's giants? Frye, in the light of the *Scienza Nuova,* recovers through Blake that naturally poetic language of the giants, and formulates it as a universal poetics, a grammar of archetypes.

Though allegorical forms may appear to be sophisticated archaisms when found in art, Frye's criticism promotes them to archetypes. What this universalizing transfer from art to the science of art involves is not really examined by Frye: in the *Anatomy of Criticism* he postulates a break or epistemological shift that differentiates art as experience from art as knowledge, and makes the latter teachable as "criticism." It is as if he had found a philosopher's stone that could transform the archaic and local qualities of art into quick gold. One has the feeling that Frye stands to Blake's poetic *materia* as Jung to his alchemical sources.

This redemptive purification (if we think of Jung) is precisely what does not take place in Benjamin or Kenneth Burke. In Benjamin's famous phrase, "Allegory exits empty-handed"; allegorizing, though driven by a desire for transcendence, remains skeletal, grimacing, schematic; an emblem, not an archetype; the no man's land between what can and cannot be represented; and it marks imagination off—but expressively—from all worldly instruments, including words. As for Burke, the turn from words to the Word (the Logos) is the very place in which both artist and critic dwell. Criticism does not complete this turn; if anything, it deconstructs it (though Burke doesn't use this term) by showing that words remain words while striving for definitive, transcendent status. Religions may found more than a rhetoric, but criticism remains "logological," exposing the rhetoric of whatever it studies.

If Burke's view of the formal study of literature is less pure than Frye's, his understanding of the rhetorical dimension, or of what Frye names "the verbal universe," is at least as extensive. "Logology" is a science that considers even religion as an instance of the "terministic enterprise." What's in a term? How do words become concepts or institutionalize themselves? Every institutionalized form of discourse remains, for Burke, either a persuasive strategy or a complex structure of words. The first view leads him to a "dramatistic" understanding of life and art; the second to an unformulated theory that is not covered by his definition of logology as "words-about-words." For this definition seems to point to a metalanguage, whereas Burke is actually striving to formulate the motive for criticism itself, the nature of *that* institutionalization. He often, therefore, bursts in with fascinating afterthoughts about his own writings, whether fictional or critical. His criticism is basically about how words become terms and myths. Himself an immensely inventive terminologer —Bloom has learned from him—he stays *in the turn* between terms and words, and so creates a perpetual-motion effect. Moreover, by echoing words to himself and by accepting Freud's theory of overdetermination, he makes every phrase seem doubly permeable, open to carnal as well as spiritual motives. (*Motive* always has the sense, in Burke, of that which moves a person or his work, whether the force exerted is intrapsychic or sociopolitical.) That echo-aspect or potential bivalence allows Burke to demystify spiritual concepts by a "thinking of the body" that does not devalue them.[2] His critical writings engage the duplicity of words and do not strive for final synthesis, conversion, or its scientific equivalent: a postulate, like Frye's, separating the study of art from the immediate experience of art. Writing criticism is itself a way of establishing an immediate relation to words: the words of others, which remain words about words, the words in oneself, which also remain words about words.

The immense desire to come clean in writing, which moved William Carlos Williams, Ezra Pound, and so much "American" literature in the 1920s, a desire for nothing but the spent word and its effect on the writer himself ("There is no writing but a moment that is and dies and is again wearing the body to noth-

2. "Metaphysical speculations on corporeality had an immediate motivational force, with Augustine, in connection with his attachment to the women who, whatever their contribution to him as steps along the way, don't even rate names. . . . Intimacy with a woman must always argue special intimacy with some word or words like or nearly like the sound of her name. So probably [the names of the women] are there, shining out like unseen stars, ambiguously split perhaps between terms in the constellation of the divine and terms for the problematic body" (*The Rhetoric of Religion*, p. 83).

ing"—W. C. Williams): this exhausting quest for a nonallegorical purity left its mark on Burke, both in his closeness to words and in his knowledge that they never come clean, that they are as devious as dreams that seem to be perceptions but are already interpretations. Burke's enterprise develops into a critique of pure thinking as well as of pure poetry. Not only is everything motivated; it is overmotivated; its freedom and its force reside in that surplus. Art, Blake said, passes a Last Judgment on us; so language exposes us, our state of mixed-up blasphemy and blessing, of carnal and spiritual goads. Burke is attracted, like I. A. Richards in the 1930s, to Coleridge, who had planned a great work on words about the Word, the *Logosophia,* and who was benightmared by the "concealed offense" lurking in his words and dreams. But it is symptomatic that Burke gave up trying to draw a philosophy of literary form from Coleridge and that his most sustained reading of a text is found in the chapters on Augustine's *Confessions* in *The Rhetoric of Religion* of 1961. Augustine had tried to come clean in words; yet his church, his great unified vision, is built on the cloaca of a "verbal action" without which the theology would be neither persuasive nor possible. Frye had shown that a foundering poet could still be a founder: Burke shows that a founder cannot escape the leading power of words in talking about the Word. "Speak the word only," as in Eliot's "Ash Wednesday," is a deeply ambiguous phrase. The Logos should be redemptive, a real foundation, but it may be no more than a motive. "In Ara Coeli the steps lead every possible where, solving nothing but leading."[3]

This leading is terministic but not terminal: it has to be motivated or remotivated by meanings, purposes, philosophies. These motivations gather into a "grammar" and a "rhetoric"; and in the literary thinker, Burke, Frye, and more peculiarly Augustine, the most discernible unifying motive is the notion of a *sacred book*—yet one created out of everyday, profane experience. A book, a word, a creation as profane yet holy as Williams's

3. R. P. Blackmur, "Ara Coeli and Campidoglio" (1958), in *A Primer of Ignorance.* Since I cannot formally take up Blackmur's work, I quote this as a fragment to suggest how close he stands to the same issues, and how deeply his prose meditates Eliot as well as Yeats.

Roman Eve who is, from the beginning, living sculpture. "Venus Capitolenus: There is a separate marble, buried in the sand, lost, returned to light or there new—that exists there is that to take, the chisel starts from the navel of the man who is—"[4]

Yet differences exist within that primal fantasy. For Burke, what is being created or recreated is a drama rather than poem or book: a dramatic action, to be precise, ritually unifying the community by a structure of participation we can still glimpse in the sacred plays of the Greeks. The question of purity coincides with that of purification, and with the power of drama to achieve it. Burke's *Philosophy of Literary Form* (1941, but written in the 1930s) views poems, novels, and social tracts as all in the service of a dramatic action of this ancient kind, having catharsis as its goal. The critic exposes that goal which can be achieved by good or by sinister means, by the use or abuse of dramatistic ratios and bastardized religious motives.

Books are always battles, mental war, but are they acceptable substitutes for conflict? Burke's motto for *The Grammar of Motives,* "ad bellum purificandum" ("to purify warfare"), leaves it unclear whether war can be removed, or only cleansed of darker ends. The analysis of what "war" means, why it is a permanent feature of human existence (the war to end all wars having proved to be, by 1939, just another war) is conducted by Burke in terms that are anthropological and theological rather than narrowly political. Or *symbolic*—even if he does not achieve a clear definition of symbolic action. "The author would propose to replace the present stress upon men in rival international situations by a 'logological' reaffirmation of the foibles and quandaries that all men (in their role as 'symbol-using animals') have in common" (*The Rhetoric of Religion,* "Introduction"). The importance of religion in all this is that while it has been looked upon as a central and unifying principle, it has also been, historically, the leading cause of discord, war, and bloodshed.

Actually, then, Burke sets purgation against purification. For

4. "Rome," as published in *The Iowa Review* 9 (1978): 12–64. The MS dates from 1924; it is interesting to know that Williams was in touch with Burke at this period.

it is, precisely, the religious or transcendent strain, the desire to live an ordered life, or to be cleansed of the guilt of disorder, that welds, as he states in one of the squib-like poems he likes to insert, Order and Sacrifice:

Order leads to Guilt
(for who can keep commandments!)
Guilt needs Redemption
(for who would not be cleansed!)
Redemption needs a Redeemer
(which is to say, a Victim!).

Order
Through Guilt
To Victimage
(hence: Cult of the Kill) . . .

Symbolic action, clearly, does not purify, at least not like a cult of the kill. It is a repetition that makes us aware of a *common,* even *vulgar,* hence *comic* rage for order. To call for purity is to perpetuate a visionary disease instead of opting for purgation by using the peculiarly human tools called symbols, of which the "verbal principle" is recognized even in religion by the term "Logos."

That words may purge but do not purify leads, of course, especially in Puritan kinds of religiousness, to a more naked poetry, or to no poetry at all. The puristic strain is most visible and most productive in Milton, where the relation of the poet to his sources, scriptural or classical, is so precarious that the question of election or vocation emerges in agonizing form. Is all this labor really spiritual rather than vain and worldly? Will it be justified, a labor crowned by grace?

The specter of a discontinuity between labor and grace, artistic genius and religious truth, threatens the Christian-Humanist synthesis and forces the poetic genius back on its own. The latter becomes aware of itself as primal and creative, even when unjustified and reprobate. Blake daringly resolves the conflict between poetry and religion in favor of the Poetic Genius which he asserts to be the source, while the Jewish and Christian Testaments are an "original derivation" from it. (The Classics are merely a derivation from that derivation.) Indeed, "the Religions of all Nations are derived from each Nation's different reception of the Poetic Genius, which is everywhere called the Spirit of Prophecy." The struggle for an American reception of the Poetic Genius, from Emerson, Whitman, and Emily Dickinson to William Carlos Williams, continues this line of thought; and insofar as it has to choose, it prefers itself primal and reprobate rather than Christian and Humanist.

We have not seen the last American Puritan. D. H. Lawrence's *Studies in Classic American Literature* (1922) expresses that truth as violently as Williams or Pound—or, for that matter, Van Wyck Brooks. The Puritan tradition, reinforced by the founders of America, continues its embrace. Burke struggles out of it, like a fly in ointment or religious unction; whereas Frye, raising Blake's identification of poetry with divinity to a legitimating axiom for literary studies, accommodates more easily both Scripture and its extension into a secular canon, what we call literature.

The fact that religion or society condemns the poetic genius in its midst cannot change, according to Frye, this identity of literature and divinity. Culture-politics of the repressive kind exists, but is an evil child, vision gone bad, as Blake's epics demonstrate. What is crucial is the relation of art as a whole to society as a whole. The critic sees, of course, the present weakening of religion as a structure of belief, yet hopes that the identity of imaginative religion with art will modify the impotence of both in modern life. Frye completes Arnold by returning to Blake, who said that the imagination is eternal; and he corrects Eliot by arguing that what is important in religion can be communicated, especially today, only through art. "The arts, which address the imagination, have, ever since the Romantic movement, acquired increasingly the role of the agents through which religion is understood and appreciated. The arts have taken on a prophetic function in society, never more of one than when the artist pretends to depreciate such a role, as, for instance, T. S. Eliot did" (*The Modern Century*).

Should we set Burke against Frye? With his catastrophic view of the history of religious and purifying ideals, Burke cannot legitimate art as an after-religion. Humorous (in the old sense) rather than unifying, he turns to the drama and particularly Shakespearean drama to find some paradigm of true community. Where, if not in Shakespeare, do we find represented both the vicious cycle of order and guilt, the "Iron Law of History / That welds Order and Sacrifice," and a hoped release from it? The relation of literature to politics, including modern political religions, from Puritan theocracies to the totalitarianisms of Left or Right, is Burke's burden even when he seems to be literary in the most technical sense. Let us imagine, then, what Burke might have said on behalf of Shakespeare in explaining to a politicized age a "trifling" song from *The Tempest*:

Ariel's Song
Come unto these yellow sands,
And then take hands:
Curtsied when you have, and kissed
The wild waves whist:
Foot it featly here and there,
And sweet sprites bear
The burthen . . . Hark!
Hark!
Burthen [*dispersedly*]. Bow-wow!
Ariel. The watch-dogs bark:
Burthen. Bow-wow!
Ariel. Hark, hark, I hear
The strain of strutting chanticleer
Cry—
Burthen. Cock a-doodle-do!

It is airy, like Ariel; and it passes from revel to dirge (the second, even more famous song, "Full fathom five thy father lies . . . Those are pearls that were his eyes . . .") by the gentlest sea- and see-change. We are made to intuit the mood of Ferdinand, who thinks his father shipwrecked in the tempest and seems to hear the waves soothing his loss and their own fury. And we are made to forget the bad vibes of Caliban, his equation (in the previous scene) of speaking and cursing—for it is always language itself ("My language! heavens!" is Ferdinand's cry on hearing Miranda speak) that is recovered and rediscovered in this play.

A delicate balance is created between so many things: woe and wonder, dreaming and waking, curse and blessing.

Yet even out of context that first song has a charm of its own. It suggests, capped by a curious refrain, the lighthearted integration of animal spirits, a unity that preserves in sublimated form the hierarchic order being "silenced" by a ritual dance which is pure moonshine, which takes place before dawn. "Bow" in "Bow-wow" is the command of the barker, the one who calls the tune, invisible *magister ludi*; but it is also what Ariel takes it to be, a barking sound: peremptory, disruptive, mocking. It is the voice of clown-master or King of Fools; it is, more generally, the lunatic fringe of rhyme or rhythm, sheer performative energy of language, onomatopoeia, mimicry. It cannot be resolved into orderly meaning but signals a discordant ending, a discontinuity between the real and the elfish as dawn breaks. Cock-crow, next, with its edge of obscene incitement ("cock a-doodle-do") reinforces barking, as the sun rises on a barnyard world and a pecking order that imposes once more the "burthen" of labor and language.

Where, then, is Shakespeare's paradigm of community? What we seem to have is the opposite, a momentary charm, a pure interlude, fraying into impure noise and silly puns. The lyric, like the magic circle of Romance itself, cannot really hold up time. Break or bark of day returns, and the adult nursery form is undone. This is true, no doubt; poetry does not, cannot, bridge the painful distance between master and slave, freedom and servitude.[5] But it does bridge, in Shakespeare, the distance between literate and illiterate on the basis of a shared imaginative belief or desire: Ariel's song is mythmaking in a learned *and* folkloric way, it is motivated by courtly *and* popular tradition. There is, moreover, something extravagant in the whole scheme of this Romance, which the burthen asks us to share: wishing to appeal to the entire audience (like Prospero's epilogue), it turns an antithetical pun into a piece of nonsense verse as if meaning in language were less important than a performative and contagious

5. On the issue of freedom and bondage as, through such Shakespearean songs, they influence Shelley's lyrics, see Barry Weller, "Shakespeare, Shelley and the Binding of the Lyric," *Modern Language Notes* 93 (1978): 912–37.

energy. Even "ding-dong, bell," the closing refrain of the second song, is not as congruent as it seems. It alludes, of course, to the death-knell being rung. But one can imagine Ariel, or the invisible conductor, gesturing at that point for a bell-sound from the musicians. The play-acting, that is, spreads out from the visible scene to the "wings": to the extended stage of life, where all are actors, the audience too; and to the offstage master of these charms, to Prospero or Shakespeare himself. There is a vanishing point where the master-slave relation is dissolved, or where we all participate equally in the human condition.

Great art is radical: our understanding of this fact has been advanced by Frye and Burke when it comes to religion. But art's contribution to the political sphere remains difficult to formulate. What kind of "act" is art, independently of its subject matter, which can range from the most conservative beliefs to libertine thought, from Ariel's "airy tongue" to satirical rage? Historical evidence is inconclusive. Sometimes a writer hits home, like Brecht; more often not. Intent and reception, program and influence, seem to have separate destinies. Thirties-minded critics (I steal Kenneth Burke's phrase), like Edmund Wilson and Burke himself in America, Adorno and Benjamin in Germany, Malraux in France (indeed, almost every leading intellectual was involved) struggled constantly with the issue of art and politics.

On one level there is no mystery: art slanders an established order, good or bad, by not conforming. Its very existence is often a resistance, it gives the lie to every attempt to impose a truth by state-sponsored power. Shelley's Beatrice in *The Cenci* is an absolute symbol for this resistance. But on another level there is a mystery. However opposed art may be to religion, hierarchy, or the very idea of the sacred, it exhibits the kind of energy, concentration, and compulsive structure we associate with its despotic opponents. Fueled, psychoanalysis would say, by the Unconscious, it is the product of an exceptional alliance between conscious and unconscious or driving thoughts.

Even apparently conformist art can burst, with grotesque power, through the eggshell of its beliefs. But this precarious alliance of conscious and unconscious thoughts shows up in other areas too: in religion and politics especially. What we appreciate as exemplary in art we admire and fear as "charismatic" in public life. If it is hard enough to tell charlatan from genius in art, it often seems impossible to distinguish between creative and destructive portions of the spirit in a significant politician or religious leader.

Art cannot escape that shadiness, that ambiguity; but once published it also cannot cease exposing itself. No formula may preempt what the effect of its openness will be. The reader-critic is deeply involved in not allowing art to be shunted aside or co-opted by the newest ideology. Take the formula, as old as Herder, that the greatness of English literature (he was thinking particularly of Shakespeare) was its ability to build on folk traditions, to avoid the sterilizing discontinuity between learned and unlearned art that had afflicted French Classicism. But the phenomenon of the *Anstreicher,* as Brecht called Hitler, of the artisan and man-of-the-people who would form a powerful coalition of all classes and transform work into a joyful, satisfying activity akin to art—that ideology is not wholly distinct from the animus in my previous account of Ariel's song from *The Tempest.*

A scrutiny of the religious motives underlying such words as order, unity, and community is essential, therefore; and it was practiced by the Frankfurt School, which understood the appeal of totalitarianism in terms of an upsurge of messianic or religious politics, and connected demagogic movements with a rhetoric that relied on what Burke called "a bastardization of fundamentally religious patterns of thought." Burke used this phrase in his essay on Hitler's *Mein Kampf*—an analysis contemporary with the work of Benjamin and writers conveniently grouped as the Frankfurt School. But religion is itself a mixed matter, a complex phenomenon not easily reduced to ideals of purity, totality, or ascesis. For Nietzsche, these ideals were indeed religious but also in the service of an ultimate will to power. Totalitarianism, moreover, according to Adorno and Horkheimer, is a "progressive" consequence of the Enlightenment, which *believed* in Reason and used "dialectical" perspectives to dominate the disorder of history by means of a concept of uniformity and the purging of all nonrational—in effect, nonbureaucratic, nonconformable—ideas.

It proved to be a counterreligion, a religion of absolute secular progress.

The relation of ideals of purity to concepts in literary theory will be discussed in the next two chapters. I want to focus, for the moment, on the difficulty of reducing art to political statements and on the obviously related problem of discerning its sociopolitical influence. I have hinted that these difficulties come from the fact that it is too radical. But how is this radical character of art to be conceived?

Burke, in the analysis of *Mein Kampf* already mentioned, suggests a connection between rhetoric as a strategy of persuasion and rhetoric as the art of endowing voice with absolute magnitude. Those impatient with the "contrary voices" of parliament, or similar "houses of confusion," Burke remarked, find it tempting to "wish for the momentary peace of one voice, amplified by social organizations, with all the others not merely quieted, but given the quietus." It is surely this "sinister unifying" of all voices that cannot extend to art, except through overt repression or *dirigisme*. Ariel, in his song, incorporates by a delightful and dispersed mimicry the voices that break in; but even if it is argued that it is he, after all, who directs and plays his own song, those impure echoes and puns remain, testifying to an energy of sound, a discordant concord of voices, that cannot be further reduced. Such voices, even when internalized or subdued as "inner" voices, show a potentially compulsive, eruptive character. With psychoanalysis, moreover, we have moved closer to understanding the role of images of voice in the total psychic life of the person, so that the concept of inner voice itself becomes a bridge helping us to connect the driving genius of artist, religious leader, and politician.

Revolutions could be considered as festivals in which these voices break out and cannot be contained. They become pentecostal, but in a political way. The voices inflame, and fire is but their objective correlative. Paradoxically, therefore, the engagement of the Romantic artists with the French revolution—as of Milton with the Puritan revolution—can hinder our grasp of art's relation to the sociopolitical sphere if the political event is given priority or made the exclusive focus. For the radical character of art is then overshadowed by a fixed point of reference that excludes too much else in thought. What is meant by the radical character of art, in isolation or in conjunction with other types of radical activity, can only be demonstrated by a close analysis of the rhetorical and symbolic dimension. (Carlyle attempted something of this nature in his books on Cromwell and the French Revolution.) This analysis is not possible without literary experience: we must learn not only to read between the lines but also to hear the words, the words in the words, and the images of voice they suggest. The institution of writing itself, at the level of complexity that literature reveals, is presupposed, and the link between writing and ideation can no longer be ignored.

The productive force of close analysis has already enabled certain Romantic and post-Romantic writers to enter our consciousness in new and startling form: Rousseau, Blake, Wordsworth, Shelley, Hölderlin, Michelet, and Nietzsche have benefited. Others, Ballanche, Emerson, Thoreau, Melville, Hugo, are being revalued. After a painful separation that limited, supposedly for its own good, the understanding of literature—"literature" became only that, and was resolutely dissociated from thought-systems of a religious, political, or conceptual kind—we are returning to a larger and darker view of art as mental charm, war, and purgation.

Can we ever conceivably accept the claim that poetry rather than politics is fate, that "poets are the unacknowledged legislators of the world"? The charged word here is "unacknowledged." The influence of poetry operates, Shelley suggests, by finer than didactic means, and through a medium that is not generally perceived to be in the service of "power" or "the world." Its laws are unknown or unacknowledged, therefore; but they exist nevertheless and exert their influence by way of a "language within language" that constitutes the effective part of poetry. This doctrine could lead to a manichean or gnostic type of allegory relying on a caricature devil-god for its sport, like the Jupiter of *Prometheus Unbound,* whom Shelley gets rid of as expeditiously as possible. Yet if Shelley's poems can recrudesce into antiorthodox allegory, they are essentially hymns to an Unknown Spirit, to whom he gives various names, but who seems as uncodifiable as the *agnostos theos* of Acts 17:22–30,[6] or the spirit of poetry itself.

How difficult it is to capture a politics of the spirit as radical as Shelley's is shown by his reception; and here I return a moment to Bloom, whose first book, *Shelley's Mythmaking* (1959), helped to restore the "ineffectual angel" to prominence. The term "mythmaking" recalls the debt to Frye. Bloom trumps Eliot with Shelley just as Frye had trumped him with Blake: Shelley too is inserted into the line of great poets from whom a "total form of vision" might be derived. But already there is a difference marked by the reentry of a German source—German-Hebraic rather than German-Greek. Shelley's religion was too radical for a Christian-Humanist synthesis, so Bloom turned to a Jewish version of late German Romanticism: to Martin Buber.

Mythmaking, as Bloom conceives it, is by no means a synthesis or redemptive iconography. It is a lyrical and apostrophic movement that never leaves the area of words or dialogic exchange. Like Buber's "I-Thou," fundamental words of desire, of an apostrophe that remains open because the desired "Thou" is a relation and not an object and cannot be fixed or imaged except as a naturalized and neutered "It," so an intuition of the discontinuous, fickle, yet transcendent character of relational bonds saves Shelley from a belated and superficial allegory of love and a sentimental worship of past myths.

Bloom's use of Buber is heuristic and enables a firmer description of the radical quality of Shelley's poetry. There is, even within Shelley's lighter lyrics, a Hebraic depth, an echo of the unmediated strain of prophetic verse that inspired the "Protestantism of the poets" in Reformation England. Yet how important are these markers, "English," "Protestant," "Hebraic," "Romantic"? To juxtapose Buber and Shelley disorients historical reflection. What is recovered tends to cover the fact that historical reflection is not value-free: it imposes as well as recuperates, it substitutes one ideology for another—or it engages the untriumphant scholar in a fine and fruitless dialectic, calculating the

6. See Eduard Norden, *Agnostos Theos,* especially pp. 56 ff.

influences, establishing by fiat what is positive and what negative, and aiming at a doubtful synthesis.

As long as we practice what Nietzsche called monumental history[7]—and this kind of history is presupposed by most interpretive criticism—we must also examine what is involved in our intensive care and even canonization of certain writers. Criticism is always valuation in this regard, even if it claims to suspend valuation. The automatic valuing of works of art over works of commentary, for instance (encouraging close reading of the former but considering it vainglorious to give such attention to the latter) betrays a subtle idolatry. It monumentalizes a dead man's relics, turns them into the icon of a power that continues to operate its reversals and obliterations (what Shelley has named "thought's empire over thought") by means of the very act—criticism—being downgraded.

Bloom's understanding of Shelley remains deeply inconsistent, therefore: the critic's historical reflection makes Shelley's poetry a source of value by placing it in a monumentalized tradition. Though Shelley stands, according to Bloom, in a free relation to the mythmaking "spirit" present before all myth, this freedom is said to be in the great tradition of English visionary poetry since Spenser. It is a freedom *over* rather than *from* sources. The emphasis is on making rather than on myth; and the breaking in that making, the revisionary deformation, does not yet question the precursors. It is directed only against the reductive language of religious or political systems that legitimate "nature" as a god term (an adjunct to acts of uniformity) despite their claim to be spiritual.

By historical reflection the precursors are saved; their suspicion of "nature" makes them all Hebrews in the spirit, and they will be typed, eventually, as gnostics. Bloom's second book, *The Visionary Company* (1961), shows the ambivalent and at times antagonistic relation between the Romantics (who had been defined as nature poets by the Academy) and nature. "The bells, I say, the bells break down their tower," Hart Crane wrote in the lyric from which the book's title is derived; Bloom sees the

7. In "On the Use and Abuse of History" (1874). Nietzsche also uses the term "iconic history-writing."

Romantic imagination trying to break through to religion, or imagination breaking all forms. Especially the forms of a "religion of nature," with its false consolations, including the concept of art as a second nature, as organic, restitutive, naturally supernatural. There is only what Bloom in his later and openly gnostic phase will call "catastrophe creation."

In *The Visionary Company* Bloom is fighting the Academy and making a new case for "Romantic" poetry. To assert that the bells haunting Crane with their vocal, assaulting power have no precise referent (not even that of "imagination," or imaginative energy freeing itself from religious containments) would have brought on the old charge of Romantic mysticism or irrationalism. Yet the truth is we don't know what the bells say or what they mean. That may be part of their terrible effect. Angelus or death-knell, who knows what "dark, aerial power / Commission'd, haunts the gloomy tower"?[8] Theirs is a language-denying language, if we associate language with articulate meaning. The nearest we come to a referent, an identity, is "banked voices slain!", which suggests that the bells are images of voice that will not let the poet be, that remind him of the ghostly power of poetry, of the astonishing resonance of its language. For these voices there is no quietus: the poet is their "sexton slave" and his verse merely their accommodation.

Poetry, then, may be as fragile as nature in respect to imagination or radical inner speech—utterance of an apostrophic yet nonreferential kind. A structure of deception reveals itself, without yielding a new relational object, unless it is criticism itself as a movement of undeception. Bloom begins to be suspicious of the "freedom" of visionary poetry, its promise of a self-generated myth or unmediated visionariness. In his first book, that freedom had already been qualified; in *Blake's Apocalypse* (1963), his third book, Bloom still insists on the freedom of the Romantic poet who creates new myths from old or "revises" in a tran-

8. The suggestive force of these fragmentary verses by William Collins reminds one of Hart Crane's comment in his essay "Modern Poetry" that "some of the most intense and eloquent current verse derives sheerly from acute psychological analysis, quite independent of any dramatic motivation." The dramatic motivation was perhaps a tradition that a Bell of Aragon tolled spontaneously before a King of Spain died.

scendent way Milton and the Bible. Yet this "protestant" liberty mingles with a gnostic theme: the poet's suspicion of both imagination and nature, so that the notion of precursor poet (blocking *imago*) and demiurge (usurper god) converge. In the series of books inaugurated by *Yeats* (1970) and *The Anxiety of Influence* (1973), Bloom turns the gnosis against Blake, Yeats, and post-Miltonic poets, to show that they cannot escape belatedness and self-deception. Blake's "apocalypse" is a brave but spurious myth of freedom, a "folie du jour," a day-mare intrinsic to desire. Freedom is but a masked or unacknowledged influence.

Thus, having demystified nature by means of the Romantic emphasis on imagination, Bloom demystifies the imagination, and with it poetry itself. He asserts a negating triumph of (past) art over (present) art, as well as of life over art. He demonstrates that the influence of poet on poet is as inescapable as of father on son. Emerson's liberating insight that "the originals are not original" is translated back into the burden it denies: we are belated, and whatever we do is a compromise formation. The deceptions of "spirit," "imagination," or "desire" are marshalled into categories, depressed into ratios that show how literal and unavoidable is our debt to the past. Like a Gothic tale the theory constricts and chills us. The elation of theorizing proves to be a form of mania itself, but the punishment here is visited upon the poets as well as the critics.

Which is only just; for it was Modernist American poetry, William Carlos Williams and Hart Crane even more than Eliot, that perpetuated this creative error, the illusion of a "progress of poetry." Rejecting Eliot's whisper-style, his de-cadences, Williams and Crane foresee not only an independent American literature ("The American Sublime" or "The Great American Novel") but also an absolute beginning purely of the imagination, beyond plagiarism or the "opera" of voices that at once inspires and decomposes Crane.

By an understandable reversal this quest for unmediated voice or vision brings to light all unacknowledged mediations. Bloom's undeniable contribution to literary studies is his ear that recovers the "banked voices slain." But to do merely that, to list echoes and allusions, would be a depressing variant of source study, and a puzzled affirmation of the phenomenon of intertextuality. What happens is quite different: Bloom, a new Amphion, uses *the voice of the critic* to keep the tower of literature from becoming a tower of Babel. His theories are a function of this voice; it builds despite itself, on bricolage. The mediated immediacy of art is acknowledged by one theoretical formulation or another. Art is "catastrophe creation"; or art is the unresolved conflict of one radical principle, the desire for self-origination (equivalent to self-divinization) with the contrary fact that we are born rather than self-made, in literature as in life. While other critics, like Paul de Man, rehearse that impasse, exposing without judging the illusion of unmediated expression, Bloom orders it as a typology of lies (poets are liars) also named "revisionary ratios."

"The Case of Shelley": in 1952 Frederick Pottle's essay with that title set the stage for a reconsideration of Shelley's poetry. The problem was Shelley's antireligious yet radically spiritual character. Each of the major Romantics, however, puts us to a similar test. Sometimes, as in Wordsworth, the poet's imagination tries to break through to religion, even to established religion. But ever since the Romantic movement, and inspired by Milton or Dante, "the arts have taken on a prophetic function in society" (Frye); and this is not an academic matter only, even if the debate on the relation of religion to art is carried on chiefly in the Academy. From Matthew Arnold on, English literary studies have been preoccupied with this issue.

There is no point in asking who is the most radical of them all: Blake or Wordsworth, Shelley or Keats. But the history of reception, in Shelley's case, shows how disruptive his poetry has been to monumentalizing and religious ("Line of Vision") perspectives. A politics of the spirit is not subject to punctual verification; and in Shelley that politics is so closely identified with the peculiar alchemy of his language that it often does not seem to require a precise historical placement. Paul de Man goes so far as to invest Shelley's power purely in language as it discloses its own spirit. Shelley's *The Triumph of Life* reveals, according to him, "the positional power of language considered by and in itself."[9]

"Positional" includes "positing" and "impositional": the word reflects an old distinction between "natural" and "positive" law. Extending de Man one could say that when Shelley claims that poets are unacknowledged legislators, he means that they promulgate laws that cannot be recognized as having positive (human and subjective) force because they act on us like natural (unconsciously or inescapably suffered) events. In language, what seems natural is always positive or the effect of a "positional power."[10] Despite a similarity between Shelley's words and ordinary language, the poetic use of those words displaces their ordinary meaning so completely that language appears as a power "by and in itself," like the sun in *The Triumph of Life*. "The sun," writes de Man, "does not appear in conjunction with or in reaction to the night and the stars, but of its own unrelated power." Sequence or family resemblance, in this Humean analysis, do not alter the fact that each force or figure is replaced—obliterated—by the next, and what is really disclosed is the disjunctive, impositional presence of language. "The previous occupants of the narrative space are expelled by decree, by the sheer power of utterance, and consequently at once forgotten."

It should be remembered that we are dealing with narrative or verbal space as it imposes on a reality we cannot know any more than, according to Kant, the thing in itself. The only thing to be known is this powerful, impositional action of language—and since we are in the era of Rousseau, Kant, and the French

9. All my quotations are from "Shelley Disfigured" in *Deconstruction and Criticism*.

10. From a Husserlian point of view, de Man seems to transfer "thetic qualities" (*Ideas*, pars. 113 ff.) to the "act" of languaging. But "positional" is a loaded word: it may participate in the effort to overcome falsely progressive (Hegelian or dialectical) theories of art and to respond to the claim of Saussurean semiotics that there are no "positive" terms. The whole question of what is "positive" and what "negative" has complicated itself to the point that in 1975 a group of scholars associated with the University of Konstanz issued a collective volume entitled *Positions of Negativity* (ed. Harald Weinrich). The application of "mathematical" concepts in philosophy is discussed by Coleridge, with reference to Kant, in the *Biographia Literaria*, chaps. 12 and 13. For the positive/natural antithesis, see also Nietzsche's early (circa 1869) fragment on the Origin of Language.

Revolution, de Man's implication is that the revolutionary mentality follows rather than founds this consciousness of language. His insight points to a *coup de force*—on the part of the critic as well.

This coup has to be repeated as monotonously as the Mallarméan *coup de dés* that will never abolish chance. However radical, even revolutionary, the terms of discourse are—here they recall the divine fiat ("sheer power of utterance"), or Bloom's emphasis on lying usurpation, or Nietzsche's on the will to power, or endless statements on a crisis in modern letters—the political notion of *coup* is deprived of all but its illusory or imaginative force. Political revolutionaries are the unacknowledged poets of the world—but more naive than the poets, more trusting in the effectiveness of a unique or single imposition.

Language rather than politics is fate; politics is part of a counterfeit Great Tradition that arrogates to itself the impositional strength of performative language. Yet de Man's own position has become too absolute. For we can hardly forget—despite that "coercive forgetting" induced by the "sheer power of utterance"—that even in Shelley power tends to be associated not with language but with "spirit," the very word found in the opening lines of *The Triumph*:

> Swift as a spirit hastening to his task
> Of glory and of good, the Sun sprang forth
> Rejoicing in his splendour, and the mask
> Of darkness fell from the awakened Earth—

The word "spirit," so common in Shelley, makes even language an Ariel: the free (or freed) servant of an *unknown* power. Here the sun declares a glory that may not exist, except as a self-fulfilling prophecy. We cannot know who the taskmaster is, or even the ground of rejoicing. The sun must lose itself in its own splendor. This chaste haste, this springing forth is indeed spiritual ("swift . . . spirit . . . sun"), or epiphanic rather than natural: it is as close as poetry can come to evoking within a description of natural process an act of free precipitation.

If Shelley is depicting something that might be gathered into a word or a figure, it is *enlightenment.*[11] But does the "spirit" of language give light to the sun, or does the spirit of prophecy? Or are they the same spirit? The allusion to Psalm 19 ("The heavens declare the glory of God. . . . In them he hath set a tent for the sun, / Which is as a bridegroom coming out of his chambers, / And rejoiceth as a strong man to run his course") strengthens the declarative zest of verses in which causality and relationality, and perhaps an entire structure of gradualism and subordination, yield to a more imperative sense: that of self-origination, or at least self-tasking. Shelley projects a sublime yet recurrent event, which never happens or happens all the time. He does this, moreover, in a context that embraces other great speech acts, poetic or prophetic: texts like the Psalms, Dante, Milton, Wordsworth. Their mode of presence, or mode of absence, if you wish—freely to be evoked rather than necessary and constraining—is part of the enlightenment of language itself, which sublimates the very style of visionary allegory it repeats.

Shelley exhibits but does not ultimately name, with one name, this enlightenment. He does not identify it completely with the historical movement we call the Enlightenment, or with revolutionary political action as such. He leaves the unknown as the only knowable thing, as "the influence which is moved not, but moves." Poetry is the nearest name he comes to, as at the end of *A Defence of Poetry.*

What de Man must be saying, then, is that a genuinely poetic text makes the negative ("freedom," "random and mortal action") emerge from the very positivity, the impositional power of language. (Like Freud's Unconscious it negates without knowing the negative.) *The Triumph of Life,* even as a title, is a positive irony of this kind, for Shelley depicts a dance of death, or the triumph of life over the living. Unrelatedness mimics relation; usurpation wears the face of succession; death becomes the father of tradition. The phenomenality of things, their evanescent imprint, is inscribed repeatedly—trace upon trace, trace after trace—on the groundless ground of the mind. Hence Shelley's typical efface-

11. "Enlightenment is humanity's exodus from its self-perpetuated minority [*selbstverschuldete Unmündigkeit*]." This is Kant's famous opening statement in an essay replying to the question "What is Enlightenment?" (1784).

ments, which focus in *The Triumph* on the dead Rousseau who is evoked only to be revoked, given a face to speak through (per-sona) only to be effaced. And the reader repeats this pattern: the reader, also maddened by mortality, continues "the endless prosopopoeia by which the dead are made to have a face and a voice which tells the allegory of their demise and allows us to apostrophize them in our turn. No degree of madness can ever stop this madness, for it is the madness of words."

> . . . it is necessary to level the existing structure of the *Apollinian culture,* as it were, stone by stone, till the foundations on which it rests become visible.
>
> —Nietzsche, *The Birth of Tragedy*

De Man continues the critique of historicism found in Nietzsche, Benjamin, and Derrida. Historicism is monumentalizing despite itself, and stands in the way of accurate historical perception. Yet "historical," in this context, is but a word for "mortal," or that which threatens lasting monument or totalizing mind. "The image caught in the focus of allegorical intuition," Benjamin writes in his book on the German tragic drama, "is fragment, rune. Its symbolic beauty flees as the light of sacred learning falls on it. The false glow [*Schein*] of totality departs." He who ruins may read. Monuments are a denial of mortality, hence of history: a denial that ends in a defacement like that recorded in Shelley's "Ozymandias":

> . . . Two vast and trunkless legs of stone
> Stand in the desert... Near them, on the sand,
> Half sunk, a shattered visage lies, whose frown,
> And wrinkled lip, and sneer of cold command,
> Tell that its sculptor well those passions read
> Which yet survive, stamped on these lifeless things,
> The hand that mocked them, and the heart that fed.

A foundation carries nothing, a visage lies shattered nearby. They mock the represented power of the subject, but also the hand that "mocked" (imitated) them. The giant if ruined forms of the pagan imagination persist into the nineteenth century as an amalgam of Roman and Egyptian fantasies, complicated by

Northern mythology. A capricious art arises, involving among others Piranesi and Fuseli, Collins, Blake, and Keats, before reaching a sort of culmination in Wagnerian opera. This giantism, however, even in Vico, is a divinatory reanimation rather than a historical archeology. "Transmutemini, transmutemini," Robert Fludd wrote, inspired by alchemical metaphors, "de lapidibus mortuis in vivos lapides philosophicos" ("Let us be transformed from dead stones into living, into philosopher stones").

What justifies this *new science* of history is, as in Shelley's sonnet, "those passions read / Which yet survive." Only the passions are lasting; and reading them leads at best to an uncomfortable kind of monumentalizing, which evokes both their sublime and their all-too-human nature. This monumentalizing art is Shelley's inheritance, and he tries to respect its subject, the passions, while forging a subtler, a verbal and musical, mode of representation.

"Those passions read . . ." What of writing itself as a passion? Does not writing jeopardize its own totality: book-monument, verbal icon, enshrined Logos? Shelley's case exhibits the ease with which the very force of writing, one that subverts its own monumentalizing tendency, is ignored or misunderstood. Critical scholarship of Shelley has remained allegorical despite itself. His counterallegorical or antirepresentational "music"—that "subtler language within language"—has not been heard.

A major problem of contemporary criticism is summed up by the question: can there be nonallegorical kinds of reading? Or allegorical only in Benjamin's transvalued sense? This question goes deeper than the problem of ideology, or whether interpretation, however objective in format or content, is tacitly expressive of a *parti pris,* an unconscious or semiconscious politics of culture. It goes right through this problem of ideology to that of theology. For we have seen that criticism is monumentalizing (or totalizing) even when it does not seem to be allegorizing; and that a contrary criticism (sometimes called "deconstructive") finds itself approaching the point where it must break with representational values: the point where theology too abandons allegorical commentary or complicates it so much by levels and modes that it becomes a continued act of figuration.

Allegorical commentary, especially in theology, can be marvelously inventive: one figure displacing another, a ruin of riches, as also in startling moments of Donne or Shelley or Shakespeare. Derrida and de Man reduce this continuous figuration to the concept of *writing*; and they fashion a mode of criticism helplessly ironic in its emphasis on displacement, on words rather than the Word. Philosophy too is seen by them as a mode of writing that tries to achieve the break with representational values through scrutinizing or purging all figures; but philosophy remains a bleached sort of poetry, figurative discourse despite itself.

Here Nietzsche is a key, or an important intermediary. Nietzsche had associated figuration with the Apollinian world of appearances (i.e. representation), with phenomena "imitating" in image or concept a Dionysian music, "the inmost kernel, or heart of things, which precedes all forms" (*The Birth of Tragedy,* especially sections 5 and 16). A "yawning gulf" opens, according to Nietzsche, between the spirit of music and the delight in representational form which that spirit antithetically provokes. Yet is there, one must ask, such difference between writing and music —music as an art-medium, delivered from metaphysics and the Wagnerian context? Or is music not representation that has broken with representation, and that *like all art* is carried by the "passion" of this break, or rather of this breaking, since the break must be repeated, and yields the *form* of art itself as a function of that repetition?[12]

Art as a radical critique of representation—of the conventions that have become a second nature, by which we see what we see, by which we conduct the business of life—can only be challenged by those who live its death, that is, its very integrity as an anti-representational medium. It is they who are driven to insist that art multiplies rather than destroys representation; that it creates fresh modes of perception; that it provides "feet" for thought as real yet imaginary as Blake's: "And did those feet in ancient times / Walk upon England's pleasant green?" As in Blake, the action takes place near a breaking point marked by enlightened superstition; by the figure, for example, of spirit of place or *genius loci,* that gains its vigor through art's struggle with historical place.

12. This is the direction in which I would have to revise my discussion of "Pure Representation" in *The Unmediated Vision* (1954).

Concerning feet: nothing can stand on itself, not even art; nothing can stand without continuing to move, to displace itself, to create its own rotational and gravitational field. Most criticism reposes, however, like baroque entablatures, on plaster giants, on tacit ideological distortions of history, often borrowed and literalized from art itself. The problem with criticism is not that it is necessarily more abstract or allegorizing than art but that it does not show enough of itself while claiming to show all. It is, in short, less radical. "Where are human feet? For lo! my eyes are in the heavens," is the cry of one of Blake's giant forms; this cry for imagination's human base is not Romantic but the voice of every radical position.

Frye turns the cry into a slogan that motivates the systematic enterprise of criticism. Literature is said to "incarnate" imagination, to become its ideal human body. Frye, then, does not break with representation by means of allegory: he uses allegory, rather, to create accommodating archetypes and to achieve an integration *avant la lettre* that weakens the force of the letter by reducing it to the status of catalyst or vanishing agent. Frye comes close to understanding why theology, and now critical theory, is forced to break with representational values by means of the very instrument—traditionally denominated as allegory—that is also used to save appearances. But he continues to save the appearances, and to draw everything into an encyclopedic, monumental, totalizing system.

Criticism deracinates itself when it evades the issue of "representation" in its many, including theological, aspects. Marxist thought, being countertheological rather than atheological, at least keeps the issue alive. It is not afraid of quoting scripture (the idealist or metaphysical tradition) for its purpose. Yet its own god-terms become oppressive and scare the "practical" or clean-thinking Anglo-American critic. After Richards, questions of belief or truth are separated from literary thinking. The idea that literary statements are "pseudo-statements" diverts the heavy traffic, Hegelian or Heideggerian, scientific or theoretical, into an endless detour called "Philosophy of Rhetoric." So diverted it does not even have to be denounced.

Recent "practical criticism" is even more hygienic: it substitutes the issue of "communication" for that of "representation," and limits the mixed richness and rigor of critical discourse. The latter is carefully—neoclassically—separated from poetic and philosophical kinds of writing. But neither the strength nor the fallibility of a literary text, neither its authority nor its self-questioning, can be understood when the literary element is screened out and confined to literature as distinct from philosophy or criticism. However cleansing this stylistic scruple may be, however essential to the demystification of monumental or totalizing perspectives, its very purity exhausts the writer, who often collapses on a word within the words. Capitalize or foreground any word, the word *Word* itself, and you recreate a sublime or allegorical form: a quasitheological, hypostatized entity. On the back of this hunch, as on the back of giant or dwarf, the supposedly purer discourse is carried on.

CHAPTER FIVE

Purification and Danger 1: American Poetry

a reply to Greek and Latin
with the bare hands . . .
—W. C. Williams, *Paterson*

Art is a radical critique of representation, and as such is bound to compete with theology and other, ritual or clinical, modes of purification. "The pure products of America / go crazy," William Carlos Williams wrote; and it is necessary to admit from the outset that the word "pure" has many meanings, some ambiguous, some downright deceptive. Though my theme is purity, and more specifically language purification in American poetry, one could easily write on "Seven Types of Purity." Empson's *Seven Types of Ambiguity* was, in fact, a response to doctrines of "pure poetry" around him.[1] Our new, hypothetical book would start by explaining purity in the strictly rhetorical sense: *sermo purus, Latinitas, katharotes, kathara lexis, Ellenismos.* I am not as learned as I

1. In America Kenneth Burke is sensitive throughout his writings to the "pure poetry" movement, and interesting polemical analyses can be found in R. P. Warren's "Pure and Impure Poetry" (1942), reprinted in *Selected Essays;* and Frederick Pottle's *The Idiom of Poetry* (1941), chap. 5. George Moore's *An Anthology of Pure Poetry* had been published in 1924; in his introduction Moore contrasts didactic verse or thought with "Greek" innocency of vision, claiming also that "Shakespeare never soiled his songs with thought." This antididactic strain in definitions of purity goes over into New Critical precepts, and is strongly influenced by Flaubert, Mallarmé, Gide, and the French Symbolists generally. See the extracts bearing on "purification" in Ellmann and Feidelson's *The Modern Tradition.* This perspective, however, leads back to Hegel's (later, Pater's) understanding of Hellenic "purity" in art, and to Schiller's famous essay on *Naive and Reflective Art* (1795–96).

pretend: this comes right out of the magisterial compendium on literary rhetoric by Heinrich Lausberg. It allows me to make the point that a first definition of purity would already involve historical notions: of Latinity and Hellenism, of classical norms in opposition to Oriental or so-called barbaric features of style.

When the vulgar languages, the national vernaculars, developed their own literature, they were surrounded by classicist censors and snobs. The native product was often denounced as foreign, incult, Asiatic. Voltaire found many of Shakespeare's and Dante's expressions "barbarous." The decorum of the diction itself was taken to be the meaning. It is a nice irony that in our own time Leavis and Eliot attacked Milton's grand style for the obverse reason: their claim was that Milton, unlike Shakespeare, violated the spirit of the vernacular. How complicated and fertile in its tensions this battle over style could become is suggested by the fact that those suspicions of native developments were often fostering a different kind of rejuvenation, a renaissance of the Classics. Contaminated antiquity was to be purified by being reborn in its pristine *vetustas* and *majestas*; this aim of the Renaissance Humanists competed with the birth of a modern, vernacular literature. The break with Latin as an idealized father tongue, an Adamic yet a learned language, was so traumatic because it came at the very time the mother tongue was being cultivated.

Dante, for example, promoted his native dialect not only in the *Commedia* but also in two prose tracts, the *De Vulgari Eloquentia* and *The Banquet*. The first was written in Latin; and they spoke with a cleft tongue in favor of Latin and the vernaculars. Two centuries later, Du Bellay's treatise on the enrichment of French was one of the important Renaissance apologies aiding the rise of the national vernaculars as sophisticated media, but it was not uncritical. There was a recognized need to chasten the vernaculars, to purge them of national or local idiosyncrasy and to make them as elegant as Latin. Against their greening was set a weeding and a pruning: a Latinity to emerge from within.

What I want to emphasize is twofold. It was a poet, Malherbe, who proclaimed, "I will always defend the purity of the French tongue," and it was a poet, Mallarmé, who set out once again to "purify the language of the tribe." Purity is not a scholarly imposition. It is intrinsic to the care of the language we now speak. A "lingua franca et jocundissima" is always being challenged by some ideal of purification: the very Latin Stevens here uses against itself, or scientific standards of correctness, or "de-babelization" (C. K. Ogden's word) through an artificially engendered language, a "Universal Character." Moreover, the issue of poetic diction—an *English* version of the *French* concern for purity—is not a one-sided but a rich and baffling subject. (Owen Barfield's *Poetic Diction* and Donald Davie's *Purity of Diction in English Verse* are still exemplary books in this area.) Good poetic diction is felt to be a language within language that purifies it, restoring original power; bad poetic diction is felt to be artificial rather than natural, a deadening if ornamental set of words and rules. Literary history shows, however, how impossible it is to uphold this distinction between repressive artifice and natural virtue, between conceptions of language that stress an original purity and strength and those that impose an immaculate "classical" or "Aryan" ideal.

Any call for purification or repristination is dangerous. For it is always purity having to come to terms with impurity that drives crazy. The situation is familiar; and whatever the motive for purity, language and religion are its major battlegrounds. The language of religion especially; but also the religion of language itself, language as a quasireligious object when a new vernacular is developing. And American poetry, still striving to break with Anglophile burdens in the 1920s, and more puritanical than it knew, was making the vernacular into a religion.[2]

There is a Nyakyusa saying: "The dead, if not separated from the living, bring madness on them." Ritual helps this separation, according to Mary Douglas in her fascinating book, *Purity and Danger*. Literature is ritual in this sense. William Carlos Williams, writing in the 1920s, after the charnel house of the First World War, in which the dead had risen to claim the living, proclaimed that America had to separate itself from "a civilization of fa-

2. For American reflections on purity of style before the twentieth century, see *The Native Muse: Theories of American Literature*, vol. 1, ed. Richard Ruland (New York: E. P. Dutton), esp. pp. 32–33, 76–77, and 182–83.

tigued spirits," from the defiling if urbane and polished plagiarisms of European culture.[3] Williams can justify even Henry Ford in this light. "My God, it is too disgusting," he writes, thinking of Ford (who said "History is bunk") as the solution. And he adds: "Great men of America! O very great men of America please lend me a penny so I won't have to go to the opera."

He means to *"Lohengrin* in Italian SUNG AT MANHATTAN—", that is, to this artificial international culture, this elitist hybrid art totally alien to native America. Instead of supporting opera, let the commercial industrial complex support real works, and pay the artist a tithe to create the new culture, or as he says satirically, to "capitalize Barnum." The circus metaphor catches something; for the culture that would emerge had plenty of trained animals and clowns (TV before TV) yet lacked the good old animal guides, Blake's "Animal Forms of Wisdom."

For the moment we are still in Williams's grain, looking for a penny to escape the "Traditionalists of Plagiarism," who perpetuate their dead culture through the starspangled absurdity of multinational opera. (In Germany, through the genius of Brecht, a Threepenny Opera does develop.) But are we not also, already, with Allen Ginsberg—thirty years, a generation later? A Ginsberg who is equally broke, though trying to "make contemporarily real an old style of lyric machinery," "W. C. Fields on my left and Jehovah on my right," crying howly, howly, howly, ready to abandon the false India of America for a true one more holy in its stink:

> America, I've given you all and now I'm nothing.
> America two dollars and twentyseven cents January 17, 1956.
> I can't stand my own mind. . .
> Asia is rising against me,
> I haven't got a chinaman's chance.
> I'd better consider my national resources. . .
> America how can I write a holy litany in your silly mood?
> I will continue like Henry Ford my strophes are as individual
>   as his automobiles more so they're all different sexes.
>
> ["America"]

3. I quote from the following sources: *Spring and All* (1923), *The Great American Novel* (1923), and "Marianne Moore" (1925). The text used is that presented in *Imaginations,* ed. Webster Schott.

Where am *I* going, you wonder. It is my purpose to convey a sense of the impasse that came with the Spring Cleaning that Williams undertook in *Spring and All,* and other works of language purification. The impasse was not unproductive: it patented an American type of sublimity. Since then we have not gotten tired of hearing about the American Sublime; its capaciousness, spaciousness, greatness, newness; its readiness to take on experience and remain sublime. Despite ecological and economic disasters that mock these ideals and bust their adherents, the goldrush of every latest poem recycles the agony, redeems the dirt.

Is the pattern, then, all that different from the familiar one of the old European codgers, of William Butler Yeats, for instance, who embraced the "desolation of reality" after the circus animals, his illusions and histrionic attitudes, had gone? At the very time Williams is thinking of "capitalizing" Barnum, Marianne Moore is "translating" Old World "Animal Forms of Wisdom" in her own way. Her splendor too is Menagerie. Compulsively we wash our hands of the old culture, of its *opera* (in the sense of masterworks as well as the baleful Wagnerian instance); we denounce it for being sublime junk, an artificial resuscitation of decadent art; we ritually strengthen ourselves for a rejectionist type of verse close to improvisation and prose poetry, but it never refines itself into actual gold. Dirt and paydirt become one. That puristic turning away from opera, why does it produce so much soap opera? Warmed-over Whitman, confessional poetry? Or why, at best, only golden projects, elaborate scales, played on bluesy piano or jazzed up guitar, all prelude it seems, as we wait for the human story to commence?

Stevens is one of these preludists, a sublime improviser; he too is purging Europe from America, but enjoying and exploiting the thought that it can't be done. The purification, if it is to be, must be more radical than cultural concepts imply. No ideas but in things, was one of Williams's slogans. The idea is that things are cleaner than ideas; and Stevens replies: "How clean the sun when seen in its idea, / Washed in the remotest cleanliness of a heaven / That has expelled us and our images." Where would that cleaning, purging, expelling, end? The paradoxes are many. Williams realizes that the affected words are not purer than before. "I touch the words and they baffle me. I turn them over in my mind and look at them but they mean little that is clean." The dirt of Europe may have been removed, but now the words are plastered with muck out of the cities. When he does write an exemplary poem, antithetical to his prose, with its involuntary waves still tiding after Whitman ("We have only mass movements like a sea"), when he gives us

> So much depends
> upon
>
> a red wheel
> barrow
>
> glazed with rain
> water
>
> beside the white
> chickens

it is marked less by purity than by neatness and composure.

I slow down to look more closely at this well-known poem. It is a sequence of pauses filled by words. It is as if language had only nonnatural sentences, and Williams were seeking a natural sentence: properly rhythmed, punctuated, by the mind pressing against what it perceives. Yet the caesuras here are too sharply, too keenly placed to be only rhythmic pauses. They are deliberate cuts—as deliberate as cutting in the movies or surgery—and place things "beside" each other, avoiding plot or temporal climax. The cutting edge of the caesuras, moreover, here turned inward, suggests an outward-turned force that excludes or could exclude all but its own presence. There is meaning, there is an object focussed on, but there is also something cleaner than both: the very edge of the pen/knife that cuts or delineates these lines. "A word is a word most," Williams wrote, "when it is separated out by science, treated with acid to remove the smudges, washed, dried and placed right side up on a clean surface. . . . It may be used not to smear it again with thinking (the attachments of thought) but in such a way that it will remain scrupulously itself, clean perfect, unnicked, beside other words in parade. There must be edges."

The cleanliness, however, of Williams's phrasing depends so much on what is edged out that we become more interested in what is not there than in what is. The red wheelbarrow moves us into the forgetfulness of pure perception, but also suggests someone can't stand his own mind; it is as functional a carrier of the cultural surplus or whatever nonplusses clean thinking as Ford's slick cars and other vehicular gadgets made in America. A wheel is a wheel, however glossy, however intricate: the earth itself is a wheel we forget. Gilded chariots or red wheelbarrows are equally soothers of memory, anti-mnemonic like a pastoral nature that hides its motives. The strength of *pure* poetry resides, then, like all poetry, in the impure elements it cuts out, elides, covers up, negates, represses . . . depends on: and the strength of *impure* poetry in the very idea of purity that makes it go—and go like—crazy.

I am as susceptible as anyone to the dream of a clean-perfect language: one that no longer mixes images and meanings, desire and memory; that cuts off, leanly, the attachments of thought; that does not contaminate life with dead matter, or the new and the old. I would like Williams's wheel to be my will, and to carry me beyond mere instrumentality: I'd like to think of it as at the navel or omphalos of a spontaneously constituted place of affection, not barren like the backyards of hospitals, even if relieved by that red and white. I'd like those contagious colors, in fact, to carry me by unconscious metaphor beyond the suggestion of disease into a world where "it seems sufficient / to see and hear whatever coming and going is, / losing the self to the victory / Of stones and trees" (A. R. Ammons, "Gravelly Run"). Even here, of course, one cannot lose the self entirely: a certain glaze meets one's gaze, "air's glass / jail seals each thing in its entity." Yet in such a prison one could live happily enough as god's spy or transparent eyeball. No Hegel or Heidegger there to turn a wheelbarrow into a philosophic tool. Best of all, I'd like that wheel to depend, to swing low, and carry me "up" and "on," and make me forget what I am now doing, namely, playing with words that do not stand on themselves but rest on other words. That red wheel, that red barrow, archaic mound of adamic or decomposing flesh, that wheelbarrow left there to cart manure, culture, cadaver, whatever: I want it to compost spiritually, to become words forgotten by words, as nature by nature when Ammons writes: "the sunlight has never / heard of trees." *There* is purity: in that "Nothing that is not there and the nothing that is" (Stevens, "The Snow Man"). "Gravelly Run" ends on the run, as it were, and frosty, as befits a self-purifying landscape, or verses that recall the link of nature poetry to epitaph:

> stranger,
> hoist your burdens, get on down the road.

> exposing his gifted quite empty hands
> —Geoffrey Hill, "In Piam Memoriam"

American poetry, then, like that of older vernacular traditions, is enmeshed in the paradoxes of purifying its words, of constituting itself as a Palladium in the city of words. This relativizing conclusion is unsatisfying, however; it says nothing about why poets have become absolute for poetic purity, martyrs to the art like Mallarmé or Emily Dickinson. I want to discuss the latter of these near contemporaries by looking closely at two lyrics written about three years apart. Read in sequence, their quest for purity appears in a revealing and frightening way. We glimpse, as in the early Williams, and originally in Wordsworth, the link between nature poetry and language purification; between questions of representation and purity of diction; and we understand that nature enters not as the pretext for sublime self-projections but as a privative and admonitory force. The language of nature replaces the dead language of classical or poetic diction; but the language of nature proves to be as monumental as what it replaced. It is a voice speaking from landscape as from a grave; a modern classical idiom in the making; a hieratic vernacular inscription. The burden hoisted by the stranger, or the promise to be kept, includes this purification of the vernacular.

Here is the earlier of the lyrics (783):[4]

> The Birds begun at Four o'clock—
> Their period for Dawn—
> A Music numerous as space—
> But neighboring as Noon—

4. The text of the poems as well as their numbering is taken from *The Poems of Emily Dickinson*, ed. Thomas H. Johnson (as cited in my acknowledgments).

I could not count their Force—
Their Voices did expend
As Brook by Brook bestows itself
To multiply the Pond.

Their Witnesses were not—
Except occasional man—
In homely industry arrayed—
To overtake the Morn—

Nor was it for applause—
That I could ascertain—
But independent Ecstasy
Of Deity and Men—

By Six, the Flood had done—
No Tumult there had been
Of Dressing, or Departure—
And yet the Band was gone—

The Sun engrossed the East—
The Day controlled the World—
The Miracle that introduced
Forgotten, as fulfilled.

There is a plot. Two events, perhaps three, are coordinated, and form a beginning and an end. At four the bird song starts, at six it has stopped. That the sun has risen is the third event, unless contemporaneous with the second. But this plotlike division of time, and these numbers, four, six, are in stylized opposition to the multiplying "force" or flood of the passing music. There is something uncountable despite the counting, the bookkeeping; and it extends to a sun that arrives on the scene with "engrossing" power.[5]

The temporal sequence, then, is deceptive. "Their period for dawn" already suggests the birds have their own dawn within a scheme of "Independent Ecstasy" (stanza 4): their song, neither sanctifying nor theatrical, neither expressly for God nor for Society, cannot be subordinated to an "end." Nor is it subordinated

5. Dickinson likes to use "counting house" terms: her lexicon, Noah Webster's *American* dictionary of the English language, includes the economic sense of "engross" (s.v. 4 in the first, 1828 edition) as well as "to copy in a large hand" (s.v. 5) and "to take or assume in undue quantities or degrees; as, to engross power" (s.v. 6).

to sunrise, since it is said to be "neighboring as Noon." The sun is already in the music. When the sun is mentioned in the last stanza, it is depicted as risen: already in place. Its exact position or power in the scheme of things cannot be calculated any more than the "miracle"—the numerous music—that came and went. The presence of Day is a second "miracle" that replaces the first so completely that the first is "Forgotten, as fulfilled."

The relation between "forgotten" and "fulfilled" is the depth-charge of this small poem; but on the surface Dickinson's lyric carries a moral message as clear as its plot. Nature has style, Nature has the right decorum. Its daily miracles are enacted unselfconsciously. Joyful and strong they may be, but never self-regarding. The birds "expend" their voices, the sun "engrosses" the world. It is a lavish economy, without inhibition or Puritan restraint. "Engross" may imply an overbearing result, but from intrinsic power rather than from a striving for effect. As a statement about devotional verse, or religious rhetoric, the lyric is impertinent: do we need, it hints, a mode of worship that is pretentious, inmixing self-regard or the wish for applause? Yet Dickinson's lyric is itself not beyond reproach: though it exalts unselfconsciousness, its "palpable design" conveys a moral that is witty at best, childish at worst. How *neat* all this is, including her verses! "No Tumult there had been / Of Dressing, or Departure." But neatness is not a major virtue. It is a form of cleanliness in a religion that puts cleanliness next to Godliness.

To purify words about God is Dickinson's apparent aim. She can do more, as we shall see: she can purify God of words. Here she plays an old game, and confuses cleanliness with purity. Almost every religion claims to institute the right worship, the right words. Evangelical religion, in particular, is often fanatic about purity of diction. The peculiar and fascinating thing is that in Dickinson's lyrics nature and style are the same, a divine etiquette. Nature teaches art to hide art for the sake of unselfconsciousness. What is described here is not Nature, but *a mode of being present* that at once values and cancels the self. If there is "imitation of nature" it focusses on how to rise, that is, come to presence, come into *the* Presence.

That sunrise may be sunset, that "the King / Be witnessed" only "at" death (465) makes no difference to the poet. For the "I" is always in a state of mortification: it is both a witness, a selfhood, and purged from or transmuted by the act of witnessing. "The Absolute removed / The Relative away" (765, written circa 1863); the pun on "Relative" suggests that there may have to be a separation from family as well as from time. What o'clock it is becomes irrelevant, therefore; and when the first-person form is used it expresses incapacity: "I could not count their Force," "Nor was it for applause / That I could ascertain." The strong, elliptical ending, "Forgotten, as fulfilled" is as close as one may come to an absolute construction: if it relates to anything it must be the eclipsed "I." The apparent referent, of course, is song, "the miracle that introduced"; but that song is really the poet's, whose presence is elided, "Forgotten, as fulfilled."[6]

The more we ponder this lyric, or its pseudoprogression, the more curious it appears. Is the desire to come to or into Presence so strong that it verges on a death wish? Could we read stanza 5 as intimating: May the departure we call death be as orderly! Could we interpret the hiatus between stanzas 5 and 6—no explicit causal connection joins the vanishing of the birds with the risen sun—as a space death has made or could make? With the last stanza something other than common day seems to be evoked. It is as if the daily event we call sunrise had been quietly displaced by divine day. Do we, after all, reach "Degreeless Noon" (287) "Without a Moment's Bell" (286)? Is the natural silence also the preternatural, as the sun's absolute presence obliterates everything else?

Dickinson's ellipses bear study, though they put an interpreter in the uncomfortable position of arguing from silence. This silence becomes typographic in one formal device, baffling, but at least obtrusive. In many poems an idiosyncratic mark—dash, hyphen, or extended point—replaces the period sign and all other punctuation. It can appear at any juncture, to connect or dis-

6. Sharon Cameron's *Lyric Time: Dickinson and the Limits of Genre* (Baltimore: Johns Hopkins University Press, 1979) has exact remarks on the stanzas as "flashcards" suggesting "the absence of any trace left from a previous moment/ picture." See her discussion of "The Birds begun" and "At half past three" on pp. 176–78. She calls "begun" a "strange preterite" (perhaps, I would add, a nominative absolute or pseudo-infinitive, though the 1828 Webster lists *begun* as an alternate preterite form) and points to the complicated grammar of the poem's last line.

connect, generally to do both at once. It is a caesura or *coupure* more cutting than that of Williams. It introduces from the beginning the sense of an ending and both extends and suspends it. The semantic value of this hyphen is zero, but it allows the asyndetic sentences to become an indefinite series of singular and epigrammatic statements. The zero endows them with the value of one, with loneliness or one-liness as in an amazing poem that begins "The Loneliness One dare not sound" (777).

Why does this formal mark, this hyphen with zero meaning, have intraverbal force? Perhaps because it both joins and divides, like a hymen. Perhaps because it is like the line between dates on tombstones. It may be an arbitrary sign or it may be nakedly mimetic. In any case, the decorous proposition that nature is style is radicalized: this elliptical, clipped mark evokes style as nature. That hyphen-hymen persephonates Emily. At every pause, which it institutes, it can remind us of her wish to be a bride of quietness. "Title divine–is mine!" (1072) But her only title may be her epitaphic lyrics, that sum up a life by brief inscriptions, very much like titles. The briefest inscription would be the letters E. D. and a set of hyphenated dates. The hyphen-hymen matters more than the dates, for what is crucial is the moment of juncture: dawning/dying, an unviolent transition from natural to supernatural, like waking into a dream, nature not being put out but "Forgotten, as fulfilled."

We come to Dickinson's later, less readable poem (1084):

At Half past Three, a single Bird
Unto a silent Sky
Propounded but a single term
Of cautious melody.

At Half past Four, Experiment
Had subjugated test
And lo, Her silver Principle
Supplanted all the rest.

At Half past Seven, Element
Nor Implement, be seen–
And Place was where the Presence was
Circumference between.

How dry and bookish, as if a computer had been given a number of words, and instructed to produce a minimal narrative! Only that narrative remains from the earlier version, though more stark, more outlined; the pathos and the moral play are gone. The sun too is gone, and the personal focus of reference. In this emptied landscape abstractions nest a "single Bird," the remnant of a purification whose motive we are trying to find.

Now one-stanza-one-act is the formula; and this new, unlavish economy extends to theme. A single term, a single note, rather than a numerous and multiplying music begins the action; then the bird sings freely; then it has ceased. One, two, three.

The time indicators, which periodize the event, terminating its three parts like a stop watch, heighten the contrary force of the poem's last word. That last word is like the first of each stanza, "At Half past. . . ." It marks what lies *between* integers.

The between remains: something not whole, not at once. Yet the drive toward atonement is haltingly continued in this poem, which is paced without auction or augmentation—without pseudoprogression. *Half past* is repeated, and half past is a turning point that does not turn. The first of these poems was written close to the age of thirty-three; the second three years later.

Though "between" sticks out, is it a middle or a mediation? Other words too stick out, despite their effort to blend. They resemble each other as terms, even when their meanings are separable. So "Experiment," "Element," "Implement" rhyme obscurely. It is hard, moreover, to hold onto the distinction between "Place" and "Presence." A nonrepresentational quality suffuses everything and counterpoints the temporal markers—we don't even know, for sure, whether morning or evening, sunrise or sunset, is the period, because all mention of light is omitted. We could be listening from the grave.

Not quite: "silver Principle" contains a hint of light breaking. Yet the paradox remains that light breaks what it should illumine. Something, at the end, is not seen that was seen before. The very words become obscure. What *visibilia* do "Element" and "Implement" describe? Does "Element" refer to sky or bird or the music itself? Since "Implement" follows, we assign "Element" to a range of meanings exclusive of "Bird." The technique, if we can so designate it, approaches modern devices that Hart Crane called "as independent of any representational motive as a mathematical equation."[7] The earlier lyric had as its subject a problematic coming to or into Presence; now it is a coming into absence or indeterminacy.

The only way to resolve the indeterminate meaning of "Element" and "Implement" is to remember the earlier lyric and its conclusion: "Forgotten, as fulfilled." This suggests that "Implement" may have its etymological meaning of *implere,* that which fills, and "Element" could denote either what is filled or the beginning, the first term, in contradistinction to the last. "Neither beginning nor fulfillment is seen" (at the end), is what the stanza says. The meaning of the two poems is comparable.

If so, how do we interpret the later poem's shift toward verbal abstraction and a nonrepresentational method? Hart Crane thought that between Impressionism and Cubism poetry as well as painting was moving away from religion and toward science. This largish and imprecise speculation does not help too much. For the themes of Dickinson's lyric are neither religion nor science. Words as words have moved to the fore, words that are about to be "terms"—fixed, as if by rigor mortis. The clock strikes for them too. If they escape that fixity, that transformation of language into *last words,* it is because they still evoke, in their very abstraction, past meanings, referents at once mathematical, musical, chronometric, experimental, teleological, even typological.[8]

The poem, therefore, never progresses; it is still moving, at

7. See his "Modern Poetry" (1929), published in *The Complete Poems of Hart Crane,* ed. Waldo Frank (New York: Liveright, 1933).

8. *Implere figuram* is the term in theology for the *kairos* moment, when history moves "from shadowy Types to Truth" (Milton). The shadowy types are Old Testament figures or events, the Truth their repetition with fulfillment in the New Testament. This figural or typological perspective was extended to secular history in general: its happenings were similarly conceived as types or emblems for a superseding truth. The pattern of "Forgotten, as fulfilled," since it embraces "Implement" as well as "Element," last and first, suggests a metatypological perspective, an overcoming of typology. Cf. Robert Weisbuch, *Emily Dickinson's Poetry* (Chicago: University of Chicago Press, 1975): "the bird song is a foreshadowing type of the day, and yet we suspect that the introductory 'forgotten' miracle is granted superiority over its fulfillment" (p. 122 and p. 193, n. 20). Roland Hagenbüchle's "Dickinson Criticism," *Anglia* 97 (1979): 452–74, may be consulted for others who have dealt with the issues of reference and indeterminacy.

the end, toward a "single term." This term is not found in the dictionary: the dictionary, perhaps, is in search of it. At present, or *at* any moment that can be fixed with the mock precision of "Half past," it is merely a cipher, a divine clue. An expected *god-term* (to borrow from Kenneth Burke) supplants all the rest and places what was life and time in a radically displaced position: into a place for which the names Death or Purgatory have been used, though they are not definitive. If we take this "term" seriously, then time may be transformed at any moment: by a cockcrow that is taps, or a single note that is the trumpet call of the Apocalypse. As you lie down, each bed is a grave. "The Grave preceded me—" (784). As you rise up, a bird is the prelude to revelation. The structure of human life, from this phantomizing perspective, is a chiasmus, a crossing over from nothing to all and vice-versa: from life to death, from death to life, absence to presence, and so on. "Love—is anterior to Life— / Posterior—to Death— / Initial of Creation, and / The Exponent of Earth—" (917).

Looking back at both poems, we can spot where that chiasmus rises up and phantomizes as well as founds the terminological work. "And Place was where the Presence was" is two-faced, since it could be an expression for sheer vacancy or sheer plenitude. Place is the absence of a Presence that had been; *or* Place coincides with Presence. The one meaning does not merely coexist with the other as a type of ambiguity: the one meaning is the other, so that both remain occupying, in the same words, the same place. That is the unsettled and interminable state of affairs which "Circumference between" seems to fix forever.

Let me conclude by exploring this cryptic phrase. It is again an "absolute" construction, which we cannot attach to specific meaning or referent. To play a little, we might say that it makes reference circumferential; it so broadens it by abstraction that referentiality itself, or the representational force in words, is simultaneously evoked and revoked. Representation itself is "between" us and Presence. Or representation is the only Presence we have. "Myself—the Term between—" (721).

Whether or not this impasse (founded in the religious sensibility, but removed from institutionalized words that refer us to religion) is the residual meaning, the absoluteness of "Circumference between" is like a shudder, a cold shower perhaps. Faith and Hope, that rely on "the evidence of things not seen," are emergent at this point; yet there is no overt sign of this, and it is hard to imagine what sustenance they could find in such a void. The silent sky has returned, and the landscape is washed out, though we don't know if by radiance or if by darkness. All we can do is explore the impasse by means of those terminating words.

Circumference is a periphery, away from the center, whether the figure thought of is spatial (a circle) or temporal (the earth's circuit around the sun, bringing back the beginning or the whole event just recounted). "Circumference between" could point to earth (life on earth), or the clock itself in its roundness: that repeated watching and waiting which is a religious duty as well as a symptom of alienated labor. "Circumference between" could be that displaced place for which the Christian name is Death or Purgatory, and which intrudes "between" us and God, eternally perhaps. Circumference as that which interposes could be the most abstract cipher of them all, zero, or whatever nonrepresentational figure can hold together, in some imageless image, the juncture of life and death, death and life, self-presence and the divine presence. "I could not see to see—" (465). If we ask what "be seen" at the end, as at the end of this poem, the answer would have to be: nothing, *or* all, *or* their juncture as zero.

The two endings, then, "Forgotten, as fulfilled" and "Circumference between" are simply a hyphen-hymen written out, or last words *not* given to the void. They help us to understand why the poetry Dickinson brings forth is so lean. It would not be wrong to ask how she can be a great poet with so small a voice, so unvaried a pattern, so contained a form of experience. Is her desire for purity perhaps the sign of a sensibility easily exhausted, depleted by smallest things that inflate: "You saturated Sight—" (640)? Whereas, with many poets, criticism has to confront their overt, figurative excess, with such purifiers of language as Emily Dickinson criticism has to confront an elliptical and chaste mode of expression. The danger is not fatty degeneration but lean degeneration: a powerful, appealing anorexia. She herself called it "sumptuous Destitution" (1382). Since this is certainly prompted by her interpretation of Puritan scruples about language-art—"Farewell sweet phrases, lovely metaphors" (George Herbert)—we cannot dismiss the possibility that she so identifies with an ascesis forced upon her, that instead of the milk of hope she substitutes the "White Sustenance— / Despair" (640). Her criticism of Puritan culture, or of the God of the Puritans, would have been to make herself a visible reproach by becoming so invisible, by wasting the substance of poetry with such deliberation and precision, like a saint. Yet not believing in saints or mediations, only her poetry can stand for her: representation, not mediation, is her hope. Her words, always tending toward last words, may be an act of resistance: her literal acceptance of Puritan decorum figures forth the uncompromised life of the words that remain.

> Capacity to terminate
> Is a Specific Grace
>
> —Emily Dickinson (1196)

I am not good at concluding; I would prefer at this point to lose myself in the thought that poetry, like life, goes on, despite this amazing, dangerous quest for purity, manifested in Dickinson's endgame of words. I would prefer to quote John Ashbery, for example, because he is more relaxed, always convalescing it seems, converting what was oracular and blazing into divine chatter:

> Light falls on your shoulders, as is its way,
> And the process of purification continues happily.
>
> ["Evening in the Country"]

The burden of light, in Dickinson, despite her attempt to maintain decorum, seems heavier. Like Mallarmé, she is a crucial poet, a dangerous purifier, the offspring of a greater Apollo. In the German tradition Hölderlin, Rilke, and Celan have a similar relation to a purity more radical than what went under the name of Classicism. These poets are so intense—Shelley is another—they place so great a burden on the shoulders of poetry, that language breaks with itself. Mallarmé said he wanted to take back from music what belonged to poetry; that is one way of describing a break with representation more complete than conventional or classical form allowed. That form is but a second nature, a cleansing and not a purification. A more radical Classicism had to be discovered: that of Dionysos or, according to Nietzsche's interpretation of Wagner, Dionysian music. Theology may inspire but it no longer mediates this break with representation. Poets having expelled the old gods, their images, their phraseology—in short, poetic diction—and, having instituted a more natural diction, the process of purification continues, not so happily, and the purified language proves to be as contaminated as ever. We see that the poetic diction once rejected had extraordinary virtues, including its nonnatural character, its lucid artifice, the "mirror-of-steel uninsistence" (Marianne Moore) by which it made us notice smallest things and ciphered greatest things, and gathered into a few terms, magical, memorable, barely meaningful, the powers of language.

CHAPTER SIX

Purification and Danger 2: Critical Style

> For if the sun breed maggots in a dead dog, being a God, kissing carrion . . .
>
> —*Hamlet* (Dr. Johnson's edition)

A strange thought comes to Emerson on reading Carlyle's *Sartor Resartus.* It is an uncleanly book, a rag-bag philosophy, conceived (Carlyle jokes) among the Old Clothes shops of London, though rising to transcendental flights of fancy. "There is a part of ethics," writes Emerson, ". . . which possesses all attraction to me; to wit, the compensations of the Universe, the equality and the coexistence of action and reaction, that all prayers are granted, that every debt is paid. And the skill with which the great All maketh clean work as it goes along, leaves no rag, consumes its smoke."[1]

Undoubtedly there is something smoky or excrementitious about Carlyle's style. Such highpitched language, Emerson suggests, should burn more purely. He has no objection to enthusiasm or transcendentalism as such. Only to the "dithyrambic" style—not Emerson's term but Nietzsche's, who calls his *Zarathustra* a "dithyramb" to purity. Nietzsche had the same difficulty as Carlyle with a style that seems impure to us—unnatural, manic, pseudoprophetic. Between the ordinary subject matter of those books and their extraordinary rhetoric there is disharmony; and Erich Auerbach, noting a similar tension in Balzac and Hugo, thought it expressed the strain of taking everyday reality with high seriousness (see *Mimesis,* chap. 18). From this point of view Carlyle and Nietzsche are failed realistic novelists. They understand some-

1. Letter of 12 March 1835. The immediate context is Emerson's wish to give "the binding force of an oracular word" to Carlyle's intimation that he would visit Concord.

thing of the material and economic base of even the highest thoughts, but they cannot incarnate their perceptions in contemporary life.

Emerson's response to Carlyle had suggested a relation between style and economy. (For Emerson, of course, art reflected a *divine* economy, a cosmic production and purging of all things.) Yet the impure or extravagant element in the diction of these writers has an interest of its own: it is, as occasionally in Milton and Pope, an evacuated high style, an unauthorized tongue whose "carnival" qualities are far from empty or uncolloquial.[2] An older hieratic speech, biblical, mystical, or popular-sermonic, pierces with "Asiatic" force through "Attic" veils. Sometimes this neo-Orientalism is as vapid and stylized as the Neoclassicism it replaced. But sometimes it gathers countercultural strength and exhibits its feeding source in the material messianism of popular figuration. Yet, to judge by Carlyle and Nietzsche, this language can only be parodied, not appropriated: its weight and resonance make a fool of whatever modern writer dares impersonate it. The modern writer, consequently, parodies it so that it will not parody him.

This style, then, inherently excessive or transgressive, can only be savored in itself. It *mortifies* (often by laughter) natural language, or rather what is considered as natural by the civilized mind. Like allegory, in Benjamin's view, it disturbs classical or normative representation. Strangely physiognomic and mimic, it tends toward a sense of the corruption of the flesh that has gusto as well as disgust in it. All these aspects are clarified when Joyce heightens the style's oracular verve in one of the famous parodies from "The Oxen of the Sun" chapter of *Ulysses,* which interlards Carlyle and Nietzsche:

> How saith Zarathustra? *Deine Kuh Trübsal melkest Du. Nun trinkst Du die süsse Milch des Euters.* See! It displodes for thee in abundance. Drink, man, an udderful! Mother's milk, Purefoy, the milk of human kin, milk too of those burgeoning stars

2. Cf. Bakhtin on carnivals in *Rabelais and His World;* also W. K. Wimsatt on the Augustans in *Hateful Contraries*: "My view is that the English Augustans were, at their best and at their most characteristic, laughing poets of a heightened unreality" (p. 158).

> overhead, rutilant in thin rainvapour, punch milk, such as those rioters will quaff in their guzzlingden, milk of madness, the honey-milk of Canaan's land. Thy cow's dug was tough, what? Ay, but her milk is hot and sweet and fattening. No dollop this but thick rich bonnyclabber. To her, old patriarch! Pap!

The urbane reader finds this intolerable when offered straight. Dwight Macdonald praised Joyce for calling Carlyle's bluff. ". . . Thomas Carlyle, who racked and tortured our sweet English tongue as mercilessly as any pidgin-speaking South Sea islander; that he was considered a literary giant (instead of the inventor of *Timestyle)* shows a decline in standards; using Carlyle's frenetic, bastardized style as the transition to the death of English in the gutter was one of Joyce's happiest inspirations."[3] But do we honor style only when it reduces to a transparent or accommodated prose?

Historically, there was a standard of prose, and especially of expository prose, that the vernacular had to achieve. French Neoclassicism led the way here too; the strictures against figurative language in Sprat and the Royal Society imitated the French Academy and neoclassical ideals of diction. Today, therefore, it is as hard, if not harder, to read Rabelais and Montaigne as it is to read Luther, or English prose of the sixteenth century.

Yet prose has a way of escaping the *genera dicendi,* the Classicist doctrine of levels of style that intended to match occasion and diction. Critical prose, insofar as it had a specific level, belonged to the middle or conversational style; but that, like the middle class, was a tenuous composite, subject to dynamic shifts. It was developed for the purpose of polite conversation, in drawing room or salon, as well as for the exchange of news by "corresponding members" of a social circle or intellectual group. There might be differences of profession or of standing within a group, but there would be a common language, a vernacular of the intellect.

Plato's dialogues, Classical letter-writers, and, in poetry, Horace's *Sermones,* allowed this model of a conversational style to establish itself against technical or oracular modes of instruction. Even Gadamer's philosophical hermeneutics still holds to this

3. Dwight Macdonald, ed., *Parodies: An Anthology from Chaucer to Beerbohm —and After,* p. 524.

"Platonic" conception of a shared language that is presupposed or else created by the interpretive activity. "Something is placed in the center, as the Greeks say. . . ."[4] But Gadamer, who makes the conversational or dialogic model the very norm of understanding, evades the question posed by the grand or grotesque style with its vatic-popular roots (*vox populi, vox Dei*). In almost every significant writer of the modern period, the conversational or "friendship" style, and the oracular or priestly mode, mix uneasily. To invest conversation with the power of revelation, or dialogue with truth-inducing virtue, is a comforting, commendably middle-class, yet unstable and precarious ideal.

The problem in the eyes of Carlyle's contemporaries was not so much *Sartor*'s attack on the narrowness of British intellectual life or the introduction of a philosophical criticism. It was the style in which this was conducted. We saw that Emerson, the champion of *Sartor* in America, was perplexed by the "oddity of the vehicle." His first letter to Carlyle raised the issue. "Did ever wise and philanthropic author use so defying a diction? As if society were not sufficiently shy of truth without providing it beforehand with an objection to the form. Can it be that this humor proceeds from a despair of finding a contemporary audience . . . so be pleased to skip those excursive involved glees, and give us the simple air, without the volley of variations. At least in some of your prefaces you should give us the theory of your rhetoric."[5]

It was clearly a question of style, and no one understood the theory behind Carlyle's rhetoric. His tone is fast and loud, like an announcer at the races or a boxing match. There is a mock-heroic enlargement of events. This sort of prose had not existed in English criticism; perhaps not in German either, despite Carlyle's praise of "learned, indefatigable, deep-thinking Germany." Carlyle's impure and thunderous diction, "Rhapsodico-Reflective" (John Sterling), which addresses itself, as on the final page of his

4. *Truth and Method,* 2.2.3c ("The Logic of Question and Answer"). The poem from Rilke that serves as the book's epigraph joins the ideas of middle (*Mitte*) and playmate (*Mitspielerin*); but Rilke stresses the difficulty of reception (*Fangen-können*) in a game where the receiver has to catch a ball thrown at him (at his very center) suddenly.

5. Letter of 14 May 1834.

book, to the irritated rather than gentle reader, was the opposite of a tempered, conversational manner of writing. *Sartor* challenged the principle of decorum on which cultural commentary had proceeded: that, except for outright satire or polemics (of which Swift and Arbuthnot were the models) it should be an extension of the familiar essay or the letter to the *Spectator* or *Gentleman's Magazine*. Carlyle saw—as Proust did later in his *Contre Sainte-Beuve*—that to reduce criticism to formal conversation was to reduce literature to formal conversation, to "belles lettres."

> the ritual importance of eagle hunting among the Hidatsa is at least partly due to the use of pits, to the assumption by the hunter of a particularly *low* position . . . for capturing a quarry which is in the very *highest* position. . . . [I]n eagle hunting, conceived as the narrowing of a wide gulf between hunter and game, mediation is effected, from the technical point of view, by means of the bait, a piece of meat or small piece of game, the bloodstained carcass which is destined to rapid decay. . . . The bloodstained carcass, soon to be carrion . . . is the means of effecting the capture.
>
> —Claude Lévi-Strauss, *The Savage Mind*

Despite Emerson's fantasy and cognate ideals of language, the work of purification never consumes the evidence of its labors. *Druck* (print) and *Dreck* (dirt) do converge, as in *Teufelsdröckh*. No need to be a Lutheran to see the connection. The purest writers leave a corpse of writings: only their style can deceive, art hiding art, flinging about dung with grace (Addison's praise of Vergil's achievement in the *Georgics*), or making light of heavy. The general economics of style are still to be described, but the Emersonian vision of style is certainly alchemical as it turns excrement into the airiest beaten gold and sublimes away not only the text as a commodity but even the sense of labor itself.

Carlyle and Nietzsche, however, have a style, and even too much. They extrovert labor in a mock-muscular way. They try so obviously to lift their own spirits, which are as heavy as matter. (Nietzsche's favorite image for Zarathustra is that of a dancer, whose Dionysian *Schwermuth,* "abysmal thoughts," do not affect his joyful, quasihellenic demeanor.) Disgust itself grows wings, says Nietzsche, becomes eagle-like and is absolved (*Ecce Homo,* section 8). In this there lurks a myth of redemption and its link to Aesopian language, to "the mystery of mediation from an animal sphere."[6]

This holds even for Derrida, whose concern with purification expresses itself in *Glas* (see the reproduction on pp. 140–41) as a question of style. There is, on the one hand, Jean Genet's elegant profanity: the use of the purest, most classical French to portray criminal and obscene acts. The mother tongue, having been suppressed by an extended patronym (classical French) now exists only as an immaculately profane ideal, a specter. There is, on the other hand, Hegel's deceptive elision of the question of style: of the *Sa,* the *signifiant* (signifier) or its material/acoustic base. Hegel predicted the replacement of art by a philosophical prose that was already converting, in the *Phenomenology,* his own family romance into world-historical intuitions. This style eliminated most proper names, leaving nothing behind but an obstinate meditation on ghostly remainders. Hence the irony of Derrida's opening: "What remains, today, for us, here and now, of Hegel?"

These words, which echo Hegel's own (remarks on the "Now" at the very outset of the *Phenomenology*), may also express the fact that nothing remains of Hegel's immense and—according to its own moving principle—self-sublating labor except a certain kind of writing. What the world-spirit leaves behind, according to Hegel, is the presence of history—an internalized history, however, or the deferred "Now" of philosophical language.

This language cannot be accommodated, in Derrida's view, to a single register or level of style. Where Gadamer, claiming to follow both Hegel and Plato, sees language as "fusing horizons" through dialogic exchange, Derrida sets column against column, signifier against signified, and the act of writing against homogeneous discourse. So the word *Hegel* itself is as substantial as a proper name or signature that seals a document. But *Hegel* is

6. Mary Douglas, *Purity and Danger,* p. 199. Derrida's *Glas* takes as the first Hegel passage to be discussed the transition from "flower religion" to "animal religions" in the "Natural Religion" section of the *Phenomenology.*

also as light and high-flying as the pun that converts the name into *aigle,* and makes it appear as Nietzsche's winged *Ekel* ("disgust") that soars aloft like vatic bird into a region of pure transparency. A region where "light is speech," as Marianne Moore declares, "speech / and light, each / aiding each—when French."

Yet opacity and disgust return via Genet's *je m'éc* (see the opening of *Glas*), a charged phrase in its original context, expressing Genet's sexual nausea or fear of depletion, and challenging as an equivocal and fragmented word the purity of the mother tongue. In Derrida, the desire for purity or transparency, which was also the subject of Emerson's physicotheological reflection, becomes explicitly a question of style that mocks both the elation of *Aufhebung* and its current form as semiotics. Derrida depicts the law of exchange proposed by semiotics as yet another post-classical defeat of the project of rationalizing language, that is, making it calculable in all its parts. "Each column," he writes, alluding to the two columns on his printed page, as well as to the monumentalist aspiration of art,

> each column transports itself upward with unmoveable self-sufficiency, and yet the element of contagion, the infinite circulation of general equivalence, relates each phrase, each word, each truncated piece of writing . . . to every other, within each column and from column to column: *what has remained* [is] infinitely calculable.

There is always a residue that cannot be resolved into unequivocal meaning or recountable, accountable story. *Glas* remains a Hegelian rag. "Paper is made from the *rags* of things that did once exist" (Carlyle).

> it is significant that the same native term is used for the embrace of lovers and the grasping of the bait by the bird. . . . [A]t a semantic level, pollution, at least in the thought of the North American Indians, consists in too close a conjunction between two things each meant to remain in a state of "purity."
>
> —Claude Lévi-Strauss, *The Savage Mind*

"Where there is no differentiation," writes Mary Douglas in *Purity and Danger,* "there is no defilement." The most elementary work of taxonomy and classification goes on in language, at

quoi du reste aujourd'hui, pour nous, ici, maintenant, d'un Hegel?

Pour nous, ici, maintenant : voilà ce qu'on n'aura pu désormais penser sans lui.

Pour nous, ici, maintenant : ces mots sont des citations, déjà, toujours, nous l'aurons appris de lui.

Qui, lui?

Son nom est si étrange. De l'aigle il tient la puissance impériale ou historique. Ceux qui le prononcent encore à la française, il y en a, ne sont ridicules que jusqu'à un certain point : la restitution, sémantiquement infaillible, pour qui l'a un peu lu, un peu seulement, de la froideur magistrale et du sérieux imperturbable, l'aigle pris dans la glace et le gel.

Soit ainsi figé le philosophe emblémi.

Qui, lui? L'aigle de plomb ou d'or, blanc ou noir, n'a pas signé le texte du savoir absolu. Encore moins l'aigle rouge. D'ailleurs on ne sait pas encore si *Sa* est un texte, a donné lieu à un texte, s'il a été écrit ou s'il a écrit, fait écrire, laissé écrire.

On ne sait pas encore s'il s'est laissé enseigner, signer, ensigner. Peut-être y a-t-il une incompatibilité, plus qu'une contradiction dialectique, entre l'enseignement et la signature, un magister et un signataire. Se laisser penser et se laisser signer, peut-être ces deux opérations ne peuvent-elles en aucun cas se recouper.

Sa sera désormais le sigle du savoir absolu. Et l'*IC*, notons-le déjà puisque les deux portées se représentent l'une l'autre, de l'Immaculée Conception. Tachygraphie proprement singulière : elle ne va pas d'abord à disloquer, comme on pourrait croire, un code c'est-à-dire ce sur quoi l'on table trop. Mais peut-être, beaucoup plus tard et lentement cette fois, a en exhiber les bords

Sa signature, comme la pensée du reste, enveloppera ce corpus mais n'y sera sans doute pas comprise.

Ceci est — une légende.

Non pas une fable : une légende. Non pas un roman, un roman familial puisque s'y agit la famille de Hegel, mais une légende.

Elle ne prétend pas donner à lire le tout du corpus, textes et desseins de Hegel, seulement deux figures. Plus justement deux figures en train de s'effacer : deux passages.

reste à penser : ça ne s'accentue pas ici maintenant mais se sera déjà mis à l'épreuve de l'autre côté. Le sens doit répondre, plus ou moins, aux calculs de ce qu'en termes de gravure on appelle contre-épreuve

« *ce qui est resté d'un Rembrandt déchiré en petits carrés bien réguliers, et foutu aux chiottes* » se divise en deux.

Comme le reste.

Deux colonnes inégales, disent-ils, dont chaque — enveloppe ou gaine, incalculablement renverse, retourne, remplace, remarque, recoupe l'autre.

L'incalculable de *ce qui est resté* se calcule, élabore tous les coups, les tord ou les échafaude en silence, vous vous épuiseriez plus vite à les compter. Chaque petit carré se délimite, chaque colonne s'enlève avec une impassible suffisance et pourtant l'élément de la contagion, la circulation infinie de l'équivalence générale rapporte chaque phrase, chaque mot, chaque moignon d'écriture (par exemple « *je m'éc...* ») à chaque autre, dans chaque colonne et d'une colonne à l'autre de *ce qui est resté* infiniment calculable.

A peu près.

Il y a du reste, toujours, qui se recoupent, deux fonctions.

L'une assure, garde, assimile, intériorise, idéalise, relève la chute dans le monument. La chute s'y maintient, embaume et momifie, monumémorise, s'y nomme — tombe. Donc, mais comme chute, s'y érige.

Page 7 from Jacques Derrida's *Glas*.

all levels of speaking and writing. *Glas* incorporates this "linguistic turn" also by assimilating paragraphs of definitions from major dictionaries composed along historical lines (especially Wartburg's) and significant citations from structural linguistics. Yet linguistics, seen from the point of view of literature, is not a transcendent form of analysis that orders all things well and leaves nothing over. It is a burdensome technical discipline seeking to master knowledge through knowledge. It creates a further set of terms, or distinctions, that put new pressure on us, as if we had eaten again of the tree of knowledge. What is to be done with this superadded consciousness, these supersessive terms? Science may correct wrong ideas or remove vulgar superstitions; yet nothing, so it seems, can purify language by substituting for it an absolute diction. Though the scientific or mystical aspiration toward one language, of Adamic or Universal character, crops up in every era, historically we inherit only the *language trajectory* of this purifying desire, a residue called literature, that both represents and belies it.

The select remainders or bits and pieces, therefore, that *Glas* glues together—they come from all sides of the literary culture, from literature and linguistics as well as from philosophy—are a by-product of this differentiating activity; and they are dangerous as long as they retain a vestigial spark of identity, a resonant marginal value that provokes awareness of their factitious unity and leads to boundary transgression. In that sense *Glas* is, deliberately, all margins: instead of a well-argued commentary or shapely fiction we find a series of elaborated quotations, fragments whose "half-identity still clings to them and the clarity of the scene in which they obtrude is impaired by their presence." Douglas's last chapter is entitled "The System Shattered and Renewed"—the hidden pun in *Sartor* (taylor/teller) also points to the need of retelling, and accepting the fact that writers are in the second-hand word business. If their aim is a holistic text (a book), as well as a text that can make things whole (a Bible), then that retailed tale must function like the "kingly victim" in the sorrowful mysteries of the pangolin cult as Mary Douglas describes it. The pangolin is seen as a self-devoted victim through whose atoning (at-one-ing) the Lele overcome the impurity and ambiguity afflicting a highly formalized existence:

> The Lele pangolin cult is only one example, of which many more could be cited, of cults which invite their initiates to turn around and confront the categories on which their whole surrounding culture has been built up and to recognize them for the fictive, man-made, arbitrary creations that they are. Throughout their daily, and especially their ritual, life the Lele are preoccupied with form. Endlessly they enact the discriminations by which their society and its cultural environment exist, and methodically they punish or attribute misfortune to breaches of avoidance rules. . . . So the pangolin cult is capable of inspiring a profound meditation on the nature of purity and impurity.[7]

> Whoever speaks German knows well what a good, affectionate word that is: dear Maria [*die liebe Maria*]. . . . And I am not at all sure one can express the word "dear" so warmly and satisfyingly in Latin or in other tongues, so that it penetrates and resonates in one's heart and through all one's senses, as it does in our speech [*das ebenso dringe und klinge in's Herz durch alle Sinne . . .*].
>
> —Luther, *Epistle on Translation*

The extreme result of ideals of purity in language is glottophagia, or swallowing one's tongue. But in the immense domain of language repression glottophagia may be produced by events from personal or public history we cannot even see except in their censored form. Why does Christopher Smart write "Let Ziba rejoice with Glottis whose tongue is wreathed in his throat"? His antiphonal "For I am the seed of the WELSH WOMAN and speak the truth from my heart" implies a disturbance touching at once the mother and the mother tongue. We begin to suspect that the structure of jokes or wit or slips of tongue (the swallowed tongue) resembles that of poetic language generally. What we get to see is always a palimpsest or a contaminated form of some kind: a stratum of legitimate, sacred, or exalted words purifying a stratum of guilty, forbidden, or debased words.

Repression, then, or the "wreathed" language resulting from it, is so much part of language itself that the idea of purity must

7. *Purity and Danger*, pp. 200–01.

be projected out of historical and into mythic time, while actual speaking, writing, living, continues in a "meantime" motivated and threatened by notions of a purer speech. And the richest tangle in the "wreath" is that of divine with infantile.

The case of Smart is telling, but that of Dante is better known. We are informed that Dante called his "Divine" poem a "Comedy" because it was written in the vernacular and made use of low-style expressions restricted to the relatively nonserious realm of popular or comic art. Yet art, for Freud, was simply the maturest form of infantile wishfulness, and the adult must be ready to treat as "comic" its divinization of instincts or desires. In more strictly literary terms, what the divine comedy of art does is to save the *mammalashon*. It prevents the mother tongue from being totally displaced by some "secondary speech"—the father tongue, the conqueror's idiom, or, to quote Dante, "what the Romans called Grammar." Is that also why, in his extended Catullan lyric, "Philip Sparrow," John Skelton speaks in the person of a young girl as he exhibits the intimate yet unfulfilled promise of his native tongue?

I am but a young maid,
And cannot in effect
My style as yet direct
With English words elect.
Our natural tongue is rude,
And hard to be ennewed
With polished termes lusty;
. . . .
I wot not where to find
Terms to serve my mind.

Insofar as linguistic science, rhetoric, structuralism, etc., are "Roman" disciplines, they wean us from too great a dependence on the mother tongue. But even they, perhaps, attempt to save it in their own way—by the extreme expedient of separating off the father tongue, by developing systematically a secondary diction. There are those who claim there is nothing but Grammar or secondariness: artificial dictions or terms of art elaborated *contra naturam*. Yet by participating in the quasipsychotic rigor of that kind of systematic exhalation they could be suspected of preserving an area of purity. Something—nature, the mother, the mother tongue, or a metamaternal "language of nature"—is made inviolate by being put beyond reach. The fence or defense of discontinuity may be the strongest of them all. It seems to absolutize the separation of sacred and secular.

If pure secularism, therefore, is simply another religion, its ghost or god will appear at some point. That is why comparisons are possible between a "divine" poem like Dante's and a secular essay like Thoreau's *Walden*. Thoreau identifies the mother tongue with speech (the language heard) and the father tongue with writing (the language read). He acknowledges, like the School of Derrida, the "memorable interval" between them. He shocks us, in fact, by the extreme frankness of his preference for written over spoken. I do not recall a statement in Derrida quite so revealing from a psychological point of view as this from the famous chapter on "Reading" in *Walden*:

> The one [language] is commonly transitory, a sound, a tongue, a dialect merely, almost brutish, and we learn it unconsciously, like the brutes, of our mothers. The other is the maturity and experience of that; if that is our mother tongue, this is our father tongue, a reserved and select expression, too significant to be heard by the ear, which we must be born again in order to speak.

Thoreau does suggest an ideal return to the spoken word, but for that "we must be born again." He means us to understand that the reserve of the written word cannot be overcome in this life. Writing remains a figure: unfulfilled, "too significant to be heard by the ear." The writer of *Walden*, says Stanley Cavell, differs from Milton in knowing that his prophetic talent is not only belated but too late, from Wordsworth in not seeking the redemption of the human voice and poetry by each other; and from Emerson in not exalting oration and the sermon. The hoer-hero does nothing to make the clods calve. "He must undertake to write absolutely, to exercise his faith in the very act of marking the word."[8]

Cavell shows how this absolute writing or "American Scripture" is to be explicated. He makes *Walden* supply its own theory of the word. For Derrida too the written word is enough, and too much. Yet Thoreau introduces theology explicitly when he

8. *The Senses of Walden*, p. 29.

says that written language is born a second time, of the father. This seems to be mere metaphor, for the father tongue is represented as a natural development, a result of "maturity" and "experience." But what Thoreau actually says is that in order to *speak* the written ("father") tongue "we must be born again."

For Thoreau, then, to give up the spoken for the written gives up too much: it is fraught with such significance that what is given up returns valorized. The supernatural intimation revives, or we become unsure of the border between natural and supernatural. Marking time means marking that border as outmost sentinels: hearing nature speak. The metaphor moves toward literal status. "The face of the water in time became a wonderful book—a book that . . . told its mind to me without reserve, delivering its most cherished secrets as clearly as if it uttered them with a voice." This is Mark Twain's apprentice pilot in *Old Times on the Mississippi*; but there are voices in Wordsworth that are as intimate. The river flowing near the poet's birthplace "loved / To blend his murmurs with my nurse's song, / And . . . sent a voice / That flowed along my dreams" (*The Prelude,* book 1). Or, the "common face of Nature spake to me / Rememberable things." Or there is Michelet's sentimentally revealing comment on the Rhine. "Une immense poésie dort sur ce fleuve. Cela n'est pas facile à définir; c'est l'impression vague d'une vaste, calme et douce nature, peut-être une voix maternelle qui rappelle l'homme aux éléments . . . peut-être l'attrait poétique de la Vierge."

We know nothing literal about this "voice" or "language" of nature, yet we divine that it is the mother tongue in its idealized purity. It is the voice of waters rather than of the spirit hovering over the face of the waters. It is or is not the voice that cries bloodily from the ground in Genesis. It is a "haunting melody," or what Melville's Pierre responds to in Isabel.

> *Bélise.* Veux-tu toute ta vie offenser la grammaire?
> *Martine.* Qui parle d'offenser grand-mère ou grand-père?
>
> —Molière, *Les Femmes Savantes*

There are so many ideals of purity—anthropological, religious, racial, scientific, literary—that they tend to cross each other and to create a purity perplex impossible to disentangle completely. One can only show its power, its persistence. Purity may be a more basic category than presence. Yeats often begins with "mere images"—the "mere" indicating ambivalence. Their apparent purity, or unmediated, unreflected character, abets the illusion of presence, but the movement of the poem exposes them as forms of Romance: magic formulas, screen memories, displaced or adulterated myth.

Most narrowly construed, purity of diction is simply the absence of foreign or technical terms. Archaisms too may be proscribed, and unnecessary neologisms. Anything "barbarous" or "unnatural" is reprehended. This again suggests the motivating if deceptive ideal of a *natural* language, or rather the making of a *national* language in its image. The avoidance of foreign or barbarous terms may allow you to reveal the genius of your own language. So Luther, in his *Epistle on Translation,* mocks the Latinizing Papists. If you want to express Scripture in German, he says, you don't run to the Latin version, "you ask the mother at home, the kids in the alleys, the ordinary businessman." You learn the needful terms from their mouth.[9]

Indeed, a more historical starting point would be the growth of the literary vernaculars, of competing national languages that rival and replace Latin in the modern period. How complex the ideology of development in each country! Yet there are preoccupations that remain constant. What language was originally, and whether the vernacular can restore that "natural" tongue; or what the language of the ultimate, univocal *mathesis* might be, whether or not formed out of the vernacular; and the relation between mother tongue and a more creaturely and mysterious idiom.

Each of these aspects would need full and separate consideration: I can offer at best a few historical and exemplary facts. Take the founding of academies in the seventeenth and eighteenth centuries. Their aim was to improve the vernaculars, to give them dignity and raise them to universality. Leibnitz writes

9. *Sendbrief vom Dolmetschen* (1530).

a treatise on the exercise and improvement of German that attacks the "puritanical" extirpation of foreign words and asserts that the French model of purification may only have succeeded in impoverishing the language. Yet Leibnitz also recognized that the Thirty Years War, in which Germany was overrun by foreigners, had been disastrous for German as a language. French was now, de facto, the only model that could be imitated for culture and elegance. His proposed academy, therefore, would rehabilitate German by the careful gathering and analysis of all its resources. Conscious of the need for purification, Leibnitz's treatise went beyond it in proposing a literary vernacular characterized by copiousness (*Reichthum*) and high polish (*Glantz*), as well as purity (*Reinigkeit*).

Eric Blackall's study, from which I take the above details, substantiates Herder's comment that the genius of a nation's language was also the genius of its literature.[10] For language touches on practically everything in society; and Blackall shows not only the clash of ideals (of enrichment versus purification, for example), but how these were related to political and social aspirations. So the standard of intelligibility—clarity, lucidity, good sense—becomes more crucial as the middle class tries to consolidate its standing. While pedantry and preciousness are never attractive, they can enrich a language in its formative stage, but they are not acceptable when they exclude or stigmatize a rising class, or when that class tends to parody its own ambitions by aping the *galanterie* of what it deems fashionable. It is interesting that Gottshed, who takes up the fight against a German adulterated by French or artificially elevated terms, falls into the sartorial metaphor when he condemns "useless polluters of speech . . . who without any need hang foreign rags on our German dress, and imagine that thus they speak and write most galantly." (The very word *galant,* in fact, originally referred to clothes, so that Carlyle's "Clothes-Philosophy" simply magnifies a metaphor common in reflections on style and language.[11])

10. *The Emergence of German as a Literary Language, 1700–1775,* chap. 1 and passim. Herder's comment, "Der Genius der Sprache ist also der Genius von der Literatur einer Nation," is the book's epigraph.

11. *The Emergence of German as a Literary Language,* p. 95. That "Style is

One philosophical issue, at least, emerged clearly. Philosophy itself claimed to ground its truth on the right use of language. In England, Sprat and the Royal Society wished to curb the quasi-magical effect of strong figures, and perhaps a religious "enthusiasm" associated with that effect. One of C. K. Ogden's many arguments for Basic English goes in the same direction. Ogden not only attacks the acquisition of foreign languages as vain and wasteful (we don't always need a wardrobe, he says, a single suit may be equally good as clothing; we can leave "to minstrels of the Court the vanities of their variegated vernaculars"), he also views Basic English as "an admirable introduction to that further study of the relations of thought and language which will prove a potent antidote to all forms of Word-magic in the future."[12]

In Germany, after Luther, Jakob Boehme, and other pithy writers, a similar need for restriction was felt. Christian Wolff, for instance, substituted *Erkantnis*—a word that would play an important role in German thought—for the older *Licht der Vernunft* ("Light of Reason," synonymous with "Light of Nature") still employed by Thomasius. Wolff sought to avoid a term with misleading religious pathos, but precisely because he was sensitive to figurative expressions whose "rhetorical" force disclosed needs that philosophy could not reach or would not honor.

Blackall's account of the emergence of German as a literary language covers the period from 1700 to 1775 and ends with Goethe approaching his mature style. Yet around 1770 the achieved stability of German was being challenged once more by adversary currents. German had indeed matured rapidly toward "refinement balanced by a return to origins" (Blackall). But then the *Sturm und Drang* writers showed how precarious that balance was.

---

the dress of thoughts" was, of course, a commonplace; in one of the letters Lord Chesterfield writes to his son (24 November 1749) it is developed into: "let them [the thoughts] be ever so just, if your style is homely, coarse, and vulgar, they will appear to as much disadvantage, and be as ill received as your person, though ever so well proportioned, would, if dressed in rags, dirt, and tatters."

12. *Debabelization*, pp. 36–37. I omit from consideration two matters of importance: the seventeenth-century interest in "plain style," which is also a purification movement, inspired now by Puritan and now by scientific ideologies; and mystical currents as they affect, for example, Benjamin's "quest for a pure language" (see Martin Jay, *The Dialectical Imagination*, pp. 261–63).

Hamann certainly, and later Jean Paul Richter, injected an oracular and carnival vein—both crude and learned, as if fiber had to be introduced into the verbal diet—that worked against the "golden age," its balance of refinement and originality. (The case of the poets is even more fascinating and turbulent: Klopstock passes through a radical Nordic phase; Hölderlin struggles with a purifying "fire from heaven" identified with an unwesternized classicism that he "translates" into German; Goethe always held a conception of the word that exceeded standards of beauty, or made beauty—like Helen—ravaging as well as charming.) The question of style breaks out everywhere; and many, including Herder, look toward Shakespeare and Anglo-Saxon literature to find there an exemplary conjunction of popular and sophisticated, natural and erudite, currents of speech. Carlyle's impure, all-contaminating prose ironically treats *English* as if it were a *German* in need of the English or Saxon development Herder envied. For Carlyle Shakespeare had to come again as a Wizard of the North and bring with him not only a gala language but also a philosophy of language—a *logos* with humorous yet terrible powers.

> So dies Sansculottism, the *body* of Sansculottism; or is changed. Its ragged Pythian Carmagnole-dance has transformed itself into a Pyrric, into a dance of Cabarus Balls. Sansculottism is dead; extinguished by the new *isms* of that kind, which were its own natural progeny. . . . He who, in these Epochs of our Europe, founds on garnitures, formulas, culottisms, of what sort soever, is founding on old clothes and sheepskin, and cannot endure. But as for the body of Sansculottism, that is dead and buried.
>
> —Carlyle, *The French Revolution*

Perhaps we can, after all, make a guess at Carlyle's theory of rhetoric. In Carlyle the link between language and terror becomes itself a form of terrorism. Like many language-combatants of the era he uses the medium of style against classical humanism: its statuesque decorum. Winckelmann had infused new life into the concept of classical beauty and generalized it as a universal standard of *aesthetic* pleasure. But even Keats could not remain within this aesthetic realm: a higher, more terrible beauty beckoned. Such iconoclasm often expressed itself programmatically as a return to Shakespeare, folklore, wisdom literature, Hebraic sublimity; or as a more radical contact with Greek and Roman sources. It is an antihumanism that does not name itself: only since Heidegger and post-Nietzschean philosophy (including Foucault and Derrida) is humanism attacked by name. So strong was its Classical and Italian charm, and so persistent the fear of the religious bigotry and obscurantism it had largely replaced.

It is unnecessary to establish the exact lineage of a style I have called terrorist, but which others might view as a new type of sublimity or an emerging transcendentalism. What is clear is that Hegel's *Aesthetics* gave it a theoretical foundation. Hegel supplied the very "theory of rhetoric" Emerson found lacking, and which Carlyle had perhaps preferred to keep unconscious. Powerfully attracted to Winckelmann's understanding of ideal beauty—the supreme adequacy of Hellenic art, its balance of sensuous and spiritual, of imaginative and intellectual aspirations held within the confines of a serene form, the human body divine—Hegel insisted that Romanticism, which for him included Christian inwardness, had shattered that form forever and disclosed an abyss of negative thinking that could not be alleviated until an "absolute" philosophy healed all things. Romanticism, in brief, was not only a humanism. The beautiful illusion ("der schöne Schein") was honored, but then put aside as an illusion. There was, Hegel agreed, no greater perfection than Greek art in the realm of beauty as such: "Schöneres kann nicht sein und werden" ("Nothing of more beauty can ever be or come to be").[13] Yet as Hegel immediately adds, "there exists something higher than the beautiful appearance [*die schöne Erscheinung*] of spirit in its unmediated, sensuous form, though this be created by the spirit itself as adequate to spirit." The true content of Romantic art is characterized by "absolute inwardness," and its corresponding form by "spiritual subjectivity that has grasped its autonomy and freedom."

13. All my quotations from Hegel are taken from the Introduction to the section of the *Aesthetik* entitled "The Romantic Form of Art" (*Die Romantische Kunstform*).

How radical and terroristic—if not without pathos—Hegel can sound is made clear by a subsequent formulation, in which he defines the nonclassical or infinitizing aspect of Romantic art. It is, he writes, "the absolute negativity of everything particular, or that simple unity with itself which has consumed everything analytic-discrete, all processes of Nature, the cycle of birth, death, and revival, all limits to spiritual existence, and dissolved all specific gods into a pure infinite identity with itself."

Such sentences are themselves little abysses. Their style almost outruns grammatical closure; and while they are not terroristic in imagery or mixture of words, they raise the specter of an interminable mode of analysis that could make a ghost, or a verbalism, of every phenomenon. Language appears as a restless medium that both transcends and negates its relation to the phenomenal world—hence the terror—yet still aspires to a possibility Hegel never quite renounced: of reconciling Greek beauty and Modern spirituality in an absolute, that is, philosophical work.

> There are literary Hitlers and Mussolinis. There are writers like those animated blood-puddings who rule the German nation and stick one another with "putsches" and "purges."
>
> —Van Wyck Brooks, *Opinions of Oliver Allston*

Hegel's—and Carlyle's—*bottomless* style is disconcerting to those who found the world on nature or second nature ("Custom is the greatest of weavers," Carlyle writes in *Sartor,* playing on the common root of custom and costume); but it is positively terrifying to those who understand the political overtones. For not only does this style swallow politics as it does history (both of them foundering like "*Gigs* of Creation" in the Red Sea[14] of the French Revolution), but the French Revolution, precisely, may have motivated this style: is not Sansculottism here the manifest symbol for a bottomless revolution that terrorizes thought and freezes it into starkly defensive postures?

From this perspective Hegel's task in the *Phenomenology* is what Arnold would call an "intellectual deliverance." It is a way

14. "Never since Pharaoh's Chariots, in the Red Sea of Water, was there wreck of Wheel-vehicles like this in the Sea of Fire. Desolate, as ashes, as gases, shall they wander in the wind." Carlyle, *The French Revolution,* "Finis."

of facing or contemplating events so monstrous that they devour thought as well as themselves. The style raises, of course, a question of identification: of the involuntary sympathy of victim with aggressor, of his contamination by the destructive, devouring element, its overt display of power. Carlyle's prosopopoeias and generally the loud pitch of his style, and Hegel's tendency to make every thought interminable, could mean that the purgation has failed, that purity has embraced impurity.

Yet consider a later fighter for language like Karl Kraus. He fought journalism by means of his journal *Die Fackel* (founded in 1899). The coarsening of language and the upsurge of propaganda led him finally to the edge of silence: after Hitler came to power in 1933 he composed an issue of his journal that began "Mir fällt zu Hitler nichts ein" ("Nothing comes to me on the subject of Hitler"). But he then developed this irony, this inexpressibility topos, into a fierce tract of three hundred pages that documented Germany's corruption by quoting and analyzing Nazi news releases and the spread of propaganda. (Though set up in print, this issue of the *Fackel* was not published till 1952, when it appeared with the title *The Third Walpurgisnacht.*) Kraus is uncompromising, yet he must fight fire with fire.

Heidegger's case is more complex. His language too combats the degradation of German. Its violence is clear, but what it seeks to restore, other than a generalized sense of the power of the word, is less clear. Eliot, in *Burnt Norton,* also seeks to move us from words to the Word, though only the subtle expression of his dilemma really affects us:

> Words strain,
> Crack and sometimes break, under the burden,
> Under the tension, slip, slide, perish,
> Decay with imprecision, will not stay in place,
> Will not stay still.

Compare Heidegger, in *An Introduction to Metaphysics,* conceived at about the same time (1935): "Language in general is worn out and used up, an indispensable but masterless and arbitrarily employed means of communication, as indifferent as a means of public transport, as a streetcar which everyone enters and leaves at will." A related commonplace reinforces this. "The organizations whose aim is the purification of the language and its defense against a progressive barbarization are deserving of respect." Yet "purification" (*Reinigung*) must have had a racial overtone at this period. Heidegger compromises, or is compromised: even if he aims to repossess words like these, to turn them toward their original value, his game is a dangerous one. We are not reassured when he asserts that Western grammar emerged from a reflection on Greek and adds: "Along with German the Greek language is (in regard to its possibilities for thought) at once the most powerful and most spiritual of all languages."

No wonder, then, that the English form of practical criticism, immensely scrupulous and reserved, consolidated itself in the 1930s. Practical criticism refused every heavy date with slogans (except, perhaps, the historical location of a "dissociation of sensibility" somewhere between Donne and Milton), and every solicitation to theorize in the Hegelian or Heideggerian fashion. Theory, whether or not a vital, penetrating discipline, seemed as gross in its effect as political sloganeering. How different the *mots d'ordre* of the hour—"Ein Volk, Ein Reich, Ein Führer," from which it is not a radical step to "One Language"—and classical allusions that were called by Dr. Johnson the *parole* of the educated everywhere!

Philosophical language, then, though it questioned these loaded slogans, could be equally "terroristic." Contaminated or imprisoned by the didactic heresy, it urged, sometimes equivocally, a countertruth. It had to take on degenerate political clichés but also the idea of science as a rigorous discipline. Politics, in fact, claimed to be a science, and it extruded by exquisite casuistry overlapping and often contradictory sets of terms. There were English stirrings of theory, nevertheless: in Richards's work especially, even if "principles" sounded more modest and practicable than laws, methods, etc.; and in the defensive insistence on the intellectual and emotional toughness of art, its virtues of irony, ambiguity, dramaticity—modes of meaning resistant to ideological straitening.

> One Law for the Lion & Ox is Oppression.
>
> —William Blake

Prose always faces a higher or more extreme style, especially in the modern era when the idea of an urbane or purified *lan-*

guage of criticism has taken hold. The more we read Arnold, for instance, the more we realize that his concern is as much for the future of prose as for the future of poetry. He claims that English criticism and journalism lack urbanity; that they are "eruptive" and "aggressive"; and that while the power of English literature is in its poets, that of French literature is in its prose. He cannot admire the conceits and sallies of a Jeremy Taylor or an Emund Burke. "The ruling divinity of poetry," he alleges, has been too busy in those writers; "the ruling divinity of prose" not busy enough. Though he mentions Addison and distinguishes between the chaste and the extravagant Ruskin, Arnold chooses for his highest praise touchstones from Bossuet and Joubert, exclaiming of the former: "There we have prose without the note of provinciality—classical prose, prose of the center."[15]

The creation of this prose of the center is a neoclassical ideal imported from France, where even poetry moved closer to prose, reduced like every other art to a single principle, a single standard. This prose ideal has continued into contemporary criticism. Today there is often an identification of prose of the center with the language of criticism. Lionel Trilling, therefore, worries officially about the paradox of teaching works of literature so unlike the criticism he writes.[16] Trilling's problem is ours too; not so much because we are teachers but because the language of criticism is conducted in an accommodated style that does not even allow, or allows grudgingly, that "play of ideas" (though not of words) Arnold considered its reason for being.

I may be overstating the case; but the spectacle of the polite critic dealing with an extravagant literature, trying so hard to come to terms with it in his own tempered language, verges on the ludicrous. Hence those strange outbursts from the truly neoclassical temperaments among us: Yvor Winters's savage dismissals, Emil Staiger's wholesale condemnation of decadent Modernism. Hence also a perplexed return to the personal and oracular vein, as in Harold Bloom or Kenneth Burke. Arnold's *"modern* language . . . the language of a thoughtful, philosophic man of our days," is an intransigent middle style, a socializing instrument, one that chastens the extremes of nature.

15. "The Literary Influence of Academies" (1864), in *Essays in Criticism.*
16. "On the Teaching of Modern Literature" in *Beyond Culture.*

As for the formalist or structuralist escape from this dilemma of style, it is an evasion if it rests with a distinction between the language of description and the language of the object described, and privileges the former as a scientific metalanguage, instructive because rarefied. It is not an evasion if, as in Lévi-Strauss, it discloses the demand for order and organization in both art and science, in both languages, so to say. The effect of Lévi-Strauss's work is not to make conscious the unconscious *praxis* of groups but rather to stress "the conscious and deliberate rules by which these same groups—or their philosophers—spend their time in codifying and controlling it."[17] The interpreter enters the text: there is no pure *praxis*. All these arrangements, all these taxonomies and classifications, all these rituals and games, transcend their practical or assigned value, as in poetry too. By recognizing the principles of savage—or poetic—thought, the civilized mind takes cognizance of itself. There is a music of cognition in both.

Also sensitive to the issue are critics who remain aware of the scandal posed by Scripture. They seek a "hermeneutics of response,"[18] hoping that Scripture is not the wholly Other, or that the strain of its higher or enigmatic style will not prove discontinuous with secular literature. They insist, in any case, on the history of reception as more than passive: it has an authority of its own that supplements or invests the sacred text. But in this school too there is a tendency to bypass the problem of style by turning everything—even Scripture, even Heidegger—into ordinary language.

17. *The Savage Mind,* "History and Dialectic."

18. Cf. Cyrus Hamlin, "The Limits of Understanding: Hermeneutics and the Study of Literature," *Arion* (1978), pp. 385–419; and "Strategies of Reversal in Literary Narrative," in *Interpretation of Narrative,* ed. M. J. Valdés and O. J. Miller. Hamlin's hesitation between "reversal" and "converse" (in the sense of "conversation") is symptomatic of a theory that wishes to deal with extraordinary language in ordinary language terms. Emerson himself, faced with Carlylese, tries on occasion to understand it as conversation in its true form: "I think he [Carlyle] has seen as no other in our time how inexhaustible a mine is the language of Conversation. He does not use the *written* dialect of the time in which scholars, pamphleteers, & the clergy write, nor the parliamentary dialect, in which the lawyer, the statesman, & the better newspapers write, but draws strength and motherwit out of a poetic use of the *spoken* vocabulary, so that his paragraphs are all a sort of splendid conversation." *Journals,* V, 291.

I am describing a situation, and I have no specific remedy for it. It is only the false remedies, the quack responses, one would be opposing. If I say, echoing Spenser, that critics should have the kingdom of their language, it does not follow that one should always write in a heightened style or return to the brutality of the journals and the vulgarity of the newspapers of which Arnold complained. To read early nineteenth-century reviews of the Romantics might turn one into an Arnoldian sophisticate on the spot.

Yet critics today do not seem interested in finding an "answerable style." Perhaps they believe that an intellectual deliverance is not possible, or that the monstrous event can only be worded, if at all, by the artist. By an artist like Paul Celan, who can speak scorched words. "So sprech ich den Namen noch aus und fühl noch den Brand auf den Wangen" ("So I still pronounce the Name and feel the great fire still on my cheeks"—"Song in the Wilderness"). The question of style, however, remains: How can the critic respond to the extraordinary language-event and still maintain a prose of the center? I object only to those who rule out the question, who seek to control the situation in advance. We have as yet no principled, or theoretically founded, way of dismissing the question of critical style: of Carlylese or, for that matter, of Heidegger's and Derrida's closely written readings. If we respect the language of art, it is often because of critics whose language is but a lesser scandal.

Part II

The work of criticism is superfluous unless it is itself a work of art as independent of the work it criticizes as that is independent of the materials that went into it.

—Friedrich Schlegel

CHAPTER SEVEN

The Work of Reading

And all the Arts of Life they changed into the Arts of Death in Albion.
The hour-glass contemned because its simple workmanship
Was like the workmanship of the plowman, and the water wheel,
That raises water into cisterns: broken and burned with fire:
Because its workmanship was like the workmanship of the shepherd.
And in their stead intricate wheels invented, wheel without wheel:
To perplex youth in their outgoings

—William Blake, *Jerusalem*

In the matter of art we cannot draw up a Guide for the Perplexed. We can only urge that readers, inspired by hermeneutic traditions, take back some of their authority and become both creative and thoughtful, as in days of old. It is true, of course, that today they are less *liable* for their mistakes, and that being creative is for many a defense for whatever they do. The rabbinical or patristic exegete was creative within a scrupulosity as exacting as any invented by extreme apostles of the Catholic or Puritan conscience; he pretended not to violate the letter of Scripture or else he took pleasure in the strict counterpoint of letter and spirit, of apparent meaning and recreative commentary. The puritanism (small *p*) of so much critical writing of today, its modest but unconvincing subservience to art, comes from the realization that now it is we who put the restraint on ourselves; it is from the individual critic that the check on subjective or wild interpretation must come.

Our present condition, however, is historical and contingent; it should not be dignified into permanence by a claim that only scientific or objective criteria of interpretation can help. I know something about the situation of the critic and commentator today; I do not know what it will be in a hundred years. I know what it is today by looking at the contemporary scene rather than by attempting to predict or coerce the future. I can therefore insist that what is happening is that the reader is in fact taking back some of his authority and struggling with the problems this poses. Refusing the subterfuge of a passive or restrictive role, he becomes at once reader and writer—or takes it fully into consciousness that he is both an interpreter of texts and a self-interpreting producer of further texts. He continues to believe that certain technical criteria or forms of analysis are useful in a preparatory way, but he doubts that their scientific virtue makes of every user an efficient critic. They are not a sacrament, bestowing grace by a virtue inherent in their application.

What, then, can be specified of the act of reading today? It is *work*[1] and cannot be "justified" by an authoritarian or religious standard, or even by an empirical yardstick, such as the precise amount of literary illumination it may yield. For literature itself is probably without justification; it is in the same boat with criticism. The reading a critic gives when writing about literature simply establishes an equation that balances the authority of a given text against a produced text (commentary). Each work of reading does this anew. We have talked for a long time, and unselfconsciously, of the *work of art*; we may come to talk as naturally of the *work of reading*.

The notion of work introduces that of economic value and the possibility of a Marxist analysis. I am not ready to go in that direction, at least not systematically. We have seen the Critic become the Commissar, and this danger is one reason so many today prefer to see the critic subordinated in function to the creative writer, who is notoriously unconformable. Both fascist

1. Work that cannot be justified yet seems valuable and is freely undertaken is often called *play*: I prefer to think of speculative reading and art as "inglorious" (Vergil, *Georgics* 4.564) to indicate the uneasy conscience that has always accompanied such gratuitous activity.

and socialist labor movements, moreover, have glorified work by suggesting there is an unalienated, harmonious form of labor, distinguished from its alienated counterpart in corrupt societies. This doctrine, among American intellectuals, led in the 1960s to a claim that a new *trahison des clercs* had taken place in the universities. For if unalienated work should be found anywhere, it was in the academy. Yet the "productive scholar" fostered by the academy seemed a parody of unalienated labor. What he produced was abstruse, irrelevant, ideologically blind. It was production for its own sake; he had no joy in it and gave none.

I intend no celebration of work or aestheticization of it. On the contrary, concerning the economic aspect, I would suggest that as in work generally there is something provocative of or even *against nature* in reading: something which develops but also spoils our (more idle) enjoyment of literature. Hence the tone of weariness and the famous acedia that characterize the professional reader even when he has the force to recycle his readings as writing. "Many books wise men have said are wearisome," is Christ's sober comment in *Paradise Regained* (4.321–2). "La chair est triste, hélas, et j'ai lu tous les livres," is Mallarmé's equally sober version.

Yet it is not nature as such but the "nature" of language—or obversely the possibility of a "language of nature"—that is at issue. The most common form of antipathetic judgment is that someone does not think or write naturally, that his work is labored, artificial, ingenious. Since the neoclassical period, moreover, criticism has been primarily an "ordinary language" movement. It has helped to create the urbane and useful prose we presently write. The conversational style was made, not born: it is a historical achievement of European and English writers as they switched from Latin and avoided the temptations of precious diction and shoptalk.

The attempt to find—and keep—a "language of nature" is baffled by the fact that what is taken to be natural is a convenience: an achieved convention or *agrément*. It "pleases," but its relation to nature remains obscure. We are more in the domain of ideology than of nature. Plato's *Cratylus*—indeed Plato's hints that there may be a language of the gods as well as that of men[2]—raises the same issue in a subversive way. It may be that the conversational style, however attractive its decorum and its affranchizing and democratic idealism—its projection of a community of all classes or professions that might freely communicate on some level through the familiar essay or as men and women of letters—it may be that this style is a transitory historical episode. I would regret it, but both political and internal pressures seem to be crackling the varnish and even radically stripping the veneer of this ideal of a freemasonry or grand democratic concourse of polyphonic yet pacific persons.

At present, we continue to value literacy as liberating *and* productive. However, we have never resolved the relation of *dialogue* to *dialectic*: dialogue evokes the freely begun and ended talk of persons who must be convinced by what they hear and say and, if convinced, are not constrained to act on their conviction; but dialectic points to an intent or current, set up by means of dialogue, which may become forceful or inquisitorial and which leads necessarily to a higher, all-embracing truth. In a liberal culture, such as ours, which believes in the productive truth of dialogue and the free exchange of ideas, books tend to be overestimated. They are what we have that is best, most communicable, most easily and freely scrutinized.

Against the disappointment that may result from hoping to find wisdom in books and not finding it any more than in ourselves, there have always been satiric, religious, and moralistic consolations. It is, mostly, the literate person who turns against culture, and curses the gift, like Shakespeare's Caliban. He may also suffer, today, from what Günther Anders has aptly named "Promethean shame": his hands, which write and fabricate, cannot compete with the inhuman beauty and technologic power

2. "*Socrates:* Do you know what Homer says about the river in Troy who had a single combat with Hephaestus—'whom,' as he says, 'the gods call Xanthus, and men call Scamander'? *Hermogenes:* I remember. *Socrates:* Well, and about this river—to know that he ought to be called Xanthus and not Scamander—is not that a solemn lesson? Or about the bird which, as Homer says, 'the gods call Chalcis, and men Cymindis'? To be taught how much more correct the name Chalcis is than the name Cymindis—do you deem that a light matter?" *Cratylus,* 392, in the Jowett translation.

of the machines he has invented (*Die Antiquiertheit des Menschen*). His whole body perhaps is rapidly becoming an appendix, a vestigial concern, a servant to the servant mechanism. Books are already like gardens, a small cultivated area that miniaturizes what is lost. But what is lost is not books themselves or print-capability, but the wish, need, or motive to read what is being written in a world where publication has utterly changed its character.

Far from being an act of self-exposure, a path-breaking errand into the wilderness, questionable in the eyes of God, man, or both, writing has become in most Western countries a mixture of entertainment, confession, symbolic protest, and the endless retailing of accumulated knowledge. I do not mean to create by idealistic fiat an era where these factors did not already prevail. But it is the critical and dangerous factors that now tend to be missing. These have always been missing, in the sense of scarce: our problem today is that as the quantity of writing increases, the quality of reading should also increase to preserve the great or exceptional work as something still possible, not only as something confined to a past era and breaking out of that into present consciousness.

Can reading be all that watchful now? The more conscientious it is, the more besieged and burdened it is. Reading would have to become an endless prayer or jeremiad. Most of the time, however, it is obviously a holding action like reviewing: arbitrary, opinionated, and spotty, rather than interpretive and authenticating. The spotlight effect of reviewing holds books fast for a month or a year, but it cannot sustain or nourish them for much longer periods.

Watching or waiting for news is an instinct very deep, even religious, in us; yet what is happening at present degrades this idea of reading into a journalistic state of mind. Perhaps then the religious—better, evangelical—model was imperfect to start with. A disenchanted view would hold that there is nothing new under the sun, or that, as Emerson said, "Our giant goes with us wherever we go." But we would still have to decide whether no news is good news, or what to do with *time*.

A maieutic rather than evangelical and news-oriented understanding of reading would take us back to Plato. The Socratic dialogues cannot be reduced to a pedagogically accommodated instruction or to a remystifying of knowledge directed against the Sophists' claim that knowledge is merely know-how and should be marketed as a commodity. The dramatic and ironic quality of the Socratic dialogues, removed from the pressure of the great tragedies and their driving stichomythia, conveys a peculiarly satisfying sense of our relation to time. Socrates needs time to "deliver" the truth. So do we; his rhythm is our rhythm. It is this matter of the relation of thought to time and language—and of the relation of time and language to each other—that also preoccupies Heidegger, Wittgenstein, and Derrida, all of whom have proposed a *Sprachlehre* (a critique or doctrine of language) with therapeutic as well as maieutic aims.

Heidegger is notoriously difficult, especially for a nonphilosopher like myself, and I can only attempt to fit him into my general perspective. He suggests that language plays a role in human development greater than theories of accommodation have proposed. His emphasis falls on understanding itself, whether or not it is textualized, and on the paradox that we labor to know something which, when known and expressed by name, appears self-evident. Heidegger interprets this paradox as a sign that we have been distracted from Being by beings, that a wrong turning, which may have taken place in Plato's time and is now consolidated in language itself, has made us aliens in the world.

The paradox—or circle—of understanding is not vicious, therefore, but discloses that we are already where we want to be. We are there; and being-there (*Dasein*) expresses mankind's special status, its difficult nearness to Being. "Being is what is nearest" is Heidegger's famous formula in the *Letter on Humanism* (1947). Our problem, basically, is that of holding fast to the faculty of understanding as our one genuine source of apodictic knowledge, an understanding always in danger of being alienated by religious or scientific or practical attitudes. So, today, thinking is considered work only when "productive" of some positive, moral, or tangible good. But thinking continues to throw a questioning shadow on the pandemonium of activities, commonly labeled "work."

Heidegger is less concerned with defining or transvaluing work than with finding a resting place (*Heimkunft*), or at least sighting it, in a concept of Being that recalls the values of permanence and presence, whatever "interlunation" (Shelley's word) they suffer. Everything should be seen from the vantage point of *Dasein*; and art, whether in the form of a Greek temple or Van Gogh painting or Hölderlin poem, lodges us there. "Be still the unimaginable lodge / For solitary thinkings," Keats writes, addressing Pan in *Endymion*.

The "work" of art, then, discloses Being as this absent presence: it allows us to stand on absence, as it were. This disclosure is also what understanding as such achieves, according to *Being and Time* (1927). The essays on art of 1935 and after show that Heidegger's art theory follows interpretation theory; and that the "work" constantly alluded to is that of letting Being be, of allowing what we already know to collect itself in us and appear.

Since we ourselves are the text, there is no point to the antinomy between *Dichter* (creative writer) and *Denker* (critical thinker). The circle of understanding encompasses both the interpreter and the given text; the text, in fact, is never something radically other except insofar as it is radically near. As the "fore-structure" of the very act of reading it tends to coincide with the innermost thoughts of the reader. The question What is disclosed by reading? invokes therefore a double text that remains a hendiadys: the text referred to by the interpreter, and the text on the text created by the referring act of criticism.

Why we have texts at all—why understanding requires that detour—is a question that remains unsolved, and it allows Derrida's revision of Heidegger in terms of a critique of presence and an insistence on residues, difference, and temporal deferral. But Heidegger's practice, in his later essays on Hölderlin, Trakl, and others, also indicates something not quite subsumed by a philosophy of presence and Being. What is revealed by Heidegger's readings is the "answerable style" of the critic, whether it responds directly to the "call" of Being or to that of the poem as the "house of Being."

What remains—what Heidegger cannot annul—is Hegel's insistence on self-alienation or self-objectification as the condition for absolute knowledge. Heidegger keeps us close to the text in order to keep us close to Being, yet his very style, ruminant and quasi-tautological, not only does not substitute itself for the primary work but cannot undo the secondary and intertextual status of all writing: philosophy or fiction.

It is true that Heidegger posits—beyond the double and responsive text—a forgotten "language of Being," so estranged, so peculiarly other (like his own style) that it approaches the character of a silent revelation. His mode of interpretation is therefore far removed from what we are accustomed to recognize as practical criticism. He does not worry about "correct" readings in his effort to—harmoniously or transgressively—uncover this language of Being. The only error (since the condition of language at present is itself error) consists in closing the circle of understanding prematurely—foreclosing it—and so evading the intimate otherness of a text linked to the intimate otherness of Being itself. By such foreclosure the interpreter produces a new idolatry of the interpreted or interpreting text: a falsely objectified, or accommodated, meaning. But the aim of commentary or *Erläuterung,* writes Heidegger (and he plays on overtones in *Erläuterung* as "sounding forth," "ringing out," "purification")—the aim of *Erläuterung* is to clarify "das im Gedicht rein Gedichtete": whatever is most purely and densely poetic in the artifact. To do so requires that interpretation ("die erläuternde Rede") *break* itself and its objective ("ihr Versuchtes").[3]

Heidegger's work of reading is iconoclastic, then, aimed at language patterns repressive of an original naming of Being which may still be glimpsed in pre-Socratic thought. Later Greek thinking founded modern science and muted this naming of Being together with Nature itself. The ensuing split between thing and word, *physis* and *logos,* produced Western metaphysics, and its "language of nature" rather than of Being. Heidegger wishes to cure us of metaphysics by a recovery of the forgotten language of Being. Yet he does not pretend to give us the "rein Gedichtete" itself: he remains "unterwegs zur Sprache," on the way toward

3. See his *Erläuterungen zu Hölderlins Dichtung,* especially the preface ("Vorwort").

authentic speech, applying certain interpretive and deconstructive techniques to the language of the great poets and philosophers.

What Heidegger offers us, then, is wit (albeit heavy wit, like heavy water) rather than the mysterious naming itself. His pages are full of etymological speculation, paranomasia, and physiologic guesses. Though wordplay is not practiced for its own sake, the waywardness of Heidegger's project must throw a doubt over his achievement as a whole. He operates on the historical body of language with interesting but arbitrary instruments. Words that lodge in the hinterland of time are foregrounded, while contemporary expressions are made to appear primal or unfamiliar. The heterogeneous forms of the verb "to be" are pressed to reveal a crime against language we had covered up. He metaphorizes *Erläuterung* to make us rethink the very mode of literary commentary: how we use it to limit disturbances of the peace of language prompted by the great or the difficult poem.

Perhaps Wittgenstein's effort to have us realize that we do not *own* language is correlative. There is in him no historicizing thesis of an original unfallen language, such as Heidegger ascribed to the pre-Socratic period. But if philosophy is a matter of language use beset by pseudoproblems (nouns, for example, that become terms and block thought), it may cure itself by saying what it can say, and nothing else. There may be something that cannot be said (i.e., metaphysics), or not in words. Yet this something-nothing is precisely what worries Derrida, who does not want it to phantomize the word-work we do. Is it not better to suppose that words are inscribed for reinscription rather than for definitiveness; that all texts are infinitives; that revision, reinterpretation, rewriting are not flaws of finitude but the very kind of being (*Sein*) we have in time (*Zeit*)?

Inspired also by semiotics, or the theory of how signs are meaningful, Derrida agrees both that signs are indefinite (they defer absolute knowledge) and that they mean. The continuity of philosophy and literature is not dissociable from the interpretive process that motivates signs. Metaphysics is simply another name for a desire fatally involved with significance; with signs that aspire to renewed physiologic status, to the authority of "signatures," or the legitimacy of proper nouns whose peculiar quality is that they seem "proper" and identify directly if still arbitrarily this or that person, this or that place. So Derrida, at the beginning of *Glas,* plays with the sound *aigle* in (the French pronunciation of) *Hegel.*

At the end of the first volume of *A la recherche du temps perdu* Proust makes us explicitly aware, in a section entitled "Place Names: The Name," of the investment we have in proper nouns: in Balbec, Venice, Florence, or Gilberte. It is as if desire or disenchantment always shuttled between proper and common noun. "The sun's face was hidden. . . . The wind wrinkled the surface of the Grand Lac in little waves, like a real lake; large birds passed swiftly over the Bois [the Bois de Boulogne], as over a real wood [*bois*]." Compare Heidegger, introducing the section of *Sein und Zeit* (32) that discusses the relation between understanding and interpretation: "Das Dasein entwirft als Verstehen sein Sein auf Möglichkeiten." Here too, and without the solace of names, the prose moves ambiguously between noun elements and non-noun elements (*sein Sein* is the most conspicuous example). How much pathos in the capital letter, but how much pathos also in philosophy's effort to divest language of this fluctuating, unstable movement and so to achieve a "real character"!

The dialogic movement between primary text and secondary or interpretive discourse is another such instability. To uncover it serves to keep language from falling under a monologic spell and capitalizing itself in a few worthy (or unworthy) books. We will always have some capital or primary texts: criticism conserves even as it criticizes. Because the expanding universe of books makes us impatient for a purge—just as everyone learns to speak, everyone will learn to write, and the limits of philography are not in sight—we clutch at classics. There is a fear in us that to abandon the concept of the primary or classic work would mean ushering in chaos again: mingling great with inferior, primary with secondary or even trivial. But I am arguing against, not for, chaos. If certain works have become authoritative, it is because they at once sustain, and are sustained by, the readers they find. Only when the work of reading is taken as seriously as the work of art is confusion avoided.

Heidegger's understanding of *Erörterung* (another word for commentary, synonymous with *Erläuterung*) helps to formalize the work of reading. *Erörterung* has the same structure as Abraham's "Here I am" responding to God's call. ("And what am I, that I am here?" is Matthew Arnold's complex fusion, in "Stanzas from the Grande Chartreuse," of that response and a covertly blasphemous "I am that I am.") The patriarch's answer is more than an immediate act of obeisance. It clarifies an existential situation: it places the respondent who accepts the "point" or "charge" (*Ort* in the archaic sense of a point of convergence, particularly spearhead or battle-wedge). The answer is so forceful that each act signifies the other: *Agen-Word* becomes part of the *Word*. Heidegger's *Erörterung* is countertheological and recreates an original situation ("Ort" = origin/"Ort" = place) where language is not subdued by religion, drugged by art, or terrorized by theory and technique.

Yet Heidegger's language, in aspiring to a more original form (even if every origin is double or dialogic), becomes a special diction that violates ordinary usage. Heidegger attributes this violence to the present historical moment of discourse, as it throws off its false masters: religion, science, rhetoric. These are the "unpoetic languages" amid whose clamor poetry must make itself heard—and is being heard, says Heidegger, like a bell in the open muted by a light coat of snow. *Erläuterung* keeps the bell in the open (whereas less authentic religious or scientific discourse entombs it), though muffling its sound like snowfall. Yet we recall, against Heidegger, Kierkegaard's question whether an eternal consciousness can find a historical starting point, to suggest that Heidegger remains a pilgrim of eternity, an "ontotheological" thinker. When Derrida entitles his major work *Glas* ("passing Bell"), is he continuing Heidegger's metaphor of the bell while identifying the latter's distinction between authentic and inauthentic speech as a metaphysical, otherworldly residue? To return to another Heidegger image: if the proper, authenticating word is like a spear, it may wound; and so the desire for authentic origination (or signature or identity) which even *Erörterung* implies imports once more that psychic, sacred, or metaphysical attack on language as something at once too present and not present enough.

Wittgenstein himself never gives up the hope of solving the riddle of language, but he finds ways of turning that riddle against our simplifications. He is a word artist without charm, which makes him at least as seductive as Heidegger. His greatest difference from Heidegger is that he privileges neither philosophy (*Denken*) nor poetry (*Dichten*) by seeking their point of convergence in art. His examples in the *Philosophical Investigations* are drawn not from identified authors or literary works but from expressions in daily use: from ordinary—we might even say, anonymous—language in its confusing richness, turns, metaphorical shifts. The conditions that make speech meaningful to different types of users are excogitated as if the aura (*Dunstkreis*) of language might be reduced to a spectrum.

Indeed, however spectral the result, Wittgenstein pursues the project of language analysis; and his closest affinity may prove to be with the empirical psychology of William James, and in particular with the latter's understanding of the "halo of relations" around the image (that is, around any entity or resting place in the "stream of consciousness"). This halo is named by James the *psychic overtone* or *fringe,* and he writes:

> Every definite image in the mind is steeped and dyed in the free water that flows round it. With it goes the sense of its relations, near and remote, the dying echo of whence it came to us, the dawning sense of whither it is to lead. The significance, the value, of the image is all in this halo or penumbra that surrounds and escorts it,—or rather that is fused into one with it and has become bone of its bone and flesh of its flesh. [*The Principles of Psychology*]

James, clearly, is much freer with unanalyzed metaphors than Wittgenstein; positively promiscuous even; but this matter of the *fringe,* resembling Derrida's concept of *margin,* enters every philosophy that is aware of literature. Derrida's writing is, in this respect, strangely competitive with the modern novel, which so often becomes a stream of consciousness. In philosophy too we may find a paradoxical will to let language be, to remove from it a defensive and constrictive armor.

The contradictions that beset this will to let words be are considerable. For instance, is what should result a freer prose, or is it the dense *écriture* of Mallarmé's "poëme critique"? Derrida's style is very different from Heidegger's and Wittgenstein's. Yet each of these therapists creates verbal forms both strict and aleatory. Art and accident, art exploring the im-proprieties of language, the arbitrary relation of sound and sense, conspire to weave a new prose genre. As Derrida says: "The glue of the aleatory makes sense." This prose is a plural, for language cannot be cured by some higher authority, either in the writer or in an academy that would purge figuration from language. Human understanding is bound up with words, as Locke too realized, though what he denounced as "abusive" (figures of speech) is precisely what makes words usable. The authority of language can only be tested by close reading and resides in language itself as used and used again. Explanation gives way to explication, and explication becomes a genre that maintains the art work itself, the peculiar authority of its diction, amid the figuration or the chaos of suppositions coming from the combined forestructure of language and the interpretive mind.

Let me restate the issue in terms more familiar to the reader of literary and cultural criticism. It turns on the role of theory in close reading. What fosters the ability to read finely and closely? "You might read all the books in the British Museum," Ruskin affirms, ". . . and remain an utterly 'illiterate,' uneducated person; but . . . if you read ten pages of a good book, letter by letter—that is to say, with real accuracy—you are for evermore in some measure an educated person" (*Sesame and Lilies*). F. R. Leavis, strange scion of the branch of Ruskin, erects close reading of *English* texts into a vernacular creed. Theory for him is gratuitous and interfering and certainly unneedful.[4] Studying English is a discipline and school in itself. Such a thing as a "theory of literature" can only be a solecism, a barbarism; there might be a "theory of English literature" but that would probably be a mere equivalent to Leavis's ideas on close reading.

John Crowe Ransom, however, equally interested in close reading, noticed that Blackmur and Eliot changed their style of critical writing—perhaps insensibly—as they went on. "Looking

4. See above, Introduction, note 3.

if possible ever more closely at their texts, at the same time they have seemed to find bigger and harder and more theoretical questions. . . ." Ransom continues:

> The good critic cannot stop with studying poetry, he must also study poetics. If he thinks he must puritanically abstain from all indulgence in the theory, the good critic may have to be a good little critic. . . . Theory, which is expectation, always determines criticism, and never more than when it is unconscious. The reputed condition of no-theory in the critic's mind is illusory. [*The World's Body,* "The Cathartic Principle"]

Why then the taboo against theory in Leavis, and which may have originated with Eliot? Ransom suggests that Eliot encouraged too narrow a trade unionism of the guild. The resulting dichotomy of critic and creative writer is a defensive specialization. Eliot, of course, merely extended the Arnoldian tradition, with its anxiety that criticism would corrode creativity. The Arnoldian concordat restricted the critic to a specific role: uncreative himself, he would circulate ideas and so prepare parochial England for a second Renaissance of truly creative literature—a literature marked by "imaginative reason"; a literature, unlike that of the Romantics, which would transform rather than evade ideas.

Arnold's concordat was a shrewd political arrangement. Eliot was not happy with it: he recognized it as a stabilizing maneuver, an effort to gloss over the dissociation of sensibility and the increasingly corrosive effect on culture of the critical or self-conscious spirit. But even while attacking Arnold for averting his face from decadence, he supported the limitation on theory. The criticism of today, however, by its very existence, as well as its peculiar features, is forcing its way back into a concept of literature unduly narrowed by the anti-self-consciousness principle at work in the Arnoldian concordat.

The most peculiar feature of philosophical criticism is indeed the difficult alliance in it between speculation and close reading. Considered as a development in the history of prose, it tends to reject previous rules of expository spareness, pedagogical decorum, and social accommodation. These rules can produce benefits, but they are not absolutes. We gain something and lose something in accepting them. Combined with the narrow focus of critical pieces that make a fetish of the particular work discussed, they lead us to forfeit the range and freedom of such essayists as Montaigne, F. Schlegel, Coleridge, Emerson, Ruskin, and even Arnold himself.

Yet the critical essay, while recouping its freedom to theorize, continues to bind itself to close reading. For Arnold close reading was reserved for Scripture or the Classics: he may compare two translations of a passage from Homer, for instance. Eliot quotes closely rather than reads closely: his discriminating taste seeks the approval of the educated reader without excessive demonstration. Before 1919, and certainly before the expansion of the "English School" as a separate academic discipline at Cambridge, close reading was, if not exegetical (in the service of the Classics or Scripture), a condescending, didactic exercise for those excluded from the higher reaches of education. Ruskin's beautiful exposition in *Sesame and Lilies* of Milton's "Lycidas" and Wordsworth's "Three Years She Grew" finds its occasion in an address to a girls' school.

Paradoxically, then, the avant-garde essay insists on the priority of reading over theory even while insisting on the importance of theory. There is more labor than grace in its often tedious and detailed reference to excerpted rather than selected passages. It is a strange mixture of philosophic and practical criticism. And the philosophy or theory it engages is by no means dogmatic or conclusive, but rather a textual entity to be worked through like a poem or prose artifact. Theory is (as yet) part of our textual environment and not an independent or premature agency to unify that environment.

No wonder there are no poems to the Muse of Criticism. Does she exist? What pleasures her, or what pleasure is in her? The signs are that she is more a governess than a muse, the stern daughter of books no longer read under trees and in the fields—a pastoral image which had a certain reality for those brought up before 1950. Even Leavis does not read closely in his writings, though he expects us to have done so. He prefers his audience to be already in the know, and contents himself with spiritual winks. But the work of art has become work for us: it is part of our curacy, our living, and has to be read and transmitted in terms that include the pedagogical and technological dimension of modern life.

Aristotle said that imitation was pleasurable in itself. So it is possible that pleasure may return to the critic if he imitates older, more sacred modes of commentary. Something of this sort is indeed happening; but the pleasure of it will remain highly qualified. For our imitation of sacred exegesis is consciously archaic or a mock-up unless we believe in authority: that of the sacred text and, by extension, of our own, critical text.

Yet the "textual equation" established by the work of reading means that to read is to test the authority of authors or commentators against self-experience. Moreover, we are now forced to write ourselves down to balance the equation between us and the past, or between self and other, since authority in a nonsacred age is simply that which is written *and* survives. Our unwritten judgments could never resist the imposition of the flood of words, the paper pollution that sweeps all with it. It is like the old trial by water for witches, except now it is a trial by texts. Try and drown them: if they survive, they are guilty of witchcraft. Our authority—that is, survival—is bought at that price and remains suspect.

The involuted style of Richard Blackmur, therefore, perhaps the first of our witch critics, betrays an extreme awareness of how the mind is textured by texts and how the critic's, if not the poet's, authority is always under the shadow of imposture. Each critic usurps the mind of the town a few brief years. He manages to kill or revive some reputations. But his satisfaction is not in the political mayhem itself, which is almost a by-product, a by-fatality. If satisfaction is found it is in the thought that he has read *more* closely: that texts were not used by him as mere examples or to illustrate some high argument. Blackmur's close reading expresses a laboring mind, for which writing is travail—"A Long Way Round to Nirvana," to adapt the title of Santayana's essay on Freud's *Beyond the Pleasure Principle*. Lionel Trilling, it is true, sought to restore the essay to a certain decorum, and perhaps to exempt it from the disappearance of pleasure that he feared was the "fate" of literature. Did he succeed?

Nor is salvation to be found with those who ask for innovative criticism. The call to "make it new" is today an Epicureanism. For over a century now, and especially in France, writers have denied this kind of progress. It is strange, then, to see criticism taking up the lost cause of innovation or renovation and cheering art on to feats of transcendence and trespass, while contorting itself (like cheerleaders) into simulacra of their message.

Yet neither can art be asked to fail. Philosophies of decadence exist, but secretly they demand to be disproved: they are inverted calls for breakthrough and defiance. The contemporary emphasis on repetition (a "recollection forwards," as Kierkegaard said) means that we have recognized again the greatness, the sublimity, of the Ancients. It is we who recollect them forwards by the work of reading or the new work of art. There is no continuance by grace, nor is there an automatic pilot. Their strength is measured by our response, or not at all. That response can range from parody to the countersublime, but it always involves close writing.

Close writing, in art or criticism, is the correlative of close reading. The life of close readers has always, of course, meshed with texts. Milton's mind is deeply textual. Yet the haunting exerted by texts on the contemporary mind is perhaps more graphic and less musical than when transmission was oral. Few of us could face an audience and quote by heart large chunks of Donne or Milton. A poem is a poem is a poem; but is it still "Light to the sun and music to the wind"? The texts that course through me tend to be accompanied by a will to analysis that makes them stutter. I preserve them by elaboration, not by quotation. Like Arnold, then, the critic of today needs an anti-self-consciousness principle, but he seems to attain it only by "working through" more and more texts. His nirvana is an impasse reached after the play of mind and text, of text and text, has wearied itself.

The "it is written," both as debt and as challenge to further creativity, has been with us for a long time. Perhaps as long as literature itself. Yet in terms of a "modern" awareness, we can take it back to Flaubert and such projects as *Bouvard and Pecuchet* (1881) and the "Dictionary of Accepted Ideas." These were meant to put all future writers into a permanent state of embarrassment and so to jeopardize writing. Everything we could say would appear as already said, not in the honorific sense of having been anticipated by the Classics but in the demotic or daemonic sense of words sinking, necessarily, into mere copy, or the defiled, jargonic use Nathalie Sarraute named *tropisms.* The profoundest thought or expression would have no destiny except to be as trivialized as Freud is today.[5]

Flaubert checks the Words in Wonderland attitude perpetuated by the very phrase "creative writing." An explicit literary nihilism arises which also characterizes Nietzsche and within or against which most literary thinkers now move. The word *nihilism* sounds strange in English, but it comprises a set of attitudes that is subtle and complex and includes, for example, Flaubert's remark that he wished above all to write a book "about nothing." *Nihilism* is against *neologism* in the broad sense of the word: the possibility of saying anything new. The writer—critic or artist—is a bricoleur and has always been such. No ultimate historicizing disjunction can be made between ancient formulaic composition and "modern" methods of inner quotation.

It has been pointed out that Flaubert's *style indirect libre* (which purports to convey the words or thoughts of his characters without actually quoting them) already encouraged a slippage from direct quotation, as in novelistic dialogue, to an elegantly queasy reportage in which everything is implied as having been said, though nothing is uttered. And many recent studies have appeared of inner or hidden quotation in writers of fiction. Yet if so much is quotation, or a bricolage that seeks to overcome

5. I append a few excerpts from Flaubert's "Dictionary":
English Women. Show surprise that they have such pretty children.
Antichrist. Voltaire, Renan . . .
Blonds. Hotter than brunettes (see *Brunettes*).
Brunettes. Hotter than blonds (see *Blonds*).
Conversation. Politics and religion should be excluded from it.
Darwin. Said we came from monkeys.
Italy. Must be visited immediately after marriage.
Italians. All musicians. All traitors.
Prose. Easier to write than verse.

a condition it perpetuates, then all writing, not merely criticism, is parasitic.[6]

The claim, moreover, that literary, distinguished from critical or philosophic, language is "full" (polysemous, richly ambiguous) has to be modified. The richer or more loaded language is by quotation and allusion, the more it can subvert meaning. Puns, in which this load becomes an overload, are a special case of this subversion: however witty and explosive, however energetic their yield of meaning, they evoke in us a sense of leprous insubstantiality, of a contagion that might spread over language as a whole.

The literary nihilist is the Cheshire Cat of language. He is a mobile synecdoche: through him language bares its teeth in an empty grin. That bare grin cannot be hidden by explications backed by theories of multiple meaning that raid other fields of knowledge. As Paul de Man says, using an image not unrelated to the Cat:

> At the moment that modern critics claim to do away with literature, literature is everywhere; what they call anthropology, psychoanalysis, linguistics, is nothing but literature reappearing, like Hydra's head, in the very spot where it had supposedly been suppressed. The human mind will go through amazing feats of distortion to avoid facing "the nothingness of human matters." [*Blindness and Insight*]

"Le néant des choses humaines." That is Julie speaking in Rousseau's *Nouvelle Héloise* as she faces death with religious equanimity. Rousseau, according to de Man, did not seek to fill that human void by longing for a lost object. De Man sees Rousseau as exemplary of a consciousness that has freed itself of the allure of compensations: especially of the comfort of meaning. True literary consciousness, he generalizes, never results "from the absence of something but consists of the presence of a nothingness," which it names with ever-renewed understanding.

Thus literature cannot be explained or illumined by prevalent concepts of secularization, which are merely versions of "lost object" theorizing. Revisionist or philosophical criticism takes

6. Cf. J. Hillis Miller, "The Critic as Host," in *Deconstruction and Criticism.*

its most radical step at this point and challenges all historical explanation, all periodization, based on concepts of fall, secularization, restoration, etc. In such theories something "divine" that is lost (father, mother, God, golden age, primordial unity, unfallen language, meaning) finds its way back through the sophisticated regression or natural supernaturalism of art.

The subtle tyranny of secularization theories has made us forget till recently the analogy between criticism and theological discourse. Matthew Arnold struggled to subdue religion to literature in the name of a providential development. He predicted that only the poetry implicit in religion would remain. "The strongest part of our religion today," he said in 1880, "is its unconscious poetry" ("The Study of Poetry").

Has the prediction come true? One is tempted to reverse it, with so many psychotheological studies around. Freud's Eros and Thanatos are drives with the names of gods. The history of modern interpretation (including Freud) is also the history of the repression of allegorical exegesis. But we cannot so easily bypass two thousand years in favor of two hundred. Freud's genial analysis of the latent content of dreams already appears as yet another, and persuasive, mode of allegoresis.

Such books as Owen Barfield's *Saving the Appearances* (1957), Kenneth Burke's *The Rhetoric of Religion* (1961), and Harold Bloom's *Kabbalah and Criticism* (written as an extension of Gershom Scholem's pioneering work on medieval Jewish exegesis) indicate a new awareness of how learned or mystical systems of theology sustained and perpetuated canonical texts. The immense energy expended on this nurturance was highly imaginative: the legal and the ludic, the hallachic and the aggadic, cooperated. The same energy invests today's focus on a literature that—a crucial difference—cannot be clearly set off as holy and inspired. The will to discourse in what we have come to name *criticism* is therefore something remarkable: it has no sacred text as referent and cannot be justified.

"Justified" in the religious sense of the word—so Milton seeks in *Paradise Lost* to "justify the ways of God to men." Rationalization remains a possibility, of course, but each rationale labors under the cloud of being merely that. Literary-critical discourse, in short, is, like literature itself, a profane "troping." Whether the object of that troping is a sacred or a secular (classic) work is less important than that the consciousness of profanity overshadows at present the critical rather than the creative writer. I mean this relatively, of course. It is the critic who talks and worries more about the burden of the past. The creative writer, especially in contemporary America, is still promoting an ideology of newness and breakthrough. Yet already for Coleridge and Arnold, to choose sad if obvious examples, there are demons of the threshold who warn against a profaning of the ancient texts, even when these belong to a transcended culture. Criticism seems unable to achieve an easy conscience about the secularism it is struggling toward.

Indeed, so vast is our inheritance of an art immersed in myth and religion, so steeped is our language in their terms, that any project of secularization becomes invested with the pathos it would expel. Call for a "new language," cry for the extirpation of "the evil-smelling old logos" (Ihab Hassan), and unless you abandon words altogether in favor of nonverbal signs (and even then there is a risk of fostering symbols as cultic or quasi-magical as older hieroglyphs), the project of purification accrues strong religious overtones and appears to be a displacement of those feelings.

Aestheticism, as it developed in the nineteenth century, was part of this effort at purification. It wished to establish a religion of art and so to reverse a dependence that could not be overcome. When Malraux varied "Railroad stations are the modern cathedrals" into "Museums are the modern cathedrals," he recapitulated an old dilemma. Novalis, who said that the writer worked in words as the sculptor in stone, even when his matériel was the Bible, also suggested a religious concept of the primacy of art. Language itself is sacred: crafting or grafting it, living in the house of the great writers, has redemptive power. So Statius lauds Vergil in Dante's *Purgatorio*: "Through you I became a poet, through you a Christian." It is no accident that George Steiner has emphasized the evangelical aspect of the otherwise highly technical and disputatious process of translation. Translation is dissemination as well as imitation: every great artist contributes, like Jerome himself, to a vulgate, or what Herder liked to regard as a Bible of the Nations.

How deeply religion is connected, in present consciousness, with the "theology of the poets" is also attested by scholarly and scientific movements. The influence of Jung and of the Eranos circle is not exhausted, while that of scholars like Eduard Norden (*Agnostos Theos* and *The Birth of the Child*) has come to us mainly via the somewhat petrified form of E. R. Curtius's extension of *topoi* from ancient and medieval to modern spheres. Norden wrote: "Encompassed by the aura and atmosphere of past cultures, we live, in the Heraclitean sense, their death." Yeats could not have put it better. Ancient formulaic language is sacred language: what is Christian lives the death of what is pagan; and even if we succeed in discriminating the exact shading of interpenetrating religious formulas, the shared cultic style haunts us with a sense of underlying unity.

In Martin Buber's *I and Thou* (1916–22) two types of "founding word" *(Grundwort)* are postulated as the supreme formulas charging all discourse, sacred and secular; and Buber's "Whoever speaks a founding word, enters the word and stands in it" anticipates Heidegger's closer but pseudoscholarly analysis of a language of Being. The modern writer, of course, surrounded by all these spooky, learned treasures which generations of historicist scholars of religion have unearthed, may try to "swallow the formulas." But this is just another way of living their death.

We see, from this perspective, how belated is the enterprise of Northrop Frye. But it is also illuminating in this regard, and closest to us. Though Frye urbanely evades any *odium theologicum,* he always insinuates a sacerdotal or evangelical purpose into criticism, most clearly when, like Milton and Blake, he encourages in art the old "liberty of prophesying." His theory of formulas (archetypes) is presented as a scientific or structural project of description, but it saves art in a world split between scientific and religious (or ideological) imperatives.

Frye entitles the last chapter of his book on Blake, *Fearful Symmetry,* "The Burden of the Valley of Vision." Yet like Emerson, or Billy Graham, his mode is evangelical and lightens this burden—specifically, the yoke of imagination, creative energy as it bears down on the wary critic and teacher in the minute particulars of great writing. It bears down in bulk as well as visionary urgency. From our broadening perspective ("The cemeteries are on the march" is how Frye describes the resurrectional force of modern historicist knowledge in a later book, *The Modern Century*), it is hard to forget the illustrious dead, how much human creativity has accomplished, for good or evil. The past cries to be recognized and the present to be transformed. An anti-art arises, therefore, which is like the wilful squandering of that burdensome heritage. Eventually we fear that society itself is anti-art; that, at best, it channels creativity into the minor arts of "design" (decoration, fashion, posters, textiles, pottery) and, at worst, lures it into the pseudoworld of the communications media: advertising, propaganda, entertainment, journalism.

Frye's problem (ours too) is that major art in its very negativity or terrifying respect for exact witness cannot be co-opted. There is no accommodating it. So what can the function of criticism be? Must art remain outside of society, ineffective, a "useless passion," as Sartre named human existence itself? By a magical sleight of style, by a superb manipulation of our intellectual hopes and desires, Frye rescues criticism as accommodation. Criticism, he alleges, says nothing about the artistic experience as such—the latter may indeed be provocative, irritable, antisocial—but evolves a structure of its own to absorb the arts into society by education. For the anti-arts of advertisement, propaganda, and the culture industry cannot be driven out by the very art whose resentful shadow they are. Art can enter society only when tempered by the frame criticism provides. The emphasis shifts, therefore, to education, and to the question of whether we can break down the barriers between the academic and the creative spheres so that everything imaginative can find a place in the university—as unexpectedly perhaps as in Moses' camp.

When Moses is told of ecstatics in the Israelite camp, he exclaims: "Would to God all the Lord's people were prophets" (Numbers 11:29). How to honor yet control that prophetic energy, that speaking in tongues, is what makes all criticism social criticism. Frye's witty if understated *vision* of the critical enterprise is the most liberal theology or justification of art the modern professional has managed to devise.

Yet except for its formidable armature and professional tenor it is less explicitly redemptive than Emerson—or the Henry James, Sr., quoted by Richard Poirier in *A World Elsewhere*:

> The reason . . . why the painter, the poet, the musician, and so forth, have so long monopolized the name of Artist, is, not because Art is identical with these forms of action, for it is identical with no specific forms, but simply because the poet, painter, and so forth, more than any other men, have thrown off the tyranny of nature and custom, and followed the inspiration of genius, the inspirations of beauty, in their own souls. . . . They have merged the search of the good and the true in that of the beautiful, and have consequently announced a divinity as yet unannounced either in nature or society. To the extent of their consecration, they are priests after the order of Melchisedec. . . . [pp. 23–24]

That is patent enough, though enfeebled by its peculiar and sentimental brand of Platonism. Suddenly Frye's sophisticated armature of categories becomes more understandable, as does all emphasis on forms and genres in conservative criticism, which tends to be—let us admit it—Aristotelian. For while Henry James, Sr., seems to exalt art, he actually uses Platonism to attack it by evading the relevance of "specific forms." A higher concept of style is proposed, which Poirier accepts in principle—for he too sets something higher, language and literature, against mere techniques, mere genre—but Poirier also grounds this style in something lower, the very density of the verbal grappling.

"The problem," writes Poirier, "is stylistic. Quite locally so in the sounds and shapes of words. Genres have no instrumentality for expression. . . . What is most interesting in American literature is the attempt in the writing to 'build a world' wherein, say, even drunkenness might be the rule of day."[7] Style here is vision, "a world elsewhere," existing nowhere but in the textual quality of the text or in its "struggle for verbal consciousness," in D. H.

7. *A World Elsewhere*, pp. 11–12. Poirier means by drunkenness, as his reference to William James's *Varieties of Religious Experience* shows, a quality of time discontinuous with the sober environment in which we ordinarily live.

Lawrence's phrase. The transcendentalism of Emerson and James Sr. must become a textual fact: a fact flashing into fantasy, of course, but always conditioned by words.

The trouble with James Sr. is that he expands the concept of style so much that it coincides with Christian performance or the religious version of what Poirier calls in a later book the "performing self." Even those who only stand and wait can be said to have this style—a life-style, as it would now be called, though the idea of discontent does not surface except as a far prospect of apocalypse. Listen to Father James's description of a waiter seen transcendentally:

> He is no longer a menial, but my equal or superior, so that I have felt, when entertaining doctors of divinity and law, and discoursing about divine mysteries, that a living epistle was circulating behind our backs, and quietly ministering to our wants, far more apocalyptic to an enlightened eye than any yet contained in books.[8]

A living epistle to a new or unannounced god—is this not the claim of every avant-garde movement in letters as well as in religion? It carries us beyond the "Iceland of negation," as Emerson said, into "some new infinitude."

Our latest infinitude, of course, claims to stay within a negative dialectic. It is semiotic, differential, deconstructionist. For Emerson the moral difficulty lay precisely in being patient (on ice) while waiting for the promised end. "It will please us to reflect that though we had few virtues or consolations, we bore our indigence, nor once strove to repair it with hypocrisy or false heat of any kind." What will happen to the link of reading with watching or waiting, if we divorce ourselves from all talk

8. *A World Elsewhere*, p. 26. This angelic and sublimated image of work (cf. Milton's "They also serve who only stand and wait") is a disconcerting constant of religious or evangelical politics. To gain some distance from it one might compare it with Walter Benjamin on Abraham's patience (*Illuminations*, p. 129) and Sartre's description of a waiter in *Being and Nothingness* (1943), chap. 2, section 2, "Patterns of Bad Faith." Among discussions of the possibility of unalienated labor, important for the 1930s, are Hendrik de Man, *Der Kampf um die Arbeitsfreude* (1927) and Ernst Jünger, *Der Arbeiter* (first appearance, 1932). Also Carlyle's *Past and Present* (1843).

about "end," "promise," "unannounced god," "founding word," "living epistle"?

The emphasis on reading as a "work" that may rationalize itself as it goes on but cannot be justified is open to the charge that I have smuggled in a religious distinction. For the contrast of work and justification is especially acute in extreme Protestant movements. When Shakespeare sees Antony caught up in Cleopatra's "toils of grace," he expresses wittily, and in a conspicuously profane context, the religious paradox that opposes work and salvation, effort and grace. It presents these as an unresolvable tangle. It is, similarly, my suggestion that through the work of reading the work of art never comes to rest. Caught in our toils its grace becomes more of a toil.

What the dis-gracing of art involves is clearest, perhaps, in another medium. We all know that the most hypnotic art form today, the cinema, is also the most technical and directorial. The more "natural" a medium seems to be, the more artificial it in fact is. The naturalness of the cinema is an effect of art, not of grace. We accept that; yet the iconic illusion of the medium is so strong that the moviemakers themselves feel compelled to break it. But one can hardly be iconoclastic enough vis-à-vis either visual or verbal icons. Especially because, recently, theories emphasizing the verbal icon have predominated.

The very terms *verbal icon* or *verbal image,* which suggest that the strength of literary words lies in a graphic power similar to that of imaging, seem of doubtful validity when images have proliferated till they are manipulable signs or a picture-writing that overshadows the writing done with words. The rivalry of image and word has entered, today, a different phase. The image may be winning out over the word—the image as iconic idol, as something that will stick in mind and heart whether we trust it or not, as something that exposes itself and us.

Both semiotic and deconstructionist theories argue, of course, that there is more than meets the eye in images, and more than meets the ear in words. Meaning is not an accumulation of positive charges but rather a serialized negative, the awareness of ranges of difference within what is posited. The work of art, illuminated by the work of reading, discloses the iconoclastic within the iconic. Such an analysis may be correct in a structural sense, but it neglects the precise social and affective context. Photographic reproduction does not merely convert all symbols into signs that can then be compared and juxtaposed. It also heaps those symbols on us as homeless clichés that tease and frustrate imagination. The dump of sublimities lies all before us from which to draw *Monty Python and the Holy Grail* or interchangeable movies that retail or satirize them.

I am doubtful that we can separate the stardust or *Dunstkreis* of words from the image hoard of the movie world. "All in a mingled heap confus'd there lay / Robes, golden tongs, censer, and chafing dish, / Girdles, and chains, and holy jewelries" (Keats). We can even trace the augmented difficulty of wording images from Keats through Pater to (say) Yeats, Stevens, and Malraux. In "Leda and the Swan," Yeats struggles with an image as if it were a phantasm. The image, the unverbal icon, keeps gaining on us. Is it possible to *transprose* film as Pater did Leonardo's "Lady Lisa"? Pater's verbal refinement of ecstasy, or image-fixation, fascinates without quite convincing. Ruskin is a bit saner in the worship he accords Turner's abstractions, which set Nature (as in a storm) against merely natural images. Yet Ruskin did not end sane.

The work of reading is a sullen art reacting against modern iconomania. It may be too panicky a view that there is a contest between word and image which is being won by the latter, but I would still wish to link reading to an overall "vernacular" or "ecological" perspective that deals with human capacity in relation to its technical and formal achievements. Is imaging, now that everything can be imaged, ecstasy enough? We take our being from the monuments (however trivial) among which we live, and which we can classify but no longer destroy. The more we waste them, the more they vamp us, like portraits in a Gothic novel. We know what we have made, Vico thought, adapting the premise of a creator god; but now what we have made knows us.

Reading, like writing, is more than a technique: it is a complex and variable act with its own history. The challenge to read or inscribe or semioticize the image can be considered a form of image-breaking at a period when even the mirror of art multiplies, in a technicized compulsion to repeat, clichés of ecstasy. The readable image is the disenchanted image. But what of word and text, when they are too readable? Here the converse holds. The text, reified by certain ideologies or exploited by certain reading techniques, is made, by "deconstruction" for example, unreadable again. The unreadable text is the disenchanted text. Like Hegel's labor of the negative, the patience of critical reading points to an act, and a sustained one: when it is absent we rely on pseudoevents or a trivialized theory of reference to discharge our powers.

CHAPTER EIGHT

Literary Commentary as Literature

The school of Derrida confronts us with a substantial problem. What are the proper relations between the "critical" and "creative" activities, or between "primary" and "secondary" texts? In 1923, writing his own essay on "The Function of Criticism," T. S. Eliot accused Matthew Arnold of distinguishing too bluntly between critical and creative. "He overlooks the capital importance of criticism in the work of creation itself." Eliot's perception was, of course, partially based on the literary work of French writers since Flaubert and Baudelaire, including Mallarmé, Laforgue, and Valéry. But Eliot is wary lest his charge against Arnold, and in favor of the critical element in creative writing, be misapplied. "If so large a part of creation is really criticism, is not a large part of what is called 'critical writing' really creative? If so, is there not creative criticism in the ordinary sense?" Thus, having let the cat out of the bag, Eliot at once tries to contain the damage and deny, like Arnold, that criticism can find its own justification, and be creative or independent.

> The answer seems to be, that there is no equation. I have assumed as axiomatic that a creation, a work of art, is autotelic; and that criticism, by definition, is *about* something other than itself. Hence you cannot fuse creation with criticism as you can fuse criticism with creation. The critical activity finds its highest, its true fulfilment in a kind of union with creation in the labor of the artist.

In 1956, talking at the University of Minnesota on "The Frontiers of Criticism," Eliot is still uneasy about the "creative" potential in criticism. Characterizing his earlier essay as a reaction to the "impressionistic" type of criticism prevailing in his day, and fearing that now the "explanatory" type has become predominant, Eliot concludes: "These last thirty years have been, I think, a brilliant period in literary criticism in both Britain and America. It may even come to seem, in retrospect, too brilliant. Who knows?"

How can anything be too brilliant? Such defensiveness is neoclassical, and used to be directed against the plague of wit or glitter or enthusiasm in art. Having helped to establish, after Coleridge, that art not only has a logic of its own but that this logic is not discontinuous with the critical faculty—and that Matthew Arnold, who thought the Romantic poets did not "know" enough, should have recognized even more explicitly that art was a kind of avant-garde criticism—Eliot draws back from what seems to him an ultimate and dangerous sophistication. Criticism cannot be a creative activity. "You cannot fuse creation with criticism as you can fuse criticism with creation."

But this fusion of creation with criticism is occurring in the writings of contemporary critics. We are in the presence of something that, if not entirely new, is now methodically pursued, and without the backing of any specifically literary authority. I mean that we accept more easily the idea of a creative element in the critical essay if its author is a poet or novelist: then his authority in the creative realm carries over into the critical. So no one will deny the difficult and curiously "creative" investment of Mallarmé's prose, or the claim that "La musique et les lettres" is as interesting a piece of writing as a poem—even perhaps a poem by Mallarmé. But Derrida is no poet or even man of letters in the tradition of Mallarmé, Valéry, Malraux, Arnold, and Eliot. He is a professional philosopher as intense and focused as Heidegger. He does not tend to write critiques of the latest works of art or review segments of literary history. Other practitioners of the new philosophic criticism, such as Theodor Adorno and Walter Benjamin, are also not "creative writers" in the accepted sense of that phrase, though their criticism has often a practical cast and engages directly the notion of technology, culture, and the "culture industry."

The basic question is that of creative criticism: what to make of the "brilliance" of this phenomenon, which liberates the critical activity from its positive or reviewing function, from its subordination to the thing commented on, whether artifact or general theme. The new philosophic criticism has a scope that, though not autotelic, seems to stand in a complex and even crossover relation to both art and philosophy. To elucidate this problem I turn back to a writer who anticipates it in an essay on the essay contemporary with an early story of that most intellectual of novelists, Thomas Mann. I refer to Georg Lukács's "The Nature and Form of the Essay" (1910),[1] published at almost the same time as Mann's *Death in Venice.*

Lukács does not accept subordination as a defining characteristic of the essay. For him the great essayists, among whom he places Plato and Montaigne, use events or books merely as occasions to express their own "criticism of life"—a phrase he cites from Matthew Arnold, who had applied it to poetry. Does the essay, then, we might ask with Lukács, and the literary essay in particular, have a form of its own, a shape or perspective that removes it from the domain of positive knowledge (*Wissenschaft*) to give it a place beside art, yet without confusing the boundaries of scholarship and art? Is it at least *possible* for the essay to muster enough vigor to institute a renewal of ideas ("die Kraft zu einem begrifflichen Neuordnen des Leben") while remaining essayistic, distinct from a scientific philosophy's striving for absolute truths (the "eisig-endgültige Vollkommenheit der Philosophie")? The central question, thus, is criticism, the essay, as work of art, as art genre. "Also: die Kritik, der Essay—oder nenne es vorläufig was Du willst—als Kunstwerk, als Kunstgattung."

Lukács is aware that his position is timely, that it comes out of a movement of impressionist criticism whose great practitioners, after Romantic beginnings, were Pater and Wilde. "The Critic as Artist" is a phrase we associate with Wilde.[2] It is against this

1. "Über Wesen und Form des Essays: Ein Brief an Leo Popper." In *Die Seele und die Formen,* translated as *Soul and Form.*

2. See "The Critic as Artist" in Wilde's *Intentions* (1891), and Richard Ellmann's fine essay "The Critic as Artist as Wilde" introducing his selection from Wilde, *The Artist as Critic: Critical Writings of Oscar Wilde.*

movement that, a decade later, I. A. Richards and others launched their search for a stricter, more principled, even "scientific" or theoretically founded study of art. This occurred at the very time that Russian formalism was beginning its own quest for a rigorous definition of "literariness." In England, what Richards started at Cambridge soon became embroiled in the question of "scientism"; and while the striving for a theory of literature, or minimally for principles of criticism, maintained itself, the antitheoretical bias of F. R. Leavis and practical pressures, which make the profession of English studies short on bishops and long on country clergy, complicated though by no means killed the issue as Lukács stated it. In Germany itself, the influence of Dilthey, who had fanned the hope for a humanistic type of science standing on its own theoretical base (*Geisteswissenschaft*), diverted Lukács's question; and in the 1930s Lukács himself was to join the search for a science of literature from the Marxist side.

Let us return, now, to the diverted question: the status of the essay in Lukács's discussion of 1910. Lukács, one feels, isn't talking about the essay alone but about the inner tendency of all reflective, self-critical discourse. The chances are, in fact, that his understanding of the relation of the essay to "dialectic"—and so of a literary form to philosophy—was mediated by Walter Pater's *Plato and Platonism* (1893). By a peculiar twist of intellectual history, Lukács seems to view the German Romantics, and especially Hegel, through Pater's conception of Socratic conversation—which, looking back at Pater now, seems suspiciously like an idealized version of Oxford tutorials.[3] "The Platonic dialogue," Pater claims, "in its conception, its peculiar opportunities, is essentially an essay—an essay, now and then passing into the

3. While Pater's discussion of dialectic in chapter 7 contains strong remarks on method as a journey or an endless dialogue that always takes you a step further toward the ideal of a single imaginative act that would intuit "all the transitions of a long conversation . . . all the seemingly opposite contentions of all the various speakers at once" (cf. the evocation of a "gallery of spirits" at the end of Hegel's *Phenomenology* as well as Bakhtin's concept of "polyphony"), it also etiolates the anagogic thrust of Hegel or Plato by statements that suggest a pedagogy of the (with)drawing room: "If one, if Socrates, seemed to become the teacher of another, it was but by thinking that other as he went along that difficult way which each one must really prosecute for himself, however full such comradeship might be of happy occasions for the awakening of the latent knowledge," etc.

earlier form of philosophic poetry, the prose poem of Heraclitus." He distinguishes treatise from essay by saying that the former is an instrument of dogmatic philosophy that starts with axiom or definition, while "the essay or dialogue . . . as the instrument of dialectic, does not necessarily so much as conclude in one; like that long dialogue with oneself, that dialectic process, which may be coextensive with life. It does in truth little more than clear the ground, or the atmosphere, or the mental tablet." Socratic irony also belongs to this "tentative character of dialectic, of question and answer as the method of discovery, of teaching and learning, to the position, in a word, of the philosophic *essayist*."

These intuitions are developed by Lukács in his own way. He asserts that while the tragic mode of existence is crowned by its ending, in an essayistic mode everything, including the ending, is always arbitrary or ironic: the one question dissolves into the many, and even the external as distinguished from the internal interruptions serve to keep things open. The consciously occasional nature of the essay prevents closure. Lukács then interprets this open or occasional character in a way similar to, yet quite different from, contemporary semiotic or language-inspired explanations. Lukács says that it is ideally (and we are in the presence of a viewpoint shaped by German idealism) a counterpart, perhaps counterpoint, to mysticism's desire for ultimate issues. That the critic should talk about ultimate issues only in the guise of reviewing pictures or books is considered a deep irony. "Ironisch fügt er sich in diese Kleinheit ein, in die ewige Kleinheit der tiefsten Gedankenarbeit dem Leben gegenüber" ("The critic accommodates himself ironically to this minuteness, to the eternal minuteness of the deepest labor of thought vis-à-vis life").

How are we to understand such a strange assertion? Lukács, of course, inherited this enlarged concept of irony from the German Romantics. In *Soul and Form* there is a dialogue on Laurence Sterne that reminds us in many respects of Friedrich Schlegel. Irony, in any case, in Lukács as in German Romanticism, and perhaps in Sterne, is a kind of familiar demon, a domesticated compulsion, the will to truth or even the demon of absolute knowledge transformed by the magic of art into something close to a human and socializing grace. The essay form is a secret relative of the Romantic "fragment": it acknowledges occasionalism, stays within it, yet removes from accident and contingency that taint of gratuitousness which the mind is always tempted to deny or else to mystify. All occasions inform the essayist as they do the typological preacher, but in a purely secular way. This nontragic, nonreligious idealism could make the essayist take as his emblem a famous formula slightly altered: "Der liebe Gott steckt —ironisch—im Detail."

It is still our situation today. Perhaps all the more so, with the influx of books, artifacts, and pseudoevents. Keeping up means becoming the victim of flux unless sustained by an ironic idealism of this sort. Lukács gives no hint, however, as to whether this kind of irony can be realized. He asserts, on the one hand, that the modern essayist has lost ground compared to Plato and others, since each writer must now draw his critical standards out of himself, and, on the other, that the essay hasn't evolved enough to attain its destined form: genuine independence from naïvely representational—didactic, moralistic, review-subordinated —aims. The very "frivolity" of style that often enters the essay in the modern period is said to point to this exacerbated situation which obliges the critic to "represent" or "review" an artifact while being interested, really, in a transcendent *idea*. This is, primarily, the idea of fiction (*Dichtung*) as prior and greater than all possible fictions; and the critic, in his ironic or casual way, is exclusively in the service of that idea. He is therefore unlikely to engage in polemics or minute judgments: the fact that he carries with him the "atmosphere of the idea" should be enough to pass judgment on the individual work of art—to free it of all false, obsolete, or partial wisdom.

Just as we are about to give him up for the idealism he later exorcised, Lukács proposes a seminal and very practical definition. The essayist-critic, he adds, cannot himself embody the idea. He heralds it, wakes our sense for it, but remains its precursor. "Er ist der reine Typus des Vorläufers." Vorläufer, literally "pre-courser," "forerunner," has a resonance in German easily lost in translation. This resonance can be restored if we translate it as "provisional," the one who foresees but is a threshold figure, like Moses or John the Baptist. He can bring us no further than the penultimate stage. In a strong paragraph Lukács delimits strictly the dignity of the essay: "Ruhig und stolz darf der Essay sein Fragmentarisches den kleinen Vollendungen wissenschaftlicher Exaktheit und impressionistischer Frische entgegenstellen, kraftlos aber wird seine reinste Erfüllung, sein starkestes Erreichen, wenn die grosse Ästhetik gekommen ist" ("The essay can insist quietly and proudly on its fragmentary character against the minor perfections of scientific precision or impressionistic vividness, but its strongest achievement will prove impotent when the great aesthetics has arrived").

I confess I am drawn strongly to Lukács's essay on the essay. So much of contemporary intellectual life consists in reading these all-purpose forms, these baggy miniature monsters which like certain demons are only too serviceable. Lukács, moreover, is as plastic as Kant or Schiller in his elaboration of distinctions, each of which is given its dignity. He is never trapped by categories. Even when he has defined the essay as something intrinsically devoted to obsolescence, as a prelude or propadeutic for "die grosse Ästhetik" (he will complete his own in the 1960s), he assigns it also an independent existential value.

Though the essay as *parergon* will surely be subsumed, as in the case of Schopenhauer, by the system, yet such *parerga*, or *Beispiele,* show the system as a living, evolving entity ("seine Verwachsenheit mit dem lebendigen Leben"). So that, in a sense, they stand forever there, *beside* the system. Pater rescued "dialectic" from the philosophers and vested it in a form whose method or path was circuitous, but Lukács, more explicitly than Pater, attributes the essay form to both irony and desire (*Sehnsucht*), to a double, complementary or contrary, infinitizing. The essay lives off a desire that has an in-itself, that is more than something merely waiting to be completed, and removed, by absolute knowledge. On finishing Lukács, we have the uncanny impression that his exemplum has enacted the entire problem. This "real" letter to a friend, Leo Popper, dated formally "Florence, October 1910," is much more than the letter-preface to a book of essays, more than an essay even: it is an "intellectual poem," as A. W. Schlegel called Hemsterhuis' essays. It delimits its own position in the life of the intellect but meanwhile incorporates so much living thought that its narrower function of *Gericht* expands into the form of a *Gedicht.*

If the essay is indeed an intellectual poem, it is unflattering to observe that very few such poems exist in the sphere of literary or cultural criticism. The uneasy coexistence, in essays, of their referential function as commentary with their ambition to *be* literature and not only be about it makes for a medley of insight and idiosyncratic self-assertion. There is a charm, of course, to many nineteenth-century essays, which preserves them from this fate. Arnold or Pater on Wordsworth can be read as interesting *prose,* sustained by valid if occasionally dated remarks. We are not threatened, not imposed on, by the force of their observation, or not any longer. Pater and Arnold are now part of the heaven of English literature, like Wordsworth himself. The ideal proposed by Lukács is, however, a harder one, and as unlikely of realization as a poem that must carry along, and not shirk, a strong weight of ratiocination or of opinion with the force of fact.

How scarce this commodity is, this essay which is an intellectual poem, can be gauged by a guess that, with the early exception of Friedrich Schlegel, only Valéry habitually attained it: one thinks of his masterful construction of the figure of Leonardo da Vinci or of "Poetry and Abstract Thought," both of which, it happens, raise the issue of the relation between artistic and scientific thinking. One might add such essays as Ortega's "In Search of Goethe from Within." Certain of Freud's or Heidegger's essays are also constructions of this kind, severe intellectual poems.

Yet neither Valéry nor Ortega nor Freud nor Heidegger engages very often in the close reading of literature or the close viewing of art. Their notion of detail, when it comes to art, is less exigent, and their exposition less grainy than ours. The critical essay today, to qualify as such, must contain some close-ups: it tends to proceed, in fact, by shifts of perspective (as in some kinds of sequential art or concrete poetry) that expose the nonhomogeneity of the fact at hand, the arbitrariness of the knots that bind the work into a semblance of unity. The close-ups are not there merely to illustrate or reinforce a suppositious unity but to show what simplifications, or institutional processes, are necessary for achieving any kind of unitary, consensual view of the artifact.

The process of institutionalization or the normalization called "objective reality" is what is focused on: though not, always, to subvert it. Subversion can be one aim, as in much avant-garde criticism; yet today, on the whole, such criticism, whether in the form of radical art or advanced commentary, seeks to remove the naiveté of formalization rather than to challenge its necessity. There is, of course, no avoiding the disillusion that comes to all, when what is taken to be nature is unmasked as rhetoric or ideology or second nature—when we see leading strings maintained into maturity and becoming bonds or even chains we at best shake a little. The critical essay is critical: we are allowed to survive but not to substantialize our illusions.

A curious reversal may therefore occur in the world of letters. Often poems seem to be less demanding than essays. To be precise, poems, especially today, are there as identity marks, written because to write is part of the contemporary heraldry of identity. Many writers read merely in order to write, not in order to discover whether it is needful for them to add their testimony. The same may be true of the essayists. Yet it seems to me that the essays of the more intellectual practitioners of the art of literary or philosophical criticism make greater demands on the reader: that they ask him to read so as not to write, that they even make the text a little harder to understand and the visible a little harder to see. They increase rather than lighten the burden of tradition, in an anti-evangelical and depressing manner.

Though less distinguished in their decorum, many essays are now more exacting than the "familiar" prose which aimed, in the previous century, to expand the family of readers. Hazlitt makes you feel equal to, or different only in degree from, Wordsworth. And while this democratic ethos (which Wordsworth shared) remains valid, the virulence of nationalistic and separatist movements has taught us how dangerous it is to assume intimacy or common standards. The labor involved in understanding something foreign or dissident without either colonizing it or becoming oneself a cultural transvestite meets us fully as the reality, the otherness, to be faced.[4]

It may well be that some of the difficult critics of whom I speak (whether Adorno or Blackmur or Derrida) are frustrated poets, and this can be held against them; but they are frustrated because they realize the discipline and learning involved, and do not want merely to exploit the past. Though not paralyzed by the heavy task of emulating pastmasters or alien traditions, they know that culture has often progressed by *contamination*; and this produces an anguish and a self-scrutiny leading to a vacillating or deeply equivocal recuperation of what Northrop Frye has prematurely named "the secular scripture."[5] Frye suggests that art becomes secular by being recuperated; yet woe to him (I must add) by whom this recuperation comes! He may profane the tradition, just as the New Testament runs the risk of profaning the Old, by giving it a universality that at once redeems and cheapens the barbarous, that is, ethnocentric, element.

Like Lukács in his pre-Marxist phase, Frye places the critical essay closer to *Gedicht* than *Gericht*. With him too the "atmosphere of the idea," not any imperious or ideological truth, changes our consciousness of fact or artifact. There is some anxiety about the past in Frye, but mainly a refusal to be anxious about, and so to overdefine, the future. "To recreate the past and bring it into the present," he writes, "is only half the operation. The other half consists of bringing something into the present which is potential or possible, and in that sense belongs to the future." It is, however, hard to know what Frye means by the "potential" or the "possible" unless it is precisely that sacred and untamed element, the "wish-fulfillment element in romance," which so often has an ethnocentric basis, and which art opposes to itself as to any institutionalization.

Here, certainly, is one "bind" that makes the critical essay both severe and essential, and more than a time-serving device. It

4. Hazlitt himself, a prime political dissident, insists fiercely enough on the difference between a writer's greatness as a writer and his politics (see, for example, the ending of the essay on Sir Walter Scott in *The Spirit of the Age*, 1825). His own political philosophy assumes, however, not only a wide audience, as in modern journalism, but also one whose politics and culture could be harmonized.

5. *The Secular Scripture* (1976). My later quotation comes from this work.

is always at once timely and untimely: it stands at the very intersection of what is perceived to be a past to be carried forward, and a future that must be kept open. In Lukács's idealism, as in Frye's, the futuristic element is "desire," or whatever fuels wishing, and cannot achieve fulfillment. When institutionalized, this desire produces superstition; kept free it produces a frivolous or disinterested irony.

It is mere common sense, then, to put the critical essay on the side of irony, but this may turn out to be more defensive than correct. What lies beyond wish fulfillment or the pleasure principle is not irony but something daemonic to which Freud ventured to give the name of reality-mastery. Lukács's career as critic veers dialectically, and perhaps daemonically, toward a reality-mastery in which desire, wish fulfillment, and formal irony play only a subordinate role. The process of incorporating what continues to violate one's identity—I mean on the level of cultural conflict or exchange—may lie beyond the range of values associated with such words as *pleasure, taste, civility, irony, accommodation*. This beyond may also become the domain of the literary essay, the more urgent and severe its aim.

"I am always amused," Wilde says characteristically, "by the silly vanity of those writers and artists of our day who seem to imagine that the primary function of the critic is to chatter about their second-rate work." The problem is what to do about first-rate work, or that which is great enough to reduce all critical comment to chatter.

The English tradition in criticism is sublimated chatter; but it is also animated by its fierce ability to draw reputation into question. Even Shakespeare had once to be made safe; and Milton is restored, after Leavis, to his bad eminence. This power to alter reputations is formidable, and it shows that criticism has an unacknowledged penchant for reversal in it, which is near-daemonic and which brings it close to the primacy of art. This penchant, of course, can be dismissed as the sin of envy: as a drive for primacy like Satan's or Iago's. Yet, Lukács remarked, there *is* something ironic about the critic's subordination of himself to the work reviewed. At best he keeps testing that work, that apparent greatness, and by force of doubt or enthusiasm puts it more patently before us. He plays the role now of accuser and now of God. A judicious rather than judicial criticism will, needless to say, not try for a single verdict: like Dr. Johnson's, it will expose virtues and weaknesses, strong points and failings together. But it can also frighten us by opening a breach—or the possibility of transvaluation—in almost every received value. Even Romantic irony, therefore, seems unable to digest Wilde's insouciance. "The fact of a man being a poisoner is nothing against his prose."

Wilde means, of course, a poisoner in life, like Thomas Wainewright.[6] But can we help thinking, at the same time, of the poison or immorality that may lodge in art and that made Plato compare a certain kind of rhetor to a dangerous cook? A breach is opened by Wilde between morality and art paralleling that between morality and religion in certain pronouncements of Christ or, for that matter, Blake and Kierkegaard. This parallel may put too great a strain on art, as Eliot feared; and it may also put too great a strain on the critic, who knows that poisons can be remedies.[7] Still, since Wilde (with anticipations in Poe and Baudelaire), the theory of art has been striving to understand the daemonic artist, even the artist-criminal. Not as an empirical or social phenomenon so much but as a theory-enabling fiction that could reveal the problematic depths of *persona* and *intention*.[8] Wilde tears apart face and mask, while the modern persona theory tries to repair the breach. Yet the issue of an intention too faceless to be envisaged still defeats us; and for that reason Derrida suggests that we should substitute the word *sfeinctor* for *author*.

Nor is it an accident, then, that Derrida interests himself in Genet and the "precious bane" of his style. Derrida's *Glas,* a work in which commentary becomes literature, by interweaving philosophical discourse, figurative elaboration, and literary criticism, begins one column with Genet's evocation of a "Rembrandt déchiré." But the theme of the torn picture (viz. manuscript) does not express an iconoclasm nourished by the simple

6. See "Pen, Pencil and Poison," in *Intentions.*

7. Cf. Jacques Derrida's "La pharmacie de Platon," in *La dissémination.*

8. There is a convergence, at this point, of the problem of intention in a secular context with the same problem in a sacred context. The depth interpretations of sacred hermeneutics, whether rabbinical or patristic or kabbalistic, are based on divine revelations that are close to being faceless, i.e., "dark with excessive bright."

opposition of art-appearance and reality (*Dorian Gray*), or art and religion, or art and a claimant absolute. It expresses, rather, the insufferable coexistence, even crossover, of holiness and profaneness in art. This crossover tears us apart; and we imaginatively take our revenge by tearing at it, or prudently and hygienically—by means of a *genre tranché* critical theory—denying the crossover, and separating the daemonry of art from the civility of criticism, or discursive from literary discourse, or persona from person, and so forth. Yet everyone has known the feeling that in Henry James or Sartre, let alone Borges, criticism is not independent of the fictional drive. The more insidious question is whether any critic has value who is only a critic: who does not put us in the presence of "critical fictions"[9] or make us aware of them in the writings of others.

What I am saying, then—pedantically enough, and reducing a significant matter to its formal effect—is that literary commentary may cross the line and become as demanding as literature: it is an unpredictable or unstable genre that cannot be subordinated, a priori, to its referential or commentating function. Commentary certainly remains one of the defining features, for it is hardly useful to describe as "criticism" an essay that does not review in some way an existing book or other work. But the perspectival power of criticism, its strength of recontextualization, must be such that the critical essay should not be considered a supplement to something else. Though the irony described by Lukács may formally subdue the essay to a given work, a reversal must be possible whereby this "secondary" piece of writing turns out to be "primary."

We have viewed the critical essay too reductively, just as, in the history of literature itself, we often find types of fiction defined by arbitrary rules from which they break loose. Let us remember, too, that instrumental music, before a certain time, was strictly subordinated to text or programmatic function. Later the instruments become speculative. The same holds true of criticism: its speculative instruments are now exercising their own textual powers rather than performing, explaining, or reifying

9. *Critical Fictions* is the title of Joseph Halpern's book on Sartre's criticism (1976).

existing texts. What is happening is neither an inflation of criticism at the expense of creative writing nor a promiscuous intermingling of both. It is, rather, a creative testing and illumination of *limits*: the limits of what Hegel called "absolute knowledge" and Dewey the "quest for certainty."

I have argued previously that the more pressure we put on a text, in order to interpret or decode it, the more indeterminacy appears. As in science, the instruments of research begin to be part of the object viewed. All knowledge, then, remains knowledge of a text, or rather of a textuality so complex and interwoven that it seems abysmal. There is an "echappé de vue ins Unendliche," as Friedrich Schlegel quaintly says. Or, as Derrida puts it, the act of reading to which we are "abandoned" by the critic forbids a single theme or resolution to emerge. "Laissez flotter le filet, le jeu infiniment retors des noeuds." We see, then, that English and French waves have an inspiration in common: whatever the difference—and it is considerable—Derrida's radical attention to the skein of language is still part of the "repudiation of the metaphysics" also aimed at by Ogden and Richards in *The Meaning of Meaning* (1923). But now the starting point, in France, is the pataphysical heritage[10] as well as a linguistic critique of metaphysics, or Hegel's concept of "absolute knowledge."

There is no absolute knowledge but rather a textual infinite, an interminable web of texts or interpretations; and the fact that we discern periods or sentences or genres or individual outlines or unities of various kinds is somewhat like computing time. We can insist that time has a beginning and an end; or, more modestly, that Romanticism, for example, began circa 1770 and ended circa 1830; but this is a silly if provoking mimicry of providential or historical determinism. Such linearity is precisely what stimulates Derrida and others to cross the line: to accept, that is, the need for lineation and delineation, but in the form of a textuality as disconcerting as a new geometry might be.

Before turning again to Derrida for an example of how literary commentary is literature, two cautionary remarks. The first is that, in criticism, we deal not with language as such,

10. For a fine account of this heritage, see Roger Shattuck, *The Banquet Years.*

nor with the philosophy of language, but with how books or habits of reading *penetrate* our lives. Arnold's "The Function of Criticism at the Present Time," still a classic essay for our discipline in terms of its quality of self-reflection, takes its power from the courage of adjudicating between English and French literature—*literature* in the broadest sense, as the character displayed by our laws, our magazines, our political writings, as well as poetry and criticism.

My second caution (still thinking of Arnold) is that a hundred years is not long in the eyes of God, if endless in the eyes of each generation. One can exaggerate the newness of the present moment in criticism. There has certainly been some speed-up in the rhythm of events even if we discount such extreme statements as Péguy's, on the eve of the Great War: "The world has changed less since Jesus Christ than in the last thirty years." Arnold himself was struck by the speed-up, and his very focus on the function of criticism acknowledges it. He sees the critic aiding the creative mind to find its proper "atmosphere," which lies "amidst the order of ideas" and beyond the provincialism of its era. And he welcomed the "epoch of expansion" that was opening in England. Yet he also feared the example of France, where the Revolution had produced a commitment to "the force, truth and universality of the ideas it took for its laws." For these ideas were not really free, but imprisoned by particular ideologies, by the French "mania for giving [them] an immediate political and practical application." My caution is that things have not changed all that much since Arnold's essay of 1864; that despite the increased tempo and complexity of modern life, what was true in his contrast of France and England may still be so.

In fact, even Lukács's notion of the essayist as a precursor type may have a direct relation to Arnold. Lukács substantializes the idea of a critic and puzzles over the paradox of a type whose essence is transience. For Arnold too the critic is a precursor, but Arnold does not claim an interest in the critic as such. His view is determined by concrete historical considerations, in particular by the stirring up of ideas in the era of the French Revolution. That stirring up is part of a great stream of tendency and must be for the good, but criticism itself is not that good. Arnold therefore makes a sharper distinction than the young Lukács between precursor-critic and creative genius, insisting that criticism merely prepares the ground for the latter by stimulating a living current of ideas. It was because that current had not been sufficiently present in England when the Romantics wrote that they failed to match the glory of the writers of the Renaissance; and Arnold ends "The Function of Criticism" by foreseeing a new epoch of creativity that the movement of modern criticism will usher in. "There is the promised land, toward which criticism can only beckon. That promised land will not be ours to enter, and we shall die in the wilderness: but to have desired to enter it, to have saluted it from afar, is already perhaps the best distinction among contemporaries." To which one can only reply: Ah, Wilderness. It is precisely that purely functional notion of criticism, or that great divide between criticism and creation, which is now in dispute.

Against Derrida's *Glas,* from which I will take my example of literary commentary as literature, it can be urged that bad cases make bad law. Exceptional this work certainly is, but can it represent criticism in any save an extreme contemporary form? It is not for me to decide that question. What seems extreme today may not be so a decade or a century hence. Books have their own fate; and I am sufficiently convinced that *Glas,* like *Finnegans Wake,* introduces our consciousness to a dimension it will not forget, and perhaps not forgive. It is not only hard to say whether *Glas* is "criticism" or "philosophy" or "literature," it is hard to affirm it is a book. *Glas* raises the specter of texts so tangled, contaminated, displaced, deceptive that the idea of a single or original author fades, like virginity itself, into the charged Joycean phrase: "Jungfraud's messonge book."

In *Glas,* as elsewhere, Derrida exerts a remarkable pressure on privileged theoretical constructs, in particular those of origin, self, author, and book. It seems difficult to let go of the concept of authorial identity: of a unified person or message characterized by a name that authenticates it within a clearly circumscribed text. Yet *Glas* not only interanimates many sources (Hegel, Nietzsche, Genet) by inner quotation and surrealist wit; it not only incorporates, in particular, passages from Genet's *Journal du voleur* (1948), but does so to become a thievish book in essence.

Genet's self-identification as a thief is developed, by Derrida, to embrace all writers. We are led beyond a psychoanalytic perspective to the haunting notion of a "vol anthique" (sometimes "question anthologique," viz. "ontologique"). This ancient theft recalls Prometheus and Hermes; but since *vol* also means flight, allusion is made to Icarus or the eaglelike aspiration of religion, science, and (Hegel's) philosophy to absolute knowledge. Most literally, though, "vol anthique" is *Blütenstaub*—"dissemination"—and expresses Derrida's counterencyclopedic notion of the propagation of the word (with roots, possibly, in Novalis and the German Romantics) and the curious floweriness of Genet's style: a pastoral purification of an immoral subject matter equal yet opposite to Promethean fire. The *Journal du voleur* is made to betray a vol-ition as high as that of other myths, and which by contagion or camaraderie also informs *Glas.*

Glas, then, is Derrida's own *Journal du voleur,* and reveals the vol-onto-theology of writing. Writing is always theft or bricolage of the logos. The theft redistributes the logos by a new principle of equity, as unreferable to laws of property, boundary, etc. (Roman, capitalistic, paternal, national) as the volatile seed of flowers. Property, even in the form of the *nom propre,* is *non-propre,* and writing is an act of crossing the line of the text, of making it indeterminate, or revealing the *midi* as the *mi-dit.* "La force rare du texte, c'est que vous ne puissiez pas le surprendre (et donc limiter) à dire: *ceci est cela*" (*Glas,* p. 222).

Does it amount to more, though, than a dignifying of bricolage? Genet, Derrida, might turn out to be mere pastiche, a resynthesizing of older notions or myths. The objection Marx lodged against costume-drama revolution (resurrecting the idea of Rome in 1789 leads to the Napoleonic eagle) could be relevant There seems to be no way of killing off, by bricolage, the exemplary Grand Story. Consider Doctorow's *Ragtime,* which rags (among other things) Kleist's *Michael Kohlhaas.* Surely it is only a matter of time before that story is recovered, not as some ultimate or privileged source but as a pre-text exploding its new frame and revealing not merely its priority but the stronger understanding in it of revolutionary fantasy.

It should be stated explicitly that the intertextual bricolage characteristic of *Glas* does not recuperate either Genet or "sacred" source texts. Derrida is not directly interested in the origin, psychic or literary, of Genet's work. To be exact, the very notion of origin is understood as a (Heideggerian) *Ur-sprung*,[11] a hyperbolic leaping like that of Icarus, which sustains itself by bricolage: by the technical exploitation or reframing of correlative structures that hold it up, fuel it falsely or failingly, but still, somehow, let it spin out the line—the tightrope even—of the "glue" of "aleatory" writing. Derrida repeats as a refrain: "La glu de l'aléa fait sens."

There is, obviously, some exhibitionism in this: art no longer hides art. But only because there is nothing to hide. We know what is to be known, that every act of presence, every "ici" or "midi" is infinitely mediated, and yet as vulnerable—*coupable*—as an unmediated venture, a flight beyond what is, out of nothing, into nothing.

The line of exegesis will therefore tend to be as precariously extensible as the line of the text. The subject matter of exegesis is, in fact, this "line." Yet criticism as commentary *de linea* always crosses the line and changes to one *trans lineam*.[12] The commentator's discourse, that is, cannot be neatly or methodically separated from that of the author: the relation is contaminating and chiastic; source text and secondary text, though separable, enter into a mutually supportive, mutually dominating relation. It is hard to find the right analogy, the right figure, for this relation; better to describe what happens in the exemplary case.

11. My reference is to Heidegger's "Der Ursprung des Kunstwerks" (1936), first published in *Holzwege* (1950).

12. The cultural and historical implications of "nonlinear" thinking are very differently expounded in such writings as Ernst Jünger's *Über die Linie* and Heidegger's replique; in Marshall McLuhan's *The Gutenberg Galaxy*; in Derrida's translation (Paris, 1962) of Husserl's *Ursprung der Geometrie,* and in his *De la grammatologie,* pp. 127–31. Also in relation to the concept of time (including the historian's) in Derrida's "Ousia et Grammè," *Marges de la philosophie.* Cf. J. Hillis Miller, "Ariadne's Web: Repetition and the Narrative Line," in *Critical Inquiry* (1976).

So in *Glas* the presence of Genet is not (even on the first page) restricted to one column: it crosses the line into the commentary on Hegel. Yet to follow this crossing needs an understanding of the link between, for example, Genet's Rembrandt essay and a passage from the *Journal du voleur*.[13] Also an understanding of that *Journal* passage in its own right, as it deals with the very theme or "antheme" of *crossing the line*. Also perhaps an understanding of the volatility of the syllable "éc . . ." as it *ech*oes not only through the right-hand column of the first page of *Glas* but establishes a continuing series by drawing in "IC" and "aig/le" ("Je m'éc . . ." "Je m'aig/le")—and even "glas," if we remember that the cry ascribed to eagles is "glatir." (See illustration on pages 140–41 for the opening paragraphs of *Glas*.) By such "contagion" or "circulation infinie de l'*éq*uivalence générale," we approach, even before we reach Derrida's discussion of the "zero signification" of Genet's flowery style, what he terms "les glas de la signification" or "le texte anthographique, marginal et parafant: qui ne signifie plus" (*Glas,* p. 37). "La force rare du texte" is "à la limite, nulle" (*Glas,* p. 222).

Here, of course, the notion of transgression (of limits) and indeterminacy (of endlessly approaching the limit we call a meaning) seem to merge. It is as if two very different types of discourse—that of Blanchot, say, and that of Georges Bataille—were being melded into one. The attempt to join such disparates is itself a transgression, and one cannot—as yet—determine whether Derrida is demystifying dialectic thinking (or other types of logic) or erecting literary wit into a new logic, at once corrosive and creative.

The Genet text that quietly pervades the Hegel column is later quoted and analyzed by Derrida himself (*Glas,* pp. 211–19). While Genet denies that he decided to be a thief at a precisely definable epoch in his life, he does recall detaching himself forcibly from the companionship of army life by an act of treachery that involved stealing from a buddy. This theft, he claims, strength-

13. For Genet's essay on Rembrandt, see his *Oeuvres complètes,* 4: 19–31. The passage from the *Journal du voleur* is analyzed below. Since the "crossing" of all these texts is complex enough, I omit the additional knot provided by a section of Nietzsche's *Also sprach Zarathustra* which deals with the theme of purity via the opposition of "Adler" and "Ekel."

ened him toward the "moral solitude" he desired, and which eventually made him break all ties of affection and love. He then continues without transition:

> La tapisserie intitulée "La Dame à la Licorne" m'a bouleversé pour des raisons que je n'entreprendrai pas ici d'énumérer. Mais, quand je passai, de Tchécoslovaquie en Pologne, la frontière, c'était un midi, l'été. La ligne idéale traversait un champ de seigle mûr, dont la blondeur était celle de la chevelure des jeunes Polonais; il avait la douceur un peu beurrée de la Pologne dont je savais qu'au cours de l'histoire elle fut toujours blessée et plainte. J'étais avec un autre garçon expulsé comme moi par la police tchèque, mais je le perdis de vue très vite, peut-être s'égara-t-il derrière un bosquet ou voulut-il m'abandonner: il disparut. Ce champ de seigle était bordé du côté polonais par un bois dont l'orée n'était que de bouleaux immobiles. Du côté tchèque d'un autre bois, mais de sapins. Longtemps je restai accroupi au bord, attentif à me demander ce que recélait ce champ, si je le traversais quels douaniers les seigles dissimulaient. Des lièvres invisibles devaient le parcourir. J'étais inquiet. A midi, sous un ciel pur, la nature entière me proposait une énigme, et me la proposait avec suavité.
>
> —S'il se produit quelque chose, me disais-je, c'est l'apparition d'une licorne. Un tel instant et en tel endroit ne peuvent accoucher que d'une licorne.
>
> La peur, et la sorte d'émotion que j'éprouve toujours quand je passe une frontière, suscitaient à midi, sous un soleil de plomb la première féerie. Je me hasardai dans cette mer dorée comme on entre dans l'eau. Debout je traversai les seigles. Je m'avançai lentement, sûrement, avec la certitude d'être le personnage héraldique pour qui s'est formé un blason naturel: azur, champ d'or, soleil, forêts. Cette imagerie où je tenais ma place se compliquait de l'imagerie polonaise.
>
> —"Dans ce ciel de midi doit planer, invisible, l'aigle blanc!"
>
> En arrivant aux bouleaux, j'étais en Pologne. Un enchantement d'un autre ordre m'allait être proposé. La "Dame à la Licorne" m'est l'expression hautaine de ce passage de la ligne à midi. Je venais de connaître, grâce à la peur, un trouble en face du mystère de la nature diurne, quand la campagne française où j'errai surtout la nuit était toute peuplée du fantôme de Vacher, le tueur de bergers. En la parcourant j'écoutais en moi-

> même les airs d'accordéon qu'il devait y jouer et mentalement j'invitais les enfants à venir s'offrir aux mains de l'égorgeur. Cependant, je viens d'en parler pour essayer de vous dire vers quelle époque la nature m'inquiéta, provoquant en moi la création spontanée d'une faune fabuleuse, ou de situations, d'accidents dont j'étais le prisonnier craintif et charmé.

What theory of allusion can account for the presence/absence of this passage on the opening page of *Glas*? If "Rembrandt déchiré" inaugurates the right-hand column of the book, embedded in the left with its marginal introduction of the Immaculate Conception ("IC") is another work of art ("la tapisserie intitulée 'La Dame à la Licorne' "). *That* seems untorn, virginal; yet does not an eagle hover invisibly in the sky, and is not crossing over (the "frontière" or "ligne") accompanied by a fear mingled with the kind of emotion that, at noon, incites "la première féerie"? What is that? May we translate it "the primal fantasy"? But what is *that*?

"Je me hasardai," Genet's next sentence reads, "dans cette mer dorée comme on entre dans l'eau. Debout je traversai les seigles." Since Genet has previously told us that "par elle dont je porte le nom le monde végétal m'est familier,"[14] he is entering as "le roi—peut-être la fée" (p. 46), a *mère dorée.* He is himself the Unicorn of this heraldic moment ("je pénétrais moins dans un pays qu'à l'intérieur d'une image," admits the paragraph following the passage on pp. 50–51). Or he is the royal prisoner, if not victim, of a Mother Nature associated twice with killers of children (here with Vacher, a page or so earlier with Gilles de Rais). "La première féerie" would seem to be the "family romance" of the absent mother, torn yet most whole, criminal and virginal, unstained like Nature herself by all the blood and suffering that should cry from that ground.

No wonder, then, that the first verse Genet wrote, as a note added to page 51 informs us, was "moissonneur des souffles coupés." It is indeed a question of breath, of maintaining the line, not genetically but as a writer. Genet as "vainqueur du vent" takes one's breath away with his imitation of Nature's impassibility,

14. "Par elle," i.e., his mother, whose name "Genet" ("genêt," the broom flower) he retains.

troubled rhythmically here and there yet remaining sublimely flowery. The wind is conquered or harvested; the text sustained. "Moissonneur des souffles coupés": who is the harvester alluded to? Is it Death, or Nature, or Vacher ("tueur de bergers"), or Genet himself?[15]

The scene with its "soleil de plomb," almost its noonday demon, is like a still out of Coleridge's *Ancient Mariner,* "All in a hot and copper sky / The bloody sun at noon . . . ." But the horror is now merely a "trouble," something "unquiet" in this quiet, and the blondness of the rye is compared to the "douceur un peu beurrée de la Pologne dont je savais qu'au cours de l'histoire elle fut toujours blessée et plainte."[16] How far, yet how near, are we from a strangled cry like "*Je m'éc* . . ."?

Is that cry not a "souffle coupé," as of butchered children? A muted, self-inflicted violence, as if Genet, that child of nature, had become a "bourreau berceur" (Derrida's phrase) like his mother? The cry's reflexiveness suggests that the "souffle coupé" may also be a "souffle coupable." *Je m'aigle*: I am my own vulture. Or as Derrida puts it: "Je seigle ou m'aigle" (*Glas,* p. 211). But that is some two hundred pages after the "aigle de plomb ou d'or, blanc ou noir" has appeared on the Hegel side of the balanced page.

Something is "mal enchaîné." The eagle referred to, via the pun on Hegel's name, is a national emblem shared, or competed for, by several nation-states, but also the Promethean torment of striving for absolute knowledge, "savoir absolu." With all boundaries in dispute (between nation and nation, outside and inside, text and commentary, Hegel and Genet, German and French, literature and philosophy, left and right margins) Genet's vaunted detachment dissolves into a self-penetration, a "s'avoir absolu" erected into a specular, heraldic image of self-presence. "Hiero-

15. When we extend the notion of "ligne" to include sounds (or the "glue" that builds phonemes into words and meanings) "moissonneur" could come apart as "moi, sonneur," and lead Derrida to the theme of *Glas* once again.

16. The verisimilar yet oneiric truth of Genet's landscape is heightened by our knowledge that Jarry had set *Ubu Roi* (1896) in a Poland that continued to be ravaged by border disputes. "The action, which is about to begin, takes place in Poland, that is to say: Nowhere."

glyphics of hysteria, blazons of phobia," these are what we interpret, says Jacques Lacan.

Derrida understands Genet's "pénêtre" (*Glas,* p. 215) so well that he sounds or extends that "souffle coupé" by following a "ligne idéale" through the "mer dorée" of the "seigle" until we come to the "mère dorée" of the "sigle": the IC (close to "ici") denoting the Immaculate Conception, or "Un tel instant et un tel endroit [qui] ne peuvent accoucher que d'une licorne." This IC/ici, therefore, is as much a personal fantasy as a final knowledge: it evokes the ecstatic desire for a here and now (an "ici, maintenant") or a pure self-presence which defines the inaugural as well as ultimate state of the odyssey of the spirit toward consciousness of itself in Hegel's system.

There are those who maintain that "the corruption of the poet is the generation of the critic." Or that, as the same authority alleges, there is a danger lest the auxiliary forces of criticism become the enemy of the creative writer. "Are they from our seconds become principals against us?"[17] Yet Dryden, of course, was blasting the nit-picking, censorious or "minute" critics of his time, the overzealous schoolmasters and arbiters of taste. Today our problem is more with the critics of critics: with those that bite or bark at their own kind, not only in their "rage to get things right" but also in order to idealize creative genius or to separate out, bureaucratically, the functions of critic and artist.

The example of Derrida, therefore, is an unsettling one, even more for litterateurs than for philosophers. In philosophy there is not quite so much formal difference made between "primary" philosophizing and "secondary" criticism. There is good and bad philosophy.

Still, I want to emphasize the problem rather than pretend to solve it. It has been with us for some time; perhaps most acutely since the German Romantics, who tried to achieve a synthesis of *poetry* and *philosophy.* "Nicht auf der Grenze schwebst du, sondern in deinem Geiste haben sich Poesie und Philosophie innig durchdrungen," runs Friedrich Schlegel's tribute to No-

17. Dryden, "Dedication" of *Examen Poeticum* (1693).

valis.[18] Yet the tribute is an epilogue to Schlegel's series of fragments entitled "Ideas": as in Novalis, the synthesis could only take a fragmentary form. Hegel then turned this ferment of fragments into a living system of ideas: mobile, interpenetrating, yet consequent and systematic. Hegel, Derrida remarks in *Of Grammatology,* was the last philosopher of the book and the first of "writing." His image of the consummate philosopher or absolute spirit (see the close of the *Phenomenology*) stands to Schlegel's portrait of Novalis as fulfillment to figure.

Derrida also does not wish to sit on the fence, or hover as an eternal precursor on the border of some elusive synthesis of poetry and philosophy. He therefore produces a text: not a book, exactly, perhaps even an antibook; not an encyclopedic system, perhaps even a counterencyclopedia. But the word *text,* so current now, and suspect, means something quite specific: historically viewed, it is a development of the Romantic fragment, a sustained fragment as it were, or—seen from the Hegelian system of absolute knowledge—an essayistic totality.

To identify that which must be synthesized as "poetry" and "philosophy" may seem very general or old-fashioned. Changing the terms does not, however, change the problem. "Il n'existe d'ouvert à la recherche mentale que deux voies, en tout, où bifurque notre besoin, à savoir, l'esthétique d'une part et aussi l'économie politique." So Mallarmé. The quote is aptly chosen by Fredric Jameson as one epigraph for his *Marxism and Form.* As we read *Glas,* we are made to think more often of aesthetics and political economy than of poetry and philosophy. And Lukács's "grosse Ästhetik," foretold by him in 1910, turned out to be, in 1950–60, precisely that attempt to marry the experience of art and the lessons of political economy.

Meanwhile one can doubt that *Glas,* or Lukács's magnum opus, transcends its condition of text, of sustained fragment or essayistic totality. Any grand Aesthetics, I suspect, will turn out to be an Xthetics, where *X* signifies something excluded, some-

18. "You do not hover at the border, but in your spirit Poetry and Philosophy have thoroughly interpenetrated." Though Hegel subsumes this ideal, he engages in a devious polemic against Schlegel and Romantic irony that is well summarized in Ernst Behler's *Klassische Ironie, Romantische Ironie, Tragische Ironie,* pp. 112 ff.

thing X-ed from a previous system and now redeemed: the "ugly," for instance, or "low" or "mad" or economic factors. *X* also, therefore, signifies the chiasmus, a more powerful sign today than Aquarius or the Circle. What has been excluded is allowed to cross the line, or to be present even when absent, like a horizon. Literary criticism is now crossing over into literature. For in the period that may be said to begin with Arnold—a period characterized by increasing fears that the critical would jeopardize the creative spirit, and self-consciousness the energies of art—literary criticism is acknowledged at the price of being denied literary status and assigned a clearly subordinate, service function. There is no mysticism, only irony, in the fact that literary commentary today is creating texts—a literature—of its own.

CHAPTER NINE

Centaur: On the Psychology of the Critic

The literature of criticism exists, yet we show it ambivalence and condescension. Literary devices when found in the language of critics are viewed as a breach of decorum: we like our criticism neat, a secondary and clearly separated activity in style and function. We could echo the reply of Thamus to Egyptian Theuth, in Plato's *Phaedrus,* after Theuth has extolled Writing, which he has invented. "O most ingenious man," says Thamus, "to one is given to create the things of art, and to another to judge what measure of harm and profit they have for those that employ them."

We have no problem, then, in talking of the *function* of the critic; but to consider his *psychology* seems to inflate his importance or to complicate our sense of his role. If a critic has his own psychology, it means that he is playing a role, or that we see him struggling with an institutional demand. Should there be no stress of vocation we could as easily talk of the psychology of butcher or baker or tradesman.

Now the psychology of the butcher becomes important only when he decides to carve up people; of the baker, when he puts Max and Maurice in dough to crisp them in a titillating act of adult revenge. What then must a critic do to make us focus on *his* psychology with proper emphasis?

The "creative" butcher and baker we have mentioned overextend their art; and we admire them, at a distance, for turning the tables on those who view them only as servants to their function. It is not an exaggeration to say that the critic has become a retainer to those in our society who want not the difficult reality but merely the illusion of literacy: if he practices in an English department, he carves and trims and patches and binds the prose of future leaders destined to build or destroy the economy; and if he becomes a journalist or reviewer he flatters, cajoles, and admonishes the authors of books whose profits keep the publishers happy and his own job relatively secure. It is an understandable if not a pleasant situation, and we do not need to know more than we already do about the psychology of *that* literature professor or *that* literary journalist.

It is when these overextend their art, when they become a *little* murderous, that they also become interesting. A poor Neapolitan professor studying Roman law turns then into a magical interpreter of the history of civilization; or a Viennese Jew whose medical career advances slowly discovers that his dreams (certainly a little murderous) are interpretable, and throw light on mental illness in relation to our highest aspirations. The only critic, therefore, whom we must take seriously is one who may not yet exist: who overextends his art, having decided that his role is creative as well as judicious. His words, the critic's words, should enter the world of art even as the arts and institutions he comments on have entered his. As the work of art is an event in the history of interpretation, so the work of interpretation should be an event in the history of art.

Yet literary criticism has not produced an epochal work of this kind, unless we except Aristotle's *Poetics*. Aristotle, however, like Vico or Freud, was not primarily a literary critic. The criticism that restricts itself to the elucidation of particular texts, and defines what is literary in the narrowest formal terms, is indeed a trade, and does not leave the area of specialization it enriches. Aristotle gave us a poetics of the sacred, not simply of drama; and many of his formal terms (*purgation, discovery, reversal*) evoke what seem to be universals in our emotional and intellectual makeup. To talk of the psychology of the critic-interpreter, of one who would be of interest to us, is to talk of someone who does not exist in the special field of literature and the arts.

Something must be wrong; and Valéry's fascination with Leonardo da Vinci stems partly from the fact that here, in embryo, was an artist who considered his paintings as materials for an intellect that traded more largely, more universally. Valéry projects Leonardo as the missing ideal: the beau idéal of criticism. His every work was also a philosophy of composition. He is the critic-artist or scientist-artist. But the price Leonardo paid was few works, many of them unfinished; and for us, therefore, he is no more than a glorious chimera, someone who exists only potentially and enigmatically, like the *grande uccello* he envisaged.[1]

The natural psyche, however, interested Valéry no further than natural man did Blake: it won't fly. There has to be a construction: something made by man rivaling or riding on the principles of nature. Valéry "constructs" (it is his word) the portrait of Leonardo even as Leonardo constructed the psychic mystery of the Mona Lisa. In his famous picture of the Madonna and Saint Anne (which Freud was drawn to yet barely interpreted in his own essay on Leonardo) Mary is shown sitting on Anne's lap while the Christ child who almost sits on the lamb is held by Mary. All meld into a single creature of heads, arms, and legs. They are members of one body, and the construction makes this dependence, and interdependence, clear. Something at once monstrous yet wonderfully human comes to light: and while childish and animal elements are part of it, they are neither the base nor the apex but points in that circling and uncertain triangular mass. The enigma of hierarchy, or what mounts what, is similar to the question of the mutual dependence of criticism and art.

One reason the critic of whom we speak fails to exist is that he evades the problem of hierarchy, and its relation to body-images. He accepts too readily his subordinate function. He denies that he has a "psychology" worth considering, or, to put it differently, he represses his own artistic impulses. He stands outside the "corpus" of literature. The works of art that sustain him are overvalued as miracles of objectivity displaying a paralogical and universal, rather than psychological and personality-bound structure.

1. See Valéry's "Introduction to the Method of Leonardo da Vinci," his first significant essay, published in 1893 and provided with marginalia and additional comments later in life.

The higher or transcendental interpreter also evades hierarchy. More precisely, he turns the idea of hierarchy against a medium doomed to be transcended by mankind's evolution toward absolute knowledge. For him art ministers to a wisdom that supersedes the very making of art; this wisdom is not knowledge-lust (*libido sciendi, Wissbegierde*) but a divine aspiration delivered from lower forms of need or desire.[2] Psychology is again bypassed as this higher critic tries to free mind from all partial objects—from what I would like to call its construct forms. Books or pictures are but fixed explosives, moments in a process of dissemination, and comparable to winged words, legendary acts, or endless sketches, *zettel,* and *cahiers.* His own text legacy, insofar as it exists, evokes a restless and aspiring dialectic. Ideally, of course, nothing would remain, except in the form of a self-consuming labor of thought. Plato and Hegel gave the same name to this higher critic and it was neither critic nor interpreter. "*Phaedrus*: . . . what names would you assign him? *Socrates*: To call him wise, Phaedrus, would I think be going too far; the epithet is proper only to a god. A name that would fit him better and have more seemliness, would be 'lover of wisdom' (that is, philosopher)."

The psychology bypass was partly removed by Freud. He realized how thoroughly matters of hierarchy—in family or state or even biology—were entangled with psychic defenses and complexes. In *Totem and Taboo* he began a reflection on the strange role animal fantasies play in culture, but he did not carry it very far, and did not link it to such "totemic" pictures as Leonardo's *St. Anne.* But he made it clear that the artist had a psychology, that the artist was compelled to deal with a dependence he could not forgo. He could not forgo it without at the same time giving up his hope for mastery or, in Freudian terms, omnipotence. Freud

2. Only Emerson, perhaps, among transcendental interpreters knows that reading is based on something analogous to physical need, as in this sublime and sublimating passage from "Quotation and Originality" (*Letters and Social Aims,* 1883): "Whoever looks at the insect world, at flies, aphides, gnats, and innumerable parasites, and even at the infant mammals, must have remarked the extreme content they take in suction, which constitutes the main business of their life. If we go into a library or newsroom, we see the same function on a higher plane, performed with like ardor, with equal impatience of interruption indicating the sweetness of the act."

saw that the neuroses were asocial forms of mastery: that they denied or canceled the family nexus, which biologically speaking included the animal world. There must be other forms of mastery; and art constitutes a region, according to Freud, in which the human desire for omnipotence is still in force, but as a counterneurosis. Psychoanalysis merely defines the place of art "in the complex structure presented by the compensation for human wishes." That place is "a region half-way between a reality which frustrates wishes and the wish-fulfilling world of the imagination."

But what does the *critic* want? According to our surmise, his wish is for a successful bypass of the animal, infantile, or social basis of his needs. He is willing to give up that which makes him interesting in psychological terms for an assured and stable level of functioning. He accepts an objective or institutionalized state of dependence in exchange for a subjective state always on the point of vacillation or revolt.

But this—you may well protest—is a perverse picture indeed. What you have described is a bureaucrat or a functionary, not a critic. A critic must be critical, yet you define him out of existence as afraid of psychology and therefore exchanging the critical spirit for a stable pseudoidentity. What you have given us is the caricature of a critic, or of someone who takes refuge from the restless and corrosive character of the critical spirit, its plaguing and unremitting self-consciousness. I quite agree; my picture does represent what happens when the critical faculty bureaucratizes itself, and kicks the creative faculty upstairs. Today the so-called critics are often the dogmatists, and their dogma is that criticism cannot be creative. Yet there is no such thing as the purely critical or the purely creative; and even though I continue to believe in the separation of genres, as in the distinctness of the sexes, and though I am unhappy with certain, let us call them unisex, experiments in critical writing—which weaken the task of interpretation by spicing it up with parafictional devices—worthwhile critical writing carries with it the power to change not simply our opinion about art but also our very idea of art in relation to other activities; including criticism.

Let me indicate what happens if we accept psychology as a mode of reflection and turn it toward the critic as reader and self-reader who seeks to formalize his thoughts on the role of art in culture.

The literary critic most of us know, the academy-grown variety, is a scholar of one candle who pores over texts, and at his most sublime chants a text (although obscure) that is an answer. This image of a task both ascetic and absorbing is not unattractive. Why should it move us? Perhaps it is the counterimage or reflex to the impossible ideal previously sketched: that of the philosopher-critic who leaves behind all texts in his effort to make thinking absolute.

In literature, the image of the scholar-critic, not of the philosopher-critic, is the viable and attractive one. It involves, however, a psychology of dependence, and of deepening dependence. Books become associated with us, and we with books. We read "Shakespeare" or "Matthew Arnold," and everybody understands the metonymic relation. To explore this relation of dependence—we are all children of the book—is to begin with the act of reading, which is neither easy nor innocent. For the avid reader commits a curious yet acceptable fraud. Wordsworth describes it in book 5 of *The Prelude* when he recalls how his mind awakened to the pleasure of reading:

> For a whole day together, have I lain
> Down by thy side, O Derwent! murmuring stream,
> On the hot stones, and in the glaring sun,
> And there have read, devouring as I read,
> Defrauding the day's glory, desperate!

What is this fisher of books, instead of streams, after? He lies down by the side of the water and regards it not. He spurns it, like an ex-lover, and defrauds the sun. "La grande douleur de l'homme," writes Simone Weil, "qui commence dès l'enfance et se poursuit jusqu'à la mort, c'est que regarder et manger sont deux opérations différentes. La béatitude éternelle est un état ou regarder c'est manger" ("The great pain of human existence, a pain lasting from infancy to death, is that looking and consuming are distinct operations. Eternal bliss is a state in which looking is consuming"). Wordsworth as poet, and here as reader, is always gathering evidence to modify that pain. When ten years old, he "held unconscious intercourse with beauty / Old as creation, drinking in a pure / Organic pleasure" from the clouds and mists. Books, as a feeding source, also assuage the separation of looking and consuming: an eye that might have been dazzled or wearied and certainly laid asleep by the day's glory, is kept awake by what it devours; and if laid asleep, is so in body only, for it becomes a living soul.

Reading, then, is revenge—against the day's glory, against the dazzling senses—revenge made blissful. Yet not the psychology of reading alone but also that of writing is our concern. If reading is a revengeful turning from an outward to an inward light, so as to lessen our dependence on immediate and external stimuli, writing, as it responds with the desperate yet fragile simulacrum of creation we call a book, deepens our dependence on that inwardness. This is true of all writing, of course, not only of commentary. Writing meets a demand or absorbs it into a "murmuring stream" of its own. The specificity of critical writing lies in the fact that what is met is already in the form of literature. The illusion of direct response has to be given up; or else maintained as the direct response to an indirect response. Literature, as we learn in even the most elementary course, is a mediated as well as mediating activity. Text calls to text, and pen writes on paper, not on mind. The gratification that lies in acts of immediate and decisive understanding is delayed while we puzzle, query, ponder, revise, resist. Our wishful voice "weeps to have" what is always already lost.

> Oh! why hath not the Mind
> Some element to stamp her image on
> In nature somewhat nearer to her own?

That is Wordsworth again, lamenting the perishable medium of books. The thought also haunts Plato when he considers written speech and finds it lacking. Written discourse, Socrates remarks, is like writing in water, "or that black fluid we call ink, using the pen to sow words that can't either speak their own defense or present the truth adequately." He then elaborates the ideal of a different kind of sowing, a genuine dissemination, which he identifies with the philosopher-critic or dialectician: "The dialectician selects a soul of the right type, and in it he plants and sows his words founded on knowledge, words which can defend both themselves and him who planted them, words which instead of remaining barren contain a seed whence new words grow up in new characters, whereby the seed is vouchsafed immortality" (*Phaedrus*).

Here we glimpse the extreme ambition of the philosopher, and which the literary critic has renounced. It is to find a living element for the immortal stamp, or seed, of the mind. It is a desire for perpetuation by spiritual means, in a living respondent. The desire is simple enough, yet no desire is quite as demanding. It informs the homoerotic paideia of the Platonic dialogues; it helps to explain the phenomenon of spiritual adoption or conversion; it may touch on longings for extreme intimacy or incorporation, and even on Wordsworth's innocently incestuous "O! yet a little while / May I behold in thee what I was once." Wordsworth, to come back to him, is particularly sensitive to the narcissism of demand and response; and a famous episode, like that of the Boy of Winander (also in book 5 of *The Prelude,* though published first in the *Lyrical Ballads* of 1800) can reveal the complex self-distancing of a mind from its desire for a direct and perpetuating relation of this kind:

> There was a Boy: ye knew him well, ye cliffs
> And islands of Winander!—many a time
> At evening, when the earliest stars began
> To move along the edges of the hills,
> Rising or setting, would he stand alone
> Beneath the trees or by the glimmering lake,
> And there, with fingers interwoven, both hands
> Pressed closely palm to palm, and to his mouth
> Uplifted, he, as through an instrument,
> Blew mimic hootings to the silent owls,
> That they might answer him; and they would shout
> Across the watery vale, and shout again,
> Responsive to his call, with quivering peals,
> And long halloos and screams, and echoes loud,
> Redoubled and redoubled, concourse wild

Of jocund din; and, when a lengthened pause
Of silence came and baffled his best skill,
Then sometimes, in that silence while he hung
Listening, a gentle shock of mild surprise
Has carried far into his heart the voice
Of mountain torrents; or the visible scene
Would enter unawares into his mind,
With all its solemn imagery, its rocks,
Its woods, and that uncertain heaven, received
Into the bosom of the steady lake.
  This Boy was taken from his mates, and died
In childhood, ere he was full twelve years old.
Fair is the spot, most beautiful the vale
Where he was born; the grassy churchyard hangs
Upon a slope above the village school,
And through that churchyard when my way has led
On summer evenings, I believe that there
A long half hour together I have stood
Mute, looking at the grave in which he lies!

[1850 version]

Nature's response to the Boy's wish that the owls "might answer him" is deep and devious rather than direct. More is eventually given than was asked, too much perhaps; and the fulfillment of the boy's demand leads strangely to his death. When Wordsworth comments on the episode that it shows how Nature "plants for immortality" seeds in the celestial soil of the mind, we find ourselves back in the metaphoric field of Plato's *Phaedrus*. But Wordsworth is saying against Plato as against Rousseau that no human engineering, no paideia however subtle, can stand between the child and Nature: it is Nature, not the philosopher, whose dialectic of fruitful accidents—which includes pauses that disclose the connection between delay and gratification—acts on the untutored psyche till "the seed is vouchsafed immortality."

Yet the Boy dies; and his death, unexpected in the light of an argument that looks toward a *Bildungsroman* in little, throws the emphasis back on the psychology of the poet who is writing. The theme of development is aborted by the very perfection of an argument which insists on Nature's sole agency. The poet acknowledges that he too is powerless vis-à-vis the Boy, that he too cannot control Nature. The poet has not found an "element" to stamp his image on, though we know from the earliest manuscript that the Boy could not be closer to the poet, since he was that Boy or stood toward Nature in the described mode of relation.

We are left with two images of a speechless and untimely event: the Boy dies before mature human speech is his; and the poet looks at his grave as if he too were deprived of what the youngster had been seeking, when he made his hands into a pastoral pipe to solicit an echo from nature, and instead of a "timely utterance" provoked a "blast of harmony." Thoreau, writing about sounds, has a paragraph on owls that serves to reinforce Wordsworth's account and bring out its complexity. "I rejoice that there are owls," he states in *Walden*. "Let them do the idiotic and maniacal hooting for men. It is a sound admirably suited to swamps and twilight woods which no day illustrates, suggesting a vast and undeveloped nature which men have not recognized."

The critic explicitly acknowledges his dependence on prior words that make his word a kind of answer. He calls to other texts "that they might answer him." His focus is on the activity of the receiver, on the possibility of drawing a timely response from "trembling ears." Standards of correctness in criticism—of validity in interpretation or of adequacy of thought to thing—try to exclude arbitrary or premature harmonizations, yet their horizon envisages nothing else. That the relation of text to interpretive response may remain eccentric, that the best to be hoped for is a "blast of harmony," unsettles us in this as in so much else. There is nothing particularly interesting about the psychology of critics except their denial that their psychology is of interest: this alerts us to the fact that many of them restrict questions of value or hierarchy to what they reify as *the* literary or *the* creative. They fail to explore the relation of their own mode of discourse to that of art.

That relation is a "genetive" or "construct" form and argues by its very existence that art is not as freestanding as it appears to be. Art leans on other art, and also on criticism, and is modified by these. The prevalence of such forms in our more articulate cultural life should lead us to think about the symbiosis of text and commentary, or primary and secondary, and then about symbiosis in general. I mean by symbiosis more than the particular association of living yet heterogenous beings: it should indicate something as encompassing as semiosis.

When Freud, for example, says at the end of his essay on Leonardo that "instincts and their transformations are at the limit of what is discernible by psychoanalysis. From that point it [psychoanalysis] gives way to biological research," he refers back, unconsciously perhaps, to his starting point, Leonardo's strange childhood phantasy of the *nibio*. "It seems," wrote Leonardo, "that I was always destined to be concerned with kites, for I recall as one of my very earliest memories that while I was in my cradle a kite came to me, and opened my mouth with its tail, and struck me many times with its tail between my lips." Here biology returns in its psychological aspect, suggesting a primal, now broken, symbiosis of animal and human existence, a mutual and nurturing bond, which is disclosed by the survival in art of such primal and prophetic images.[3] The very text that started Freud's reflections was already "at the limit of what is discernible."

To think that limit is to ponder the nexus of desire and need, mind and body, parent and child, man and mammal, within a history of denial that has characterized the human animal striving to be free—that is, to forget his creaturely origins. To think that limit also means, as in Freud, to be tempted across, and to enter not only biology but also fiction. Ferenczi's *Thalassa* is a biofiction even if it calls itself a bioanalysis. Freud conceives of *Totem and Taboo* as an essay in social psychology, but when he crosses the boundary he finds himself in a prehistory of totemic kinship relations which associate man and beast as fatefully as Christopher Smart's *Jubilate Agno*. ("Let Bloom, house of Bloom rejoice with Hecatompus a fish with an hundred feet.") Specula-

3. To Leonardo's cradle fantasy compare Cicero, *On Divination,* section 36: "While Plato was an infant in his cradle, a swarm of bees settled on his lips during his slumber; and the divines answered that he would become extremely eloquent." Among Anglo-American critics who have been explorers of biofiction one should mention Kenneth Burke's studies of Coleridge and those parts of "The Thinking of the Body" that comment retrospectively on his own mythic fantasies. N. O. Brown's *Life Against Death* and its continuation, *Love's Body,* also join thinking about the "body politic" to symbolic and symbiotic perspectives.

tive psychiatry becomes biofiction: it crosses the "limit of what is discernible," moved by an intolerable sense of the lost or canceled bond, and by the very energy such splitting may have released. The kite that came to Leonardo in his cradle "opened [his] mouth with its tail," so that speech itself, like a womb, is animated.

I do not claim to know what animal fantasy opens the mouth of critics; yet Derrida's playful transformation of *Hegel* into *eagle* at the beginning of *Glas* restores a pattern of which art yields the mythic, emblematic, or onomastic remnants. These remnants move us in Leonardo as in Wordsworth. Our very use of the name "Boy of Winander" suggests a myth; Winander is not simply a background to the child's destiny but so closely connected to it that the "of" assumes genealogical importance. The Boy belongs to, even is born of, the lake. In a similar way the critic is "of" the writer he is discussing, a creation "of" the Book he is writing or writing about. Even should we succeed in purging from literary theory all genetic considerations, biological or psychological, we would be left with the ambivalence of construct forms: hyphenated or blended words or transitional objects or mixed nature fantasies that, like "critic-scholar," "critic-artist," or "Wolf-man" and Centaur, suggest something that cannot be resolved along the axis of equivalence.

CHAPTER TEN

Past and Present

Rumors abound that the New Criticism, no longer fighting for its place in the university but accepted as the standard of an urbane and teachable discipline, is being challenged by a still newer criticism. "After us the Savage God," said Yeats; and that is how the new "revisionist" or "hermeneutic" critics are being perceived.[1] They seem to profess an esoteric and personalist approach; an amalgam, encouraged in part by contemporary French speculation, of linguistics, psychoanalysis, Kabbalistic paradigms, and other dark sublimities. This higher criticism bursts upon a scene of mass education where English teachers are trying to instill a minimum of literacy and objectivity, and are now made to feel defensive by more than their students. They are being asked to consider interpretations very self-conscious in style, which move swiftly from useful commentary to hermeneutic highjinks and expand literary history to include the hinterland of medieval systems of thought with their giddy interchange of rhetorical and theological terms. Even before this the feeling had been that literary humanism was dead, replaced by coterie criticism and the unjoyous war of academic specialists.

1. The list one usually encounters includes, among others, Paul de Man, J. Hillis Miller, and Harold Bloom. Jacques Derrida of the Ecole Normale in Paris, who teaches part-time at Yale, is also mentioned. But this betrays too narrow a perspective: it is a mere polemical convenience. There are many who feel that neither a science of literature on the basis of semiotics nor the old "corrective" or "objectivist" criticism is adequate. Hans-Georg Gadamer, H. R. Jauss, Wolfgang Iser, Norman Holland, Stanley Fish, Fredric Jameson, and all who favor a more "dialogic," "dialectic," or "transactive" model for the interpretive activity might be named.

Yet, literary criticism is neither more nor less important today than it has been since the Renaissance. The humanists of the sixteenth and seventeenth centuries created the institution of criticism as we know it—the recovery and analysis of works of art. They printed, edited, and interpreted texts that dated from antiquity and that had been lost or disheveled. Evangelical in their fervor, avid in their search for lost or buried riches, they also put into circulation certain influential ideas. Perhaps the most important of these was that the authoritative version of a book is the original version, freed from interpolation and accretion. A correlative idea was that, similarly, one could rely on an original or natural light (*ingenium*) in the interpreter, an intuitive good sense that helped him to a true understanding of a text, if it was a genuine text.

These ideas were not unproblematic. Immense learning was required to distinguish the original from the falsified source, for instance, so that antiquarianism, or erudition for its own sake, was always threatening the instinctive good sense of the interpreter. Moreover, a question could arise as to the strange, even alien character of ancient texts separated by the coming of Christianity, or simply by historical distance, from the era of the interpreter. Yet these problems did not become so explicit as to be disabling. For the humanists, in short, learning did not alienate the ancient texts by emphasizing their cultural distance: it recovered them, rather, and made them accessible.[2]

There are signs that we are now nearing the end of this Renaissance humanism. The cry "to the sources" (*ad fontes*), if still echoing in the current slogan "to the text itself," is less vigorous when our thirst for the fresh or restored literary work has been richly satisfied. There are, we sometimes feel, too many sources, and they are not as pure or distinct as they seemed to

2. For a description of the birth of modern philology and of the complexities of "subreading" ancient texts in order both to converse with them and to respect the temporal, cultural, or stylistic gap between past and present, see Thomas M. Greene's "Petrarch and the Humanist Hermeneutic," in *Italian Literature,* ed. Rimanelli and Atchity. For the difference between "grammatical" and "allegorical" methods of reading as they enter contemporary hermeneutic reflection through Schleiermacher, see Peter Szondi, "Schleiermachers Hermeneutik Heute," *Sprache im Technischen Zeitalter* 58 (1976): 95–111, previously published in *Poétique* 1 (1970): 141–55.

be. Today, after all, there is no dearth of ancient texts, or of new ones. Editing, moreover, has become only too conscious of the difficulty of recovering an "original" version or edition: in Wordsworth scholarship, for example, the authority of the 1850 *Prelude,* the text approved by the poet shortly before his death, was challenged by the 1805–06 *Prelude* printed by De Selincourt in the 1920s; and the authority of this is in turn being eroded by antecedent manuscripts, the so-called Five Book *Prelude* and Two Part *Prelude.* It is equally precarious to establish the text of Emily Dickinson's poems—which of the variants are to be chosen as definitive? From another angle, Melville's *Billy Budd* has become a mine for genetic speculation. Even when no editorial problem exists, a *philosophical* issue arises as to the concept of originality itself.[3]

For the more learning and scholarship we bring to an author, with the aim of defining his difference or individual contribution, the less certainty there seems to be of succeeding in that aim. The variorum of interpretive hypotheses that grow up around him draw his meaning and sometimes his value into question, while sophisticated analysts of various critical "fallacies" insist that we can never know the genesis or intention of the work of art. The more learning, in short, the stranger the text: either because what we learn is, precisely, to respect its otherness, its historical difference, or because it becomes too richly ambiguous, polysemous, or even indefinite in meaning.

Add to this an awareness of the impact of technology, expressed in such classics as Walter Benjamin's *The Work of Art in the Age of Mechanical Reproduction,* as well as the strange alliance of this impact with a new appreciation of the composite or formulaic authorship of oral works of literature, and the notion of unique works of art, certified by the personal name of the author or located only in their place of origin (a shrine or church or original idiom), fades away into nostalgia. That strong, elated feeling of the Renaissance artist, when he thinks of his name being perpetuated through art, relapses into a new sense of the anonymity or impersonality of the work.

3. For the time being, it is enough to quote Hegel's provocative attack on all "Ur-Metaphysics": "What comes later is concreter and richer; the first is abstract, and least differentiated."

It is not unusual, in fact, to find writers motivated by the desire to distance a text into equivocation, even to neutralize it (ne-uter: neither this nor that). Instead of claiming that polysemy —or ambiguity, or whatever name is given to plural meaning— endows a work of art with plenitude and presence, they show that it is strangely emptied by a fullness that seems more and more illusory. Words not only clarify life but also carry within them, like life itself, obscurity and death. They do not recompense us for the void of pensiveness, but maintain us in it. Maurice Blanchot describes their "lure of a negative presence" in a parable style more denuded, though not less absolute, than Kafka's:

> "Is it you?"—"Yes it's me."—"You, in broad daylight [*plein jour*]."—"In the broad daylight of obscurity."
>
> When he came to him, exchanging in broad daylight salvation for obscurity. . . .
>
> He dwelt there, the house rebuilt itself around him. I saw him behind the window, in wait without hearing me, exhausting by waiting the overfullness of our words [*le trop plein de nos paroles*].[4]

I started by saying that criticism is neither more nor less important today than in the Renaissance. It was serious then, and evangelical; it is serious now, and evangelical. But it may also be turning grim instead of serious, and far less hopeful. Because of the developments sketched above, the word *dehumanization* seems more appropriate to the condition of criticism than *humanism*. There may be something increasingly desperate in our continuing attempt to honor the name of writers by prizes, academic courses, and the like. Or in the maintained illusion that genius exists, that an artist's private life must be studied by biographies (themselves honored by prizes) for clues to his difference from us. For what we find is what we already know: that Victor Hugo or Edgar Allan Poe or Edith Wharton are exactly like us, only more so. We learn that each generation, each family, has its Gothic disasters, its social problems, its follies and frivolities, its "family romance." Even the great speculative movement we call *psychoanalysis*, which is undergoing such searching critique in

4. See Blanchot's *Le pas au-delà*, p. 97.

contemporary France, simply makes us realize once more that we have mothers and fathers, or what it means to be born.

Let me elaborate on why I think a grimmer, more realistic period is at hand, which may see the disappearance of ideals implicit in the very appeal of the words *Humanism* and *Renaissance*. There is the social factor. We teach and write in a mass culture. Though Erasmus and Comenius did not neglect elementary education, literature teachers in a mass culture are obliged to become *primarily* grammarians, spelling masters, and instructors of civics. Even the revival of rhetoric as an instrument of literary analysis—the poet Hopkins called rhetoric the *teachable* part of literature—is understandable in this light.

We should not, in any case, underestimate the phenomenon of mass education. In its own way it is as disorienting and significant as other changes that have affected millions of people. I refer to the fact that, at college age, so many are dislocated into institutes of Higher Education. The energy released by this displacement is both troublesome and awesome. Its most obvious result is that we are acquiring a new and corrosive sense of the mortality of books. They are in danger of being routinized or contaminated by endless readings forced out of industrious hordes of students. A photosensitive surface can become overexposed; so a work, insofar as it is language-sensitive, becomes unreadable when subjected to a stream of verbal comments. It is this blankness of the written page that is to be feared as much as the white, virginal horror afflicting Mallarmé. But perhaps the two types of blankness are related.

For mass education "journalizes" even the greatest works, submitting them to daily theme or timed comment. Mallarmé was already aware, like Nietzsche, of the newspaper approach to reading ("das übermässige Zeitungslesen") and foresaw what it would do to the quality of our response to poetry. He wanted to secure the latter by returning to the idea of a language within language, one beyond the corruptions of daily use. But he could not foresee that, partly because of his example, the danger would also come to lie in the wholesale application of his own rhetorical method. Today our depressed consciousness that the mass mind will get us is not alleviated by the thought that our finest readers are merely demonstrating over and over again that everything natural or spontaneous in language is a rhetorical device, and that behind the appearance of originality there is bricolage, or the canny embezzlement of previous art.

Perhaps this literary nihilism is unavoidable; it may even be a matter of deep conviction: the important thing is that it not be applied by wholesale or mechanical means. There is a "hollowness" in language, an abysmal or unsoundable quality in it, which keeps the old quarrel between rhetoric and dialectic alive. But, to quote Nietzsche, this nihilism is "the most spooky [*unheimlich*] of all the guests." Contemporary writers, even when they aim at vitalism or at "making it new," simply reveal the impossibility of removing that spookiness or saturating language with meaning. To "make it new" means to counterfeit, as in Gide's novel *The Counterfeiters* (1925), which therefore aspires to deliberate flatness of style. Or as in Gertrude Stein, whose strangely angled and tautological sentences renew only the deceptions of language. In Stein the sense that every social code or idiolect enforces obliquity encourages a more radical awareness: that the disjunction between what is said and what is meant constitutes the only depth in us.

At some point, then, the idea of a historical era called the Modern—the documentable sense that reading and writing have been affected by the massive pressures, social and economic, of the present time—is modified by the knowledge that some sort of language malaise has always been with us. This does not alter the fact that in Ezra Pound, but also in other virtuosi, there is a conviction that we who have unmade language, who have used it up, can also repair it. A fresh literature or medium always arises in order to contain and limit that feeling of a hollowness at the heart of language. We certainly remain, today, in the age of Erasmus and Comenius and of the thaumaturgic power of literacy.

No one in the earlier centuries would have denied the importance of pedagogy and paideia, yet no one would have thought of them as *the* vocation of the lettered person. It was a "pastoral" activity, to be completed by some "epic" venture in the greater world of politics or in the world of letters itself. So Milton prepared himself to write a great epic, devoutly acquiring the necessary learning throughout his life. Pound goes bad in a good cause, that of relating the "pastoral" realm of letters to the "epic" of politics. In him nihilism and vitalism cohabit, and even exchange faces. In the present era, however, this sense of a structured vocation has weakened, and is in danger of collapse. After the catastrophic events of 1933–45 we are skeptical toward the liberal ideal that education—and especially education in the arts—might gradually prepare the individual for a life free of both instinctual and external (political) constraints.

The ideal of a "Republic of Letters," transitional to a civilization where labor blossoms and repression is no more, was systematically developed by Friedrich Schiller in his *Letters on Aesthetic Education* (1795), written when the French Revolution had failed to change human nature and political conditions once and for all.[5] It also flowered in post-Renaissance notions of a "freemasonry of great spirits" (Keats). But given our present sense of the momentum in science, in politics, in the psyche—totalitarian terror, atomic terror, and Freud's hypothesis of an instinctual drive unto death—given all these types of holocaust, it is hard to maintain the humanist's faith in the person: his responsibility, agency, and perfectibility.

What is the future of *this* faith, or illusion? No thinker can pass Freud, Marx, or Nietzsche unconcerned; he must find something in the mind of men like these that is more sublime than what their mind destroyed. It is not modishness but necessity that impels us to struggle with them, as Blake did with Milton, or the biblical interpreter with the devastating and corrosive evidence of historical experience.

> "I can still speak English when my business demands it."
>
> —Marlowe, in Raymond Chandler's *The Big Sleep*

Let me descend from these generalities to the first of the specific complaints against the post-new-critical critics—their demand-

5. Schiller's theory finds its most radical contemporary use in Herbert Marcuse's *Eros and Civilization*. See also the fine pages on Schiller and Marcuse in Fredric Jameson's *Marxism and Form*.

ing style. It is quite proper to question the style of any enterprise. But no one would argue that all subjects can be made easy. If one attacked, instead of a critical essay, the style of a philosophic or scientific article, this would mean that its subject was considered pretentious or even a pseudosubject. Something is being demystified or deflated.

Yet what is happening within literary criticism today is not as sensible as that. For there critics carp at critics while paradoxically accepting almost any style the creative writer throws their way. Defensive about their function, they normalize criticism at the price of mystifying creative genius. It is as if the literary field were being crassly divided into permissive creativity (fiction) on the one hand, and schoolmasterly criticism on the other.

Should we limit the role of criticism to descriptive or evaluative comments on works of art, couched in a neutral style? George Watson, whose book *The Literary Critics* (1962) is subtitled *A Study of English Descriptive Criticism,* rightly points out that there are at least two other kinds of critical activity: legislative criticism, including books of rhetoric that claim to teach writers how to write, and theoretical criticism, or literary aesthetics. And though descriptive criticism has been the glory of the English from Dryden to Empson, even it is not unchanging, as Watson's summary indicates: "Over the centuries English criticism has tended to move away from the text and then back towards it . . . it is rapidly and early stripped of all but a few of the technical terms that it inherited from the European tradition; . . . it began as a dialogue between poets and ends as a demonstration before readers."

When we look at the historical record, then, criticism is a relatively free, all-purpose genre, and closely related to the personal or familiar essay. It is a literary genre of a special sort, although I mean by this not that it should aim to be prose-poetry, but simply that it shares its text-milieu with other forms of literature while struggling with its own generic pressures of style. So, as Watson notes, English criticism is stripped early of technical terms inherited from Europe, while now, of course, technical terms are flooding back, again mainly (though not entirely) via Europe. The critical essay, in fact, is the genre that helped the English language most in expanding its range as a genuinely serviceable *prose*. Criticism is linked from the outset to a question of style: of vernacular style.

No wonder, then, that the issue of style understood as "purity of diction" keeps haunting the critic, not only as a standard to be applied to works of art but as a touchstone for his own practice. Dryden, perhaps the first English critic of note, was concerned as much with purity of diction as with the famous "rules" governing drama. He was deeply aware of the European shift into the vernacular. English could not be taken for granted as a literary medium; it had to be nurtured and disciplined. Dedicating in 1679 his version of Shakespeare's *Troilus and Cressida,* Dryden remarks:

> How barbarously we yet write and speak . . . I am sufficiently sensible in my own English. For I am often put to a stand in considering whether what I write be the idiom of the tongue, or false grammar, and nonsense couched beneath that specious name of *Anglicism*; and have no other way to clear my doubts but by translating my English into Latin, and thereby trying what sense the words will bear in a more stable language. I am desirous, if it were possible, that we might all write with the same certainty of words and purity of phrase, to which the Italians first arrived, and after them the French.

More is at stake here than a belated aping of the French. For classical purity remains deeply associated with notions of national rebirth and renaissance. It haunts almost every writer concerned with the "vernacular matrix" (W. J. Ong) and its fertility. Being a Modern might almost be defined as living in the crossfire of the contrary ideals of language purification and language "illustration." The latter is Du Bellay's word in his sixteenth-century treatise on the French language, and meant making one's native tongue illustrious by importing expressions from the more developed literatures as well as dialectal and workaday terms.[6]

6. See Ong's *The Barbarian Within.* Also relevant is the section on the study of Latin as a puberty rite in *The Presence of the Word,* pp. 250 ff. For the use of "illustrious" by Dante, see his *De vulgari eloquentia,* book 1, chap. 17. Auerbach follows up *Mimesis* with a book on *Literary Language and Its Public* . . . whose last chapter contains an exemplary description of the earlier development of the vernaculars. On purity of diction in *poetry* Donald Davie's book *Purity of Diction in English Verse* is still very much to the point. For *prose,* consult R. F. Jones's studies on the development in England of a "neoclassical standard" and George Williamson's *The Senecan Amble.*

Perhaps the only true literary history we have, Erich Auerbach's *Mimesis,* depends for the modern part of its perspective on the great vernacular shift and reactions to it. The shift blended in a remarkable way linguistic, literary, and social values. Even philosophic writing did not escape: there was always some "ordinary language philosophy" around (M. H. Abrams has happily called it a *Wittgenspiel*) as well as the quest for an absolutely logical, nonpoetic or purified kind of prose—philosophy's Latin.

Criticism too has its "vernacular matrix" problem. Do critics today, we might ask with Dryden, write English, or instead what he called "Anglicism"? The issue is exacerbated by pressures on language from two quite different quarters: scientific ideals of objectivity and democratic ideals of education. With the invasion of criticism by scientific methodologies, and our heightened intolerance of technical terms (an allergic reaction to that very scientism), the wish for purity surfaces once more, this time questioning explicitly the language of the critic. Is purity to be gained through a technical "language of description" clearly separate from the "object language" of the work of art, or is purity gained by a liberal prose that keeps itself free of technical terms? Or should we give up the entire ideal of purification, and illustrate or adorn the language of criticism until it achieves a character of its own?

The development of journalism and then of universal education also pressures language. Newspeak or mere talk or the multiplication of books can prove subversive of the very literacy being fostered. "L'idée d'écrire s'assimile à l'idée d'ajouter à l'infini, et le goût de la cendre vient aux lèvres," says Valéry. Our "mal du siècle" is a "malaise du grand nombre." Language is as exploited and abused as nature itself. Complaints like Valéry's go back at least to the rise of "Grub Street" and of political hacks and journalists in late seventeenth-century England, when democratic institutions begin to expand and censorship to relax. From this perspective Heidegger's emphasis on the saving virtues of *Dichtung* (the arts, and preeminently the art of language) is realistic rather than elitist, and continues a meditation on the fall of culture and the debasement of language that reached a visionary acme of rage in the satirical diction of Swift and Pope.

There have been charges that a new elitism is creeping into literary studies. It is said to show itself in the growing breach between sensible literary commentary and hermeneutic cerebration. The objection bears this time not only on the verbal style of the interpreter but also on his general attitude toward the text. Instead of subordinating himself to the literary work, he puffs his own activity until criticism becomes a rival of literature. Because of its allusive, dense, intertextual quality, this new *écriture* is hermetic rather than open.

These charges are based on simplification and historical ignorance. There is no reason why all criticism should be of the reporting or reviewing kind. Even if we prefer plain-style writing, should we reduce critical prose to one pattern or delude ourselves that a purely utilitarian or instrumentalist mode of communication is possible? This attitude would have expelled the more demanding critics from Plato's Republic as poets in disguise. It could even now lead to a thorough ideologizing or leveling of the critical spirit.

Anthropologists say that cultural situations, even of the most ordinary kind, may involve a conflict of codes or idioms that cannot be resolved but remain part of the drama, the cultural dynamics. The gap between plain-style criticism and hermeneutic speculation may express such a conflict of idioms which should be studied before being condemned. What follows will try to do that.

Beryl Smalley, in her classic work on *The Study of the Bible in the Middle Ages,* borrows a term from art history to describe the technique of allegorical exegesis, which went far beyond a literal exposition of the Bible. She calls it the "pierced technique" and quotes this characterization of it from a writer on early Northern art: "It is as though we were invited to focus our eyes not on the physical surface of the object, but on infinity as seen through the lattice." So, in allegorical exegesis, "we are invited to look not at the text, but through it"—which recalls William Blake's comment that the visionary poet looks through rather than with the eye.

Without claiming that literature is to the modern mind what the Bible was to medieval thought, the hermeneutic intensity of some recent critics does raise a question about the status of the literary text. Is great literature our "secular scripture," to quote the title of Northrop Frye's book? That should indeed be a central question; yet we know too little about the relation of the literary text to the life of the mind or the life of institutions to adjudicate the quarrel of plain dealers and hermeneuticists. Owen Barfield's brilliant perception on the "tarning" involved in metaphor and in accommodating legal ordinances to changing conditions, Michel Foucault's work on the archival and institutionalized character of orders of discourse, Fredric Jameson's description of hermeneutics as a means for recuperating anti-establishment texts and so maintaining contact with the sources of revolutionary energy, or Gershom Scholem's lifelong recreation of the way Jewish mysticism "saves" the Bible despite the disabling impact of historical experience, could eventually provide an answer.

Some gap between what is directly useful and what mystical or merely speculative will, in any case, always exist in every strong intellectual effort. "Think not of other worlds," the angel Raphael cautions Adam in Milton's *Paradise Lost*: cultivate rather the garden of this world and the company of Eve. Yet in literature, as in science, there is a plurality of worlds. We cannot take for granted that other cultures are like ours; we must try to enter or understand them, or else find a theory (and not just a prejudice) that allows us to overlook their existence.

We do have at present "other worlds" that tempt the interpreter—(1) the midrashic or polysemous world of biblical interpretation, where extremely bold hypotheses and strict rules of exegesis keep company; (2) existential hermeneutics, from Hamann to Heidegger, in which the authentic text is always strange and requires interpretation. The hermeneutic activity, however, does not appropriate or master the text: it removes forms of strangeness due to ignorance, while uncovering the more intrinsic strangeness that words have as words. Though interested in "extraordinary" language, it is often confusingly allied with "ordinary" language reflection, in particular with (3) transactive or dialogic theories of reading, which stress the importance and complexity of the "orders" of speech that the literary work encodes, as well as the close link between language, community, and understanding. Heideggerian hermeneutics is also sometimes found allied, via semiotics, with (4) the conceptual, even noumenal, rhetoric that Parisian movements from Claude Lévi-Straus and Jacques Lacan to Michel Foucault and Jacques Derrida are developing. This rhetoric is viewed as motivating the deconstruction of reality (social or mental) and, at the same time, as providing the only instrument for analyzing, articulating, or criticizing it.

Our understanding of what is going on is hampered, however, by the very speed of the influx of imperfectly digested theories from Europe—theories having their own text-milieu whose acclimatization in Anglo-American culture will take more time. (One should not assume, even, that they must be acclimatized; quite possibly we can discover, through such thinkers as Peirce or Burke, a native strain of thought that would parallel what challenges us in Europe.) It is also hampered by the pressure on English studies to provide cultural basics that should have been provided by all the humanities acting together.

The "service function" imposed on English departments certainly contributes to dividing literary studies into the grind of "communication" or "rhetoric" courses as against high-stepping intellectual entertainment. English is, said Blake, "the rough basement, the stubborn structure." Where is the basement now? Is there any firm or natural grounding to be relied on in the schools? Even without the social factor, criticism is bound to become conscious of itself as a form of "serious play" similar to art. For however rough the basement of literary learning may be, its ceiling is equally unfinished, and provides no shelter. We are free to fall upward. We can expect native wit or the vernacular energies to build something, whether or not it is a foundation. Yet on looking into the intellectual heavens we see a chaos: a plurality, perhaps infinity, of competing hypotheses and mind-wearying speculations.

Nobody loves a limbo. Then how do we deal with this multiplying burden of books, sources, texts, interpretations? Here we might discover a motive, even a justified role, for theory. For theory is (in theory) supposed to do away with itself, and lead to more exact, concrete, focused insight. Or it should disburden us by allowing the mind to generalize from a sample, and so to forget the abstract and impossible task of knowing not less than everything. But every new theory adds itself to the heap and increases the burden it was supposed to remove. Every theory, in short, is but another text. No wonder that so many literary thinkers have given theorizing up and concentrate on practical criticism. We are back to securing the basement.

There is, then, no way of eluding the burden except by adding to it: by fighting the Quarrel of the Ancients and Moderns all over again in a historical chaos where nothing is definitely obsolete. The practical critic may be blind to what he is doing and the hermeneuticist too aware, but each interpretation of a work of art is gained only by struggling with a *chaos of texts* that is called, euphemistically, tradition or, more neutrally, literary history.

Modern hermeneutics, therefore, which seems so highflying, is actually a negative hermeneutics. On its older function of saving the text, of tying it once again to the life of the mind, is superimposed the new one of doubting, by a parodistic or playful movement, master theories that claim to have overcome the past, the dead, the false. There is no divine or dialectical science that can help us purify history absolutely, to pass in our lifetime a last judgment on it.

The New Critics, however different in temperament and intellect, shared certain cultural concerns. They became a movement because of the intensity of those concerns, and because they brought them into the American university. Most started outside the university, and only gradually compacted with it, uncertain whether criticism should be institutionalized. Some of the greatest men of letters of that era—Eliot, Wilson, Burke—never gave up their independence. J. C. Ransom, who named the movement, expressed his ambivalence in the title of his famous essay "Criticism, Inc." (in *The World's Body*).

The post-new-critical critics are already in the university. They are tainted by the odor of academic life: secure, yes, but also service-ridden. For the university has opened its doors. There are more—and more heterogeneous—students, and intellectual life is less centralized in rigid directors of study and a few tolerated satyrs: that is, amateur critics. Diversity and interdisciplinary study are the order of the day; and the idea of a compulsory subject matter—that one should have to master, for example, a specific body or canon of books before proceeding to another one—is loosening its hold, together with other hierarchical precepts.

Perhaps diversity is one reason no one can agree on what to name this latest grouping of critics. Are they "revisionists" or "hermeneuticists" or "deconstructivists" or "Yale" rather than Russian "formalists"? And are they formalists or antiformalists? Do they really have a common program, or is their unity simply that of achieving a "critical mass" at Yale? One reviewer has talked of a new school of "Franco-American" critics, which sounds like canned spaghetti.

These designations, however, point uneasily to the presence of a foreign element. Many of the sources of the new group are as American as Emerson, Burke, and (even) Eliot and as English as Coleridge, Ruskin, Pater, and Empson. Yet the increased flow of ideas over the Atlantic, the settling in the universities of émigré scholars, the growth of comparative literature, and the hopeful internationalism of the immediate postwar era have produced a deeper awareness of Continental (not only French) currents of thought.[7]

It should be said, at the same time, that the real issue is not the Continental connection but the presence of another kind of foreign element: the new group crosses the line into philosophy, theology, linguistics, sociology, and psychoanalysis. The autonomy of the literary work or of the discipline of criticism itself is no longer a shibboleth. Structuralism, of course, helped to provide this impulse to cross the line, as did a gradually growing acquaintance with the work of the Frankfurt School (Walter Benjamin, Theodor Adorno, Max Horkheimer, and others). But the

7. The significant critics, like Kenneth Burke and Edmund Wilson, had always kept in touch with the Continent: and Eliot was, of course, strongly indebted to French developments. But a specifically philosophic type of criticism became central in the intellectual life of Continental Europe only after Heidegger and Sartre (with help from Croce and Ortega y Gasset). The group of critics here singled out is in touch with that philosophy as well as with literature more narrowly defined.

result has been bricolage, impurity, and creative ferment, rather than systematic exploration and synthesis.[8]

In retrospect, then, the New Critics fused a peculiarly "American" with a markedly "English" prejudice against mixing art with anything, especially with philosophy. Only the empirical tradition of Locke contributes to English studies. Hegel has never been received; and despite Coleridge and Carlyle, German idealism penetrated mainly into theological circles.[9] It is hard to conceive of a writer in English publishing a book like Derrida's *Glas,* consisting of a commentary on a philosopher (Hegel) juxtaposed with a commentary on a creative writer (Genet).

Add to this the essentially agrarian and organicist attitude of the New Critics, and one sees that what is at stake is still an "anti-self-consciousness principle": the use of art to limit the brooding, self-exposing, restless emission of speculative ideas, or the "French mania," as Matthew Arnold called it, for translating ideas into ideologies, into political imperatives or urgent intrusions on the private mind. Concepts of national character are dangerous or comic, but this Anglo-American conservatism expresses the wish in all of us to have a fixed identity, one easily associated with organicist philosophies. We desire to be in one place and of that place, as organic as Yeats's "great-rooted blossomer."

So art, for the New Critics, as for Yeats, saved the imagination from abstraction and the intellectual life from Hegel, Nietzsche, and Marx. The New Critics explicated the implicit in art, but only to honor that implicitness. Ideas in art were meanings, values,

8. Why the synthesis in the near-structuralist work of Ernst Cassirer did not take is one of the puzzles of intellectual history. Perhaps it was followed too quickly by the narrower, if still impressive, schematism of Northrop Frye. In this light, Jameson's *Marxism and Form,* with its final essay "Toward Dialectical Criticism," is an interesting attempt to achieve an antiformalist synthesis.

9. Santayana's "Fifty Years of British Idealism" (in *Some Turns of Thought in Modern Philosophy*) refers almost exclusively to F. H. Bradley and moral philosophy. Our generalization has its exceptions: A. C. Bradley considered the relation between English Romantic poetry and German idealism, while Owen Barfield, D. G. James, and others (including those attracted to Croce) are not ignorant of post-Kantian developments. Murray Krieger, in America, was stimulated by both Croce and Cassirer; and general hermeneutics, going back to Schleiermacher and Dilthey, is becoming a matter of debate once more. A nonidealist type of "genre criticism," moreover, related to the Chicago or Neo-Aristotelian School, and developed into a hermeneutics by E. D. Hirsch, is still a subject of discussion.

deeply rooted and contextualized words that could not be exposed to logic-chopping or all-consuming dialectics. As Matthew Arnold claimed of Wordsworth: his poetry is the reality, his philosophy the illusion.

Coleridge believed that Wordsworth could write the first "genuinely philosophical poem" in English. The question of whether Wordsworth is a philosophical poet, or the value of that philosophy when ascertained, is not as academic as it sounds. It is a kind of touchstone dividing the Arnoldian critics from those who do not wish to make so sharp a distinction between the creative element in poetry and the creative element in philosophy. Keats is another poet who has been denied "ideas" on the ground that he is for "sensation" or that his constitution was too integrated for them. To some extent these debates reflect the impasse between philosophical idealism and the Locke tradition—an impasse that Coleridge had hoped Wordsworth would overcome. Recently a new approach from the side of Wittgenstein (that strange philosophical import), in particular his later views on language, seems to revive the debate about Wordsworth's philosophy in a way that avoids the naive split between empirical and philosophical Wordsworthians.[10]

The revisionist critics are, in any case, less nervous about philosophy, abstract thought, criticism of criticism—whatever you call it. It is obvious, first of all, that concepts like intertextuality, or their methodical faith that thinking and writing, criticism and literature, art and philosophy are creative modes to be worked through in tandem or in concert, are not inimical to the emphasis on verbal concreteness, close reading, and text-centered values. Theory for them is just another text: it does not enjoy a privileged status.

For it is likely that the energy of philosophical discourse remains indebted to metaphors and literary devices, and that the very labor of expunging and erasing them is what explains our fascination with such abstract stuff. Philosophy, then, is neither

10. See Frances Ferguson's *Wordsworth: Language as Counter-Spirit* and recent essays by Charles Altieri. Stanley Cavell's *The Senses of Walden* is essential for anyone interested in the possibility of a philosophical criticism of literature. A promising native push in this direction, using William James rather than (or in addition to) Emerson, is found in the work of Walter Michaels.

feared for its antiliterary, abstracting powers nor overestimated on account of them. The revisionist's attitude toward it is consonant with that of Huizinga in *Homo Ludens*. Huizinga claims that even the most serious philosophizing cannot be totally separated from play forms:

> Gorgias' famous treatise *On Not-being*, in which he categorically rejects all serious knowledge in favor of a radical nihilism, is as much a play-phenomenon as his *Encomium on Helen*, which he himself expressly calls a game. . . .
>
> We have no wish to go into the deep question of how far the process of reasoning is itself marked by play-rules, i.e. is only valid within a certain frame of reference where those rules are accepted as binding. May it not be that in all logic . . . there is always a tacit understanding to take the validity of the terms and concepts for granted as one does the pieces on a chess-board?

This should not be news for a generation that has read Wittgenstein and debated the logical status of "colorless green ideas sleep furiously." The agonistic factor in contemporary French intellectual life, its exhilarating if exhibitionistic quality, also reinforces our sense that there is as much serious play there as in art. We cannot value, for example, Jacques Derrida, who remains a professional philosopher, without tolerating the uncertainty of a clear demarcation between play, rhetoric, and philosophy.

Yet what of the principal founders of philosophical art criticism in Europe, Heidegger and Sartre? It is hard to think of them as playful. Like Milton's sportive elephant, they occasionally "writhe their lithe proboscis," but being determined to change the entire discourse of Western philosophy they seem to forget they are only playing a game. Derrida too strikes an English-speaking reader as overelaborate and terminological. Perhaps he is "fooling" like Nietzsche, or like the Sophists, or replaying the birth of philosophy out of Plato's struggle with those confidence men, yet the *affect* (as psychoanalysts say) is not funny. Only Ortega, a third practitioner of this kind of criticism, retains a certain lightness of touch.

In England, the amateur status of criticism vis-à-vis philosophy protects it from perplexity. English (and to an extent American) criticism has incorporated itself in order to limit its liability in the sphere of sustained extraliterary thought. It is by no means ignorant of the important issues raised by social theory, play theory, psychology, philosophy of history, and so on. The relation of ritual and myth to literature uncovered by Frazer and the Cambridge Anthropologists made a particularly strong impact—all the more so because it suggested a new look for classical studies—and the Freudian school's exploration of psychic and artistic analogues to archaic rituals helped to anticipate Structuralism. Yet the impression remains that Anglo-American criticism is more prissy and defensive today than in the 1930s, when a Kenneth Burke and a William Empson emerged. Dread of philosophy's gray on gray is only exceeded by a fear of promiscuous and impure speculation. The Locke tradition rules the waves of intellectual life as strongly as ever.

What have Continental critics accomplished except to turn philosophical criticism back on itself by asking it to consider the status of its own discourse? The philosopher, the critic, and the creative writer are fellow combatants in the field of letters. Sartre's attempt in *What Is Literature?* to separate out "prose" from "poetry" as authentically and purely instrumental could not be further from Derrida's general theory of writing as *écriture*. The act of writing is too complex and overdetermined (not only by linguistic features but also by its text-milieu) for such splitting to succeed.

What is foreseen by "revisionism" is not simply the disclosure of metaphors, images, or rhetorical devices in philosophical prose. That kind of study is useful but can take care of itself. The really difficult task is, as always, the hermeneutic one: to understand understanding through the detour of the writing/reading experience. *Detour* is meant ironically, for there is no other way. The new theory, whether we approach it through Heidegger or Derrida, puts the straight line in doubt. Writing is a labyrinth, a topological puzzle and textual crossword; the reader, for his part, must lose himself for a while in a hermeneutic "infinitizing" that makes all rules of closure appear arbitrary.

Yet if the straight line or stigmatic approach is doubted, and we enter a wilderness full of ambivalent symbols and indirect signs, other formalized habits also become questionable. The "breakthrough" mentality of Modernism, for example. Or the mystique of originality that seems part of it. Or incarnationist poetics, emphasizing the "Presence of the Word." Or historical simplifications that see literature as a one-way system, moving along chronological rails.

Is that what writing suggests, even on the face of it—a graphic or typographic phenomenon? The question need not be taken literally. Yet what we mean by "taking literally" is itself a wild and worrisome matter in the history of interpretation. Something, doubtless, is always "taken" or "posited" as literal—but what kind of constructive activity is that? Can the literal be denied by the mind that posited it? Or is it not always at once denied and posited in what we call literature? Does literalism imply a Nietzschean will to knowledge or power? Are traditions and literary histories literalisms?

One can see what makes the English habit of practical criticism so attractive. It does not brood over questions that perhaps cannot be answered, although it is disturbing that they can be asked. But philosophical criticism is not indecisive. It has its own preferred writers, texts, and positions. Nietzsche's emphasis on the will, for example, and Valéry's on the act of "construction" that is common alike to imaginative and scientific thought are important. Anything that blows the cover of reified or superobjective thinking is important. The issues that keep surfacing in revisionist criticism are the relation of creative and critical, both central to the scene of writing if marginal to each other; the *ethos* of reading and writing, their relation to not only the interpretive activity in general, which Heidegger considers basic to human life (hermeneutics as our daily bread), but to the will of writer and reader, their tendency to "mutual domination"; and the role of formal genres in all this: literary commentary, narrative, canon formation, history writing. In particular, a critique of genealogical or historical reasoning—a kind of Fourth Kantian Critique—is in the making. It has already rescued the Romantic poets from Modernist snobbishness.

The question of the ethos of the interpreter—"What does he

want?" Nietzsche would have us ask—needs elaboration. To an extent what is involved is the right to one's own tongue. We wish to have our say despite or within authoritative pressures coming from the great writers of the past, institutions asking us to conform to a community model, politics that limit subtly or by force what can be said and written. Yet they would not be pressures if we did not feel the importance of living "in truth," and a truth that can or must be expressed for others, if not for all. Is there a community of readers (interpreters) larger than specifically political or factional groups? How do we picture such a community, if only ideally? What pattern of mutuality in difference does it possess?

A further question also arises. Given the likelihood of erroneous or partial interpretation because of historical change and the instability of language, is an evaluative understanding of the literary past really possible? Richards's practical criticism holds that interpretive errors can be removed by a combination of literary and ethnological expertise: by sympathetic guesses supported by scholarship. For philosophical criticism, however, this is too simple a view.

For learning can estrange the work of art by restoring the literal meaning of what we thought were figures. There is often something radically strange in the language of others. "The closer the look one takes at a word," said Karl Kraus, "the greater the distance from which it looks back." Think also of a secular mind seriously considering the miracles described by Scripture; or of a religious mind like that of Maimonides having to understand the anthropomorphisms of the Old Testament. Both are faced by the "letter that kills." Both, consequently, must either master a nondemythologized text by renewed allegoresis or find an ecstatic, if still human, kind of understanding—that unprovable kind we call *intuitive*.

The first of these alternatives, according to Heidegger, involves technocratic violence: a will to mastery common to most theological and scientific explanation. It is precisely this type of violence that has made us lose contact with things and so with authentic languaging. In the second alternative the interpreter accepts the "hermeneutic circle"—leaps into it instead of out and beyond it. Heidegger's exegesis evolves, therefore, as a game of patience drawing fresh word-perspectives out of sources (a pre-Socratic fragment, a Hölderlin or Trakl poem) that gain rather than lose in originality; both sides of the textual equation, source and commentary, become less resolved as they approach once more the condition of primal words.

According to philosophical criticism, the attempt to establish an objective or scientific hermeneutics is an act of defensive mastery. It seeks to keep an unruly, changeable language within the bounds of intelligibility. Now it is true that verbal innovation and shifts of meaning are virtues that may become vices and corrode what should be creative. But the question being raised is not whether we are for or against rules, since we all live by some. The question is how to understand the rules of language—of a game that is partially unknown and that seems to allow the most unusual moves without jeopardizing its formal or intelligible status. Our problem, thus, is less with an unstable language than with the stability sought by science. The problem comes when we turn language against itself by overestimating the purity of science. Posthumus, in Shakespeare's *Cymbeline,* assigns all mutability, and so all corruptibility, to the woman's part in him and determines to purge it. "I'll write against them [women]," he rants. Many writers, similarly, write against language to free it from mutability and the deceits thereof.

The revisionists do not descend from heaven bearing a new and rigorous truth. They are struggling with, or against, the imperative of language purification that has been with us at least since the Renaissance in a scientific or religious or parareligious form.

The New Critics tried to purify criticism while insisting on the impurity of poetry. Paradox, irony, and ambiguity characterized the language of fiction, but little if anything was said about the language of criticism. Even literary impurity had its limits, of course: it might not become Manichean or a self-conscious compositional method. The Coleridge they admired was not the be-nightmared plagiarist, but one who insisted on the unifying power of imagination, its reconciliation of opposite or discordant qualities.

Their notion of poetry, then, was more pure than they knew. Yet to emphasize, with the revisionists, the co-presence in literary works (broadly understood) of mixed or even discontinuous orders of discourse does not make a contribution in itself. A freer criticism must have, like free verse, its own formal principles. In the present ferment, however, I see mainly the *creative* force of the *critical* spirit, as it questions such honorific terms as *creative* or *primary* or *visionary*; or feels trapped by a neoclassical concept of unity; or shows how all vision is revision—the strong if negative extension of canonized texts.

Is this avant-garde criticism, then, a rearguard humanism? The post-new-critical critics remain close readers, devoted to the study of writing in all its modes, from hieroglyphics to philosophical prose. Behind them lies an empirical tradition of great talent, presently reduced to quarreling about what particular interpretation (evaluation) is or is not correct. Before them lies no reading at all, but a wasteland of books—commercially inspired objects of esteem, or therapeutic aids, or pseudoevents—or the temptation to go beyond this and even high culture to the unmediated spirit that prefers itself to all books.

The revisionists, then, try to strike a balance between solipsism (however Gnostic) and materialism (however social). They do not dehumanize study, but they are critical of humanistic cant and of easy uses of the concept of secularization. Matthew Arnold predicted that what would remain of religion is its poetry. The revisionists point out, fortified by American, Irish, Welsh, and Continental literature, that Arnold's prediction has been fulfilled in an ambivalent way. If what remains of religion is its poetry, what remains of poetry is its heterodox theology, or mythmaking.

As all poetry and indeed all writing—not only that of prima facie religious eras—is scrutinized by the critical and secularizing spirit, more evidence of archaic or sacred residues comes to light. We may not value them, but they are too prevalent and integumented to be undone. The sacred has so inscribed itself in language that while it must be interpreted, it cannot be removed. One might speculate that what we call the sacred is simply that which must be interpreted or reinterpreted, "A Presence which is not to be put by." In fact, it may be impossible to distinguish a priori between a residual past that "defiles the hands"—the writer's hands—because it is holy, and that which defiles them because it pollutes, and should be purged from consciousness and language.

It would be a great relief to break with the idea of the sacred, and especially with institutions that claim to mediate it. Yet the institution of language makes every such break appear inauthentic. It keeps us in the "defile of the word," meeting, slaying, purifying what is held to be sacred or sublime again and again.[11] The very persistence, moreover, of so many and various ideals of language purification betrays something religious in spirit, if not in name.

Yet if we turn from religion, philosophy, psychoanalysis, linguistics, and so forth to literary criticism, and acknowledge its separate status, it is because we need that garden in the wilderness. Though freer and more visionary than most admit, literary criticism directs us to objects that are clearly there, clearly human, and clearly finite—perhaps, as Valéry surmised, abandoned by the author rather than complete, yet therefore available for the finding we call interpretation.

11. Starting with Vico, there is an entire industry of critics and historians who uncover "dark italics" (Wallace Stevens) in the purified thought of the Cartesian or Enlightenment tradition. Millennialism, as it continues into the modern period, is examined in Frank Kermode's *The Sense of an Ending,* which relates it structurally but also critically to fiction-making; while the names of M. H. Abrams, Northrop Frye, and Angus Fletcher should be added to suggest that American scholarship is not behind that of Europe in noting the persistence of metaphysical or mythic ("logocentric") elements. For the "defile of the word," see Thomas Weiskel on Wordsworth in *The Romantic Sublime.*

Coda: Polemical Pieces

> Shall I not rejoice also at the abundance of the weeds whose seeds are the granary of the birds?
>
> —H. D. Thoreau

The Recognition Scene of Criticism

Wallace Martin's response to "Literary Criticism and Its Discontents" is anything but naive. Its most sophisticated device is to posit my invention of a "naive reader" and to suggest that I would place the New Critics and their heirs in that category. But when I see the movement of criticism after Arnold as exhibiting an anti-self-consciousness principle or being so worried about a hypertrophy of the critical spirit that that spirit is acknowledged only by refusing it seminal or creative force, I am not alleging naiveté but "organized innocence," or the privileged assignment of some given, intuitive (in that sense naive) power of creation to the area of art that excludes the area of philosophy or philosophically minded commentary. This defensive partition of the critical and the creative spirit, which recognizes the intelligence of the creative writer but refuses the obverse proposition that there may be creative force in the critical writer, I have named the Arnoldian concordat.

Martin's rhetorical stance is best expressed toward the end of his response. "Why do you solicit combat with opponents whose limitations are disabling?" Martin plays the game well. He knows the power of rhetoric and indeed tries to disable much in my essay except the rhetoric. Yet I prefer to think that his final question does not seek to score but rather to challenge and

This essay was originally published as a response to Wallace Martin's "Literary Critics and Their Discontents," *Critical Inquiry* 4 (1977): 397–406. Martin's essay is itself a response to my "Literary Criticism and Its Discontents," *Critical Inquiry* 3 (1976): 203–20, printed in this volume as chapter 10, "Past and Present."

draw out. It views something as a combat which others might see as a parochial or vainglorious quarrel. It misunderstands, nevertheless, and in the name of the "naive reader," my discontent with the present phase of the Arnoldian tradition in criticism. It is only with the *enabling limitations* that one should deal, and Martin often jousts and jabs at my own successfully.[1]

I am, therefore, alarmed rather than disarmed when I read his defense of ignorance. "That a weakening of language requirements and a lack of professional philosophic interest in nineteenth-century German thought left the heirs of the New Critics ill equipped for the intellectual play in which Hartman would have us indulge may be regretted, but scarcely requires apology. Most of the New Critics were poets; they did not pretend to be scholars in the European sense." It is not, in the main, the quantity but the quality of knowledge that is at issue: what kind of knowledge enables and what kind of knowledge disables literary understanding. Yet quantity is also important. Though not everyone can be a Curtius any more than an Eliot and carry in his bones not merely his own generation but "a feeling that the whole of the literature of Europe from Homer and within it the whole of the literature of his own country has a simultaneous existence and composes a simultaneous order" (*Tradition and the Individual Talent*), there is always a *burden* of knowledge that must be carried by someone.

The *omne scibile* is usually the most disabling of indulgences; and the polyglot critic who works in nine languages may turn out to be a Danny Kaye. One has to know, nevertheless, as Valéry remarked, that the one country in which French is not taught is France. To know English, similarly, we must find a

1. I think Martin complicates the local difficulties my style may present because of his desire to draw attention to the old conflict between logic and rhetoric and to place the Yale critics on the side of "a more primal rhetoric." It is not possible, here, to insist on distinctions among those polemically grouped as the Yale critics, but I doubt that any one of them believes in a "primal rhetoric." Sometimes Martin's zeal becomes inquisitorial. The idea of "falling upwards," for instance, which he thinks I misapply via de Man's article on Binswanger, I used in a 1964 essay on Marvell's sense of temporality (*Beyond Formalism,* p. 160). My not annotating the idea in the "Discontents" essay of 1976 expressed a hope for the naturalization of the idea, for the appreciation of its figurative power apart from its appearance in technical and special contexts.

way of standing at once inside and outside of it. What I question is the unwillingness of most Anglo-American critics to engage Continental thought, especially its difficult blend of theoretical and practical criticism.

The very term *practical criticism* has come to suggest that theory is something impractical, esoteric, or apart. European efforts, at least since Goethe, to grasp theory as a living and presentational mode have foundered under the doctrine that ideas in modern life are dissociated entities, products of the will or of an insufficiently refined sense of language. Science, similarly, is accepted only as the mighty opposite of poetry. How curious that teachers who permit into the curriculum the most experimental fiction are aggressively defensive when it comes to a literature that demands as much or more: the writings, namely, of great speculative thinkers like Marx, Husserl, Heidegger, Freud. I call it "literature" not only to make a polemical point but from the conviction that each thinker draws on and in turn generates a text-milieu of his own, so that it is not a matter of "knowing" Derrida or Heidegger but of reading and steeping oneself in a corpus of critical, philosophical, and literary texts that they incorporate and revise. Coleridge can be our example in this as well. If he failed, then we too should have his courage to fail.

I do not know whether the Arnoldian tradition, now often narrowed from cultural to practical matters of interpretation, could merge in some way with the Continental tradition of philosophic criticism. Perhaps here too opposition is friendship. Yet those who have had access to both are obliged to raise the question of whether we are not drifting into a "two cultures" situation. It is not, or no longer, a matter of the genteel tradition versus those who reject the Ordeal of Civility. Or, as Philip Rahv put it, of Redskins and Palefaces. Or of ivory tower cerebration and classroom pragmatics. There is, instead, a new isolationism masking under the name of Common Sense and characterizing what it opposes as Skywriting. The Skywriters march under the banner of Hegel and Continental Philosophy, while the Common Sense school is content with no philosophy, unless it be that of Locke and a homespun organicism. One side mocks a pretentious "frogology" (THE FROG IS DEAD appeared on the walls of a recent conference on semiotics, hermeneutics, etc.), the other denounces the naive or provincial donnishness of endless practical readings and their prissy and prickly defensiveness of style.

Arnold himself was far from narrow. He believed criticism made a difference. It might modify and gradually decay the class structure by its diffusion of culture. It was precisely this faith in the literary and critical enterprise which allowed English thought to resist louder claims from the Continent, of the kind that substituted ambitious theories of *praxis* for those of *practical* reflection. Yet Arnold also elaborated a thesis which allowed a narrowing to occur in our idea of the function of criticism. For him the critic was justified only insofar as he circulated ideas, redeemed English writers from their insularity, and so prepared his country for a new Renaissance of letters, a literature not of pure imagination (as the Romantics had given) but of "imaginative reason." Now in a sense this is exactly what happened: criticism may be that literature of "imaginative reason." But Arnoldian epigones use Arnold's thesis to put the critic down, to subordinate him to an ideal that attaches itself feverishly to every new—then outworn—creative writer.

The irony of seeing in criticism the outcome of Arnoldian hopes is obvious. One can't take such a position with high seriousness. But perhaps, as Lukács argued in his 1910 "Letter to Leo Popper" on the essay form (in *Soul and Form*), the very structure of the critical essay is ironic in pretending to be a commentary or critique of a work of art, rather than a work of art itself. What is exemplary in Continental thought—here Valéry, accepted by the New Critics, is as crucial as Derrida—is that it does not make a priori distinctions of a hierarchical kind between the activities of the human mind by freezing them into genres. Most works of fiction may be greater than most works of criticism, but both criticism and fiction are institutions of the human mind, and one cannot foretell where the creative spirit may show itself.

It is not impossible that a future generation will consider some critical and scholarly essays written from Arnold's time on as interesting as the poetry and fiction of the period. It is not impossible that the creative spirit may be showing itself in such books as Hegel's *Lectures on Aesthetics,* Ruskin's *Queen of the*

Air,[2] Pater's *Renaissance,* Erich Auerbach's *Mimesis,* or certain essays of Barfield, Lukács, Benjamin, and Derrida. Moreover, though criticism is not fiction but rather a genre in its own right, it is not impossible that, today, this genre may be changing its form and occupying more intellectual and creative space.

To put criticism at a Platonic remove from its object—to consider it as referring to literature without being literary—is to demoralize it as surely as art was demoralized (in theory) by the Platonic notion of its remove from the archetype. Criticism, in short, is not extraliterary, not outside of literature or art looking in: it is a defining and influential part of its subject, a genre with some constant and some changing features. Today criticism is particularly vital because it has recognized that in addition to its pedagogic or socializing function—immeasurably increased and burdensome since the advent of mass education—it should take back its free-lance, creative powers. Criticism represents the freedom that learning and knowledge ideally give; and its natural enemy is, therefore, not the artist but the journalist. The journalist would like to elect himself as the only free-spirited one; he sets up the academic critic in contrast as one whose teaching and tenure depend on the spoliation or exploitation of art works.

Many teachers, unfortunately, because of classroom pressures and an administrative structure that treats them as a business, support this journalistic leveling of their function to one thing: direct, salable communication. The modern teacher, like the ancient Sophist, is often forced to underestimate his task by accepting the role of giving a one-drachma or sixty-drachma course and claiming that he teaches a subject well enough when he has "communicated." But he then compensates for his humility (or is it humiliation?) by overestimating the uniqueness of art as something that he serves without really participating in—except

2. In *The Queen of the Air,* Ruskin, like Heidegger, often thinks back through Greek words to the "open mystery" they express. If we could articulate the difference between Heidegger and Ruskin we might have a clue to the general character of Continental as distinguished from Anglo-American criticism. While Heidegger's diction seems violent despite itself in its reconstitution of wonder words, Ruskin's prose remains full of earnest childishness, of a simple trust that things can be properly worded by direct inspection or affectionate research.

at a distance. From that distance he equates the imaginative or creative principle exclusively with works of fictional art. *There* is the true place of spiritual combat. Yet, does it take away from art to see the critic engaged in a similar quest or "combat"? Do critics not authenticate or disauthenticate the vision of life which is theirs by comparing it with that of other writers and artists?

Perhaps, then, the first part of Martin's question, "Why do you solicit combat," is more cogent than the second part, "with opponents whose limitations are disabling," which was thought to carry his point. "Solicit combat," is, of course, chivalric in its phrasing and suggests that the metaphor of combat, at least as applied to the critical enterprise, is not to be taken literally. It seems melodramatic and agonizing. But Martin surprisingly legitimates the metaphor by alluding to Hegel—"the abominable Hegel," as William Pritchard recently called him, while making the sign of the cross to keep that speculator from corrupting the civilized (i.e., English) mind.

The passage from Hegel referred to, in the *Phenomenology*,[3] is a famous one: it describes how the master-servant relation is transformed by some necessity in the opponents for mutual recognition. When Martin says that through this allusion to Hegel he wishes to "identify the level" at which any debate with me would begin, I take it he means the following. Insofar as criticism services art there is bound to be a modification of that relation: a dialectical interchange and so an implicit or actual movement toward a new relation. Martin, further, hovering between Ignatian and Kierkegaardian (or Marxist) intuitions, suggests that a provocative agent was needed to pressure the dialectic of "criticism" and "creation" to a new stage, to give reality to a situation

3. For reasons that will appear, I prefer Hegel's fuller exposition of the stage of recognitive self-consciousness (i.e. mutual acknowledgment) in *Phenomenology*, 4.A, to the parallel version Martin quotes from the *Encyclopedia*. Other texts that might have been relevantly cited include Fichte's *Wissenschaftslehre* (1794), which "constructs" the relation between self and other in a similar if less dialectical way while concentrating on the ultimate indifference of science (philosophy) and art; also Coleridge's appropriations of Kant and Fichte in chapters 9 and 13 of the *Biographia Literaria*.

in which the Yale critics had been jousting with faceless or vituperative, rather than articulate, opponents.

In brief: criticism, like literature, drives toward a recognition scene. We should be able to describe the features of that recognition scene, as Aristotle did the features of an art embedded in a larger sociality. Yet I am not at all sure that it is possible, and precisely because the social context of criticism is so often reduced by us to the academy and petty competitiveness. At present the feeling runs strong in the intellectual community that the self-conscious critics are competing not only with their colleagues but also with the artists. What we have recognized so far is not even emulation: it is envy and resentment. In that atmosphere it were best to say, yes, the critic is simply publishing his own truth and wishes to have it acknowledged.

But since the institution of criticism itself, especially academic criticism, has come under attack, I want to go further. The recognition scene, which Hegel's dialectic continually stages, and which increases without really abating self-consciousness, today involves the very existence of criticism as a more than *pastoral* mode. True, criticism can be pastoral: it can do a job, it can annotate or write helpful (and even virtuoso) commentaries on texts. But it can also write texts of its own. It need not forever continue to be a blind mouth and found itself, as in the case of Leavis, on sheer stubbornness. That simply creates a new mystique.

No "unformulated individualism," as Malraux said in 1935, the very time Leavis was resisting the necessity of a more theoretical formulation of his position, can succeed against would-be engineers of the soul. Some of us must be willing to write a theory of criticism that is not simply a new version of pastoral: a theory of the relation of criticism to culture and of the act of writing itself as a will to discourse with political implications. There is no mute inglorious Marx any more than a mute inglorious Milton. The situation of the discourse we name *criticism* is, therefore, no different from that of any other. If this recognition implies a reversal, then it is the master-servant relation between criticism and creation that is being overturned in favor of what Wordsworth, describing the interaction of nature and mind, called "mutual domination" or "interchangeable supremacy."

> Even the desire of men and women, Hegel tells us, is constituted under the sign of mediation; it is desire to make its desire recognized. It has for its object a desire, that of the other, in the sense that there is no object for desiring which is not constituted by some sort of mediation. . . . This is the case throughout the development of satisfaction, from the moment of the master-slave conflict and through the dialectic of labor.
>
> —Jacques Lacan[4]

Is criticism then so grave a matter that no claim can be made for it without seeing it under the aspect of that "high seriousness" Arnold attributed to great literature? What has happened to the element of play? Martin urges me to publish my own truth, or to confess that, lacking an audience and desiring to speak the truth not only for myself but also for others, I must create adequate opponents through the mental warfare of polemics. "It is because we want to express the truth for others, and they want to express the truth for us, that we find ourselves 'fellow combatants in the field of letters.'" He says, even more finely: "We can never know . . . whether the desire of truth is in fact the truth of desire"—the desire to create another (the Other) as friend or antagonist.

Yet this creation, out of desire, of the Other (my true theme being not the "philosophy of criticism" but the "poetics of desire") is frustrated by the playful or evasive quality of my words. For truth to be dialectical, for this othering to take place, I must engage to be I. But here my conflicts and rhetorical complexities betray me. There seems to be no "real subject." Hartman is merely art-man. "Who is Geoffrey Hartman? Can we weave from the filaments of his writing since *The Unmediated Vision* . . . a single pattern that could be called a unity? . . . As readers, we experience him not as a person but as a rhetorical 'I' who sometimes finds that his most worthy antagonist is himself."

We have heard much about the "subject" lately, how it is a

4. It may be worth pointing out that Lacan's acquaintance with Hegel was fortified by Alexandre Kojève's lectures on the *Phenomenology*, which focused on the importance of Hegel's analysis of the master-slave dialectic and which built a bridge between that "moment" and Heidegger's thought.

changeling, a shifter, a thing of shreds and quotations. I hope it is no further evasion to point out that Jacques Derrida plays with a greater "subject" at the outset of *Glas*. "Qui, lui?" he asks, and drops the H to make him appear as a mythic and theriomorphic name. "Hegel," pronounced in French, sounds like "aigle." Yet this eagle, of course, is (inter alia) the emblem of the evangelist John whose doctrine of the Logos ("In the beginning was the Word") is deconstructed by Derrida.

Such *serio ludere* is maintained throughout *Glas*. So the question raised in my previous essay remains: what connection is there between playing and thinking, playing and interpretive criticism? What kind of reality belongs to play, and especially wordplay?[5] Derrida or Lacan might answer: the "subject" before being a self is a name, like "Georg Wilhelm Friedrich Hegel" or "Jean Genet." But names are only a metonymic expression of the fact that we are born into a language that is bestowed by others and that shapes even our desires. The "truth of desire" (to recall Martin's phrase) is that even our desire is not our own, any more than a given name is. Hence that perpetual play, or battle, to disown language in order to own it. (*The Unmediated Vision* had no other argument, even if its terms were more instinctive than philosophic, terms of "desire" lusting for terms of "cognition.") Think of Blake's poem "Infant Joy," in which the newborn child is represented as naming itself in a happy, self-baptizing dialogue with the Other. The foundling founds his name. Yet this reversal simply confirms the priority or premediation of language, for Blake's lyric is a cradle song or charm or a kind of womb talk. Through this ventriloquism, which is as basic as you can get in terms of poetic or incantatory play, the infant holds, in Wordsworth's phrase, "mute dialogues with [his] mother's heart."

"In the beginning was the Word" means that there is no time of which it can be said, here time was and language was not. The subject or self is not denied but is the very locus that discloses that relation. Our striving for an absolute self or unmediated vision simply brings to light all that mediates the incurably visionary self: if we are, we are in time and in language. As in Shelley's

5. As Martin says, "These are serious questions [yet] they will be misunderstood if there is no room for play in discussing them."

bitter *Triumph of Life,* those whose imagination is not dead keep asking "What is Life?" as they discard "shadows of shadows, yet unlike themselves." They burn up in their desire for a definitive self-image as mask after mask is revealed and cast off. The "desire of truth" is indeed the "truth of desire," but the latter is disclosed only as the "untruth" of style—Derrida's or Shelley's questioning style. Recognition of the other (Lacan would say of the "Discourse of the Other") verges on recollecting that play of shadows, masks, and words: anagnorisis becomes anamnesis.

No single formalized term can encompass the issues involved. Yet there is a need at present to recover the link between literature, language, *work,* and *play.* So I wish to allude once more to Huizinga's *Homo Ludens,* which showed how combat and play (the "play of forces," we still say) are interactive to such an extent that each society or institution has its own way of dealing with the issue of hierarchy implicit in determining what is serious and what trivial, what is propadeutic-marginal and what mature and central. Recently Walter Ong recovered for us a sense of the "agonistic structures" present in institutionalized learning before the 1960s. (See *Daedalus* [Fall 1974] and *Interchange* 5 [1974].) These questions are raised now because now the understanding of such structures has lessened, and their fading has brought forward even more neurotic potentialities of conflict and competition.

D. W. Winnicott has also made extraordinary claims for the importance of play in a book called, significantly, *Playing and Reality* (1971). He is concerned, of course, with the institution of psychoanalysis rather than with art. His description of "transitional phenomena" (a term that for us, though not for him, recalls the provisional character of Schiller's "aesthetic state," or the theory of marginality developed by Victor Turner from Van Gennep's book on rites of passage) allows us to move from dolls to all kinds of "soft objects"—and if certain purists have inveighed against statues as dolls, this would prove (even without Claes Oldenburg) an eloquent relation.

My own feeling is that far as he goes, Winnicott does not go far enough: "transitional phenomena" ("transitional objects") suggests something nontransitional to follow, but perhaps the mystery of aesthetic education is in the understanding it gives of liminal or transitional states as such. Yet when Winnicott asserts that "psychoanalysis has been developed as a highly specialized form of playing in the service of communication with oneself and others" and that the "natural thing is playing, and the highly sophisticated twentieth-century phenomenon is psychoanalysis," he encourages the question: What kind of "phenomenon" is art? It was there before psychoanalysis, as Freud acknowledged. Is psychoanalysis, then, a form of art, on the basis of the "universal thing called playing"? This is not the place to fully expound or criticize Winnicott, but his casual way of stating large propositions leaves the reader charmed and perplexed, as if even his text aspired to the status of friendly teddy or "soft object."

There exist, of course, specifically literary concepts that could be associated with the idea of playing—irony, equivocation, ambiguity, even allegory. None of these are really clear in separation. The question of style subsumes them all. Style is the "line play" of critic or artist. Who is to arbitrate between in and out in a language game where the decorum of the words is the meaning? The chief problem Anglo-American critics face in reading Continental criticism is its style: the extroverted theory is too loud (the terms are heavy or inflated, the writer can't turn up the theoretical component without the rhetorical) and often also too playful. When Derrida, by paranomasia, etymological wit of a venerable kind (see Curtius's excursus on "Etymology as a Category of Thought" in *European Literature and the Latin Middle Ages* [1948]), and depersonification allegory, converts "Hegel" into "aiglc" and continues such *ablauting*, can we enjoy his play as simply an enrichment of meaning? Or must we ideologize his subversive and at times surrealistic expropriation of the stable meaning?

In Derrida the line play wishes to be undecidable. Derrida is not a Kierkegaard who seeks to transcend the aesthetic position with its ironic or playful infinitization and to arrive at a religious position with its tragic or decisive understanding of eternity. His infinitizing of meaning hovers between playing and . . . not reality, but an as yet undefinable allegoresis. This makes practical criticism an attractive antidote, as if the "English malady" (now French?) had evolved its own cure. For we do not receive from *Glas* only a sense of joy and freedom as when the well-read mind wantons in its interpretive powers and emancipates the written word from the bond of single meanings: Derrida's playfulness, voracious and melancholic, is also fed by a "milk of mourning."

The latter is his own phrase, perhaps inspired by Melanie Klein. But the Kleinian hermeneutic overdetermines the activity of play until it points to a combat in the psyche of the infant virtually as intense as that in the bosom of the theological God. A *dark little one* is revealed, a divine child whose emblem would have to unify teddy bear and eagle. It is not my purpose, however, to end with a riddle. I wish to suggest in conclusion that the notion of play is too radical to fit any totally secular and empirical scheme. It cannot be subdued, for example, to Winnicott's (or, for that matter, N. O. Brown's) benevolent nonreality or play principle that takes the hurt out of the teleological thrust of life.

In searching for a theory of literary play we come upon the metaphor of combat once more and on the psychomachia of the formalized recognition scene. Hegel's version of that scene does not include writing because of his teleological thrust beyond every partial object and toward a reality defined as "absolute knowledge." The connection between, on the one hand, naming, playing, writing, and, on the other, the *micromegas* character of childhood experience—at once insignificant (childish) and hugely significant (mortgaging the child's future)—is not taken into consciousness. There is no phenomenology of the teddy bear in Hegel: the philosopher is all eagle.[6] Similarly, Hegel has only the rudiments of a phenomenology of naming and signification (linking the "dark little one" to the micromegas quality of the sign), though Derrida draws out what there is by his magnificent, restless analysis in *Glas* of excerpts from the *Phenomenology* and the *Aesthetics.* Those passages become passages to so much else but principally to a new recognition scene not found in Hegel, and where, even when speech is left behind, writing emerges as a permanent form of life elaborating the transitional objects we call texts—which can never be left behind.

6. Eagles can't be made into soft objects, one thinks. Derrida emphasizes "l'aigle pris dans la glace et le gel" to contrast the hardness of Hegel with Jean Genet (he divides with Hegel the pages of *Glas*). Genet proves to be ambiguously hard and soft: what a doll! But then *gl* itself, the glottis-glue sound, is variable in a similar way: *aigle, glace, gel.*

Criticism, Indeterminacy, Irony

"Indeterminacy" is a word with bad vibes. It evokes a picture of the critic as Hamlet, "sicklied o'er with the pale cast of thought." It is often said to involve an attack on the communicative or edifying function of literature. A pseudoscientific or anti-humanist bias is ascribed to critics when they do not replace words by meanings quickly enough. We like to consume our literature. We like to think of critics as service stations that keep readers fueled for their more important business, refreshing them and speeding them on.

Yet indeterminacy, though not an end to be pursued but something disclosed by liberal and thoughtful reading, is more like a traffic sign warning of an impasse. It suggests (1) that where there is a conflict of interpretations or codes, that conflict can be rehearsed or reordered but not always resolved, and (2) that even where there is no such conflict we have no certainty of controlling implications that may not be apparent or articulable at any one point in time. This "tacit component" will be mentioned again. But two things should already be clear. The referential function of words in ordinary situations, where the context is easily determined, is not in question. At the same time, all statements are potentially overdetermined and have a circumference larger than their apparent reference.

A statement made in a novel, as compared to a statement made in a restaurant, is subject to a different kind of interpretation, but it is not a different statement. This look-alike (sound-alike) quality is disconcerting because the frame or setting (restaurant/restaurant-in-a-novel) is interchangeable—and often played with, in works of art. Quotation marks are a generalized frame of this kind: any phrase can be put in question, or echoed that way.

Phrases do echo crazily in some minds, and in one's own mind at times. Othello is a victim of this echoing. There is the joke of one spouse saying "Good morning" and the other snarling "You want to pick a fight?" Even when the reader has "the comfort and security of a frame of reference . . . the frames of reference are not constant, and their number seems limitless."[1] Shakespeare makes fun of a word that echoes itself: "Cuckoo! Cuckoo! O word of fear / Unpleasing to a married ear." Or, as Valéry says elegantly and generally: "La résonance emporte sur la causalité." The drawing in of strange reverberations, of unexpected contexts—frames of reference—is a mark of literature; and this "interinanimation" will always have a tacit component. (See I. A. Richards, *The Philosophy of Rhetoric,* chap. 3; Kenneth Burke, "Semantic and Poetic Meaning" in *The Philosophy of Literary Form;* and Michael Polanyi, *Personal Knowledge,* part 2.) What is inexplicit is as functional as what is patently there, though it is hard to describe in a rigorous manner the relation between marked and unmarked features, between what is provided and what elided, what is verbal and what situational, what is foregrounded and what understood.

In "The Voice of the Shuttle" (*Beyond Formalism,* pp. 337–53) I described this structure as it governs figures of speech. They have overspecified ends and indeterminate middles, so that the elision or subsuming of the middle terms (a received story, a traditional theme, a current idiom) creates a sense of mediated immediacy that provokes interpretation. But I have done no more than provide a graded progression of examples; and these may require not only modification or completion but also an understanding that cannot be totally anticipated or constrained. This understanding is like a frame or context always beyond the horizon.

Even in the absence of a competent theory, however, we should recognize the fact that with the Symbolist poets, from Mallarmé

1. Stephen Booth, *An Essay on Shakespeare's Sonnets,* pp. 186–87. Empson's *Seven Types of Ambiguity* depends heavily on the same "Shakespearean" solace.

and Rimbaud to Hofmannsthal, Yeats and Valéry, a reflection on language accompanies explicitly the writing of poetry—a poetry we are still, at present, trying to *theorize*. Iris Murdoch puts the matter well. "Precision of reference had been sometimes more, sometimes less, important to the poet; but now suddenly it seemed that the whole referential character of language had become for him a sort of irritant or stumbling block." Characteristic of Symbolist or post-Symbolist poets, she continues, "is the way in which language appears to them like a metaphysical task, an angel to be wrestled with. Their attention is fixed upon language itself to the point of obsession, and their poems are thing-like, non-communicative, non-transparent to an unprecedented degree; they are independent structures, either outside the world or containing the world."[2] This, then, is part of the context in which literary criticism moves at the present time. The poets were there before Saussure.

"In our time," Paul Ricoeur has said in *Freud and Philosophy*, "we have not finished doing away with *idols* and we have barely

2. *Sartre: Romantic Rationalist*, pp. 29–30. More sustained attempts to theorize the symbolists are Edmund Wilson's *Axel's Castle* and Charles Feidelson's *Symbolism and American Literature*. Murdoch views Sartre basically as an anti-Symbolist writer (romantic, on the one hand, rationalist and scientific, on the other); Wilson's attitude toward the Symbolists is ambivalent; Feidelson more positively repatriates the movement. On two kinds of indeterminacy, an older type related to the "undetermining" effect of meter, and a modernist type related to "the intractable energy of the images" and the ellipsis of logical connections, see J. C. Ransom, "Wanted: An Ontological Critic," in *The New Criticism*. Van Wyck Brooks's chapter on "Coterie-Literature" in *Opinions of Oliver Allston* attacks Modernism (without naming it) as an extreme and elaborated Symbolism, partly expatriate, partly international mystification. He utters, strange to say, exactly the same kind of charges against the New Criticism (considered an adjunct of coterie-literature) as are heard today against deconstruction or related theories. Namely (1) an emphasis of form over "responsible" content and meaning; (2) a self-inflating concern for personal prestige; (3) doubting life and magnifying the death-drive; (4) making literature a game, "an intellectual pastime for dilettanti"; (5) overvaluing technique and the scientific method; (6) undervaluing all other "humanistic" issues. Brooks is important, though, for bringing emphasis back to the disparaged Romantics. A significant shift in the critical spectrum comes only when a theory of Romantic poetry is recovered in the 1960s and breaks up the exclusive Symbolist-Modernist axis. Northrop Frye's *Fearful Symmetry* (1947) is still an attempt, in the wake of Yeats, to present Blake as a great precursor, a Romantic Symbolist.

begun to listen to *symbols*. It may be that this situation, in its apparent distress, is instructive: it may be that extreme iconoclasm belongs to the restoration of meaning." To some extent every developed theory attempts to separate criticism from sheer skepticism or "nihilism." But how it does this can be very diverse. The diversity is itself of interest and perhaps not totally reducible. Can we understand anything without an inner movement of assent? Is that question best approached through a "grammar" of assent or through a Husserlian analysis of the "positional" and "intentional" structures of thought? Through existential dialectics or through speech-act theory? Should we perhaps eschew all technical philosophy and be content with hints derived from fusion or identification theories, by Vico, Dilthey, Poulet, and psychologically oriented authors? For the literary scholar, is it sufficient to follow the debates concerning the relation of understanding to belief in Richards, Eliot, and the New Criticism?

In terms of systematic thought I have nothing to add. But I would like to recall that fiction itself, our very capacity for it, is what is threatened by both overskeptical and overaffirmative (dogmatic) philosophies. The destinies of fiction and criticism are joined; and the fact that criticism takes the form, so often, of commentary, is a sign of this. Even a negative commentary tends to save the text by continuing it in our consciousness. The relation of criticism to fiction, in any case, is more intrinsic than of thought to a found object. If, as in the Anglo-American tradition, we approach this issue through an insistence on meaning, I would continue to preface it as follows:

> . . . the problem of meaning cannot even be faced without considering the necessity or fatality of some primary affirmation. Religious belief is such a primary act, but a special form of it. The founding of a fictional world is such a primary act. Fiction reveals something without which the mind could not be, or could not think. The mind needs a world, a substantialized Yes. Yet every great artist rebels against this, and today his rebellion is conventional. By beginning to question the necessity of fiction, i.e. the inherently affirmative structure of imagination, he joins the philosopher who sees a truth greater than that arbitrary Yes. [*Beyond Formalism,* p. 74]

Indeterminacy as a "speculative instrument" should influence the way literature is read, but by modifying the reader's awareness rather than by imposing a method. To methodize indeterminacy would be to forget the reason for the concept. It does not doubt meaning, nor does it respond to an economy of scarcity and try to make reading more "productive" of meaning. Quite the contrary: it encourages a form of writing—of articulate interpretation—that is not subordinated naively to the search for ideas. From this perspective the apparently opposite demands for *objective interpretation* on the part of E. D. Hirsch and for *subjective criticism* on the part of Norman Holland ignore equally the resistance of art to the meanings it provokes. Reduction of multiple meaning, according to Hirsch, is achieved through the postulate of a determinate and determinable authorial intention. Holland places the reduction of meaning in the "defensive mastery" of the artist and the defensive misery of the reader. Hirsch would regulate the understanding, so that it does not waste itself; Holland would deregulate it, since the problem is not subjectivity but our overreaction to it, an excess of social rules and psychic defenses.

Though the issue of multiple meaning and its reduction is raised by both critics, they eventually leave art behind. Holland evangelizes the very difficulty of gaining an interpretation of art, suggesting that the interpretive work builds up, by way of the classroom, a community of readers who share this interpersonal, reflective experience; Hirsch seeks to rationalize literary studies by arguing that interpretation of art must abide by the rules of interpretation generally, that meanings are hypotheses subject to canons of verifiability. The concept of indeterminacy, however, explores the "blind lawfulness" (Kant) of imagination, or how art allows the understanding to produce its own form of meaningfulness. "As it must not, so genius cannot be lawless," Coleridge wrote in his *Lectures on Shakespeare,* "for it is even this that constitutes its genius—the power of acting creatively under laws of its own origination."

I realize that reduction of meaning and the role of the principle of indeterminacy would need more exposition than I can offer here. May I emphasize the following: As a guiding concept, indeterminacy does not merely *delay* the determination of meaning, that is, suspend premature judgments and allow greater thoughtfulness. The delay is not heuristic alone, a device to slow the act of reading till we appreciate (I could think here of Stanley Fish) its complexity. The delay is intrinsic: from a certain point of view, it is thoughtfulness itself, Keats's "negative capability," a labor that aims not to overcome the negative or indeterminate but to stay within it as long as is necessary.

How long, though? That cannot be abstractly answered. Forms of closure will occur, precipitated by acts of writing or reading. But it is the *commentary process* that matters: the taking away, modification, elaboration, of previous meanings. "All symbols are fluxional; all language is vehicular and transitive" (Emerson). As long as criticism is also commentary, the work of art that is its "referent" is established as a constant variable, and its successive actualization (its "history") must itself be studied, as in the reception theory of the School of Konstanz associated with Hans Robert Jauss and Wolfgang Iser.

To compile an inventory of meanings in their structural relations ("structuralism") or of the focusing and orientative acts of consciousness in *their* relations ("phenomenology"), seems rather distant from what we do as critics, even when unusually introspective. This is where the gap between the "scientific" approach to literary studies and humanistic criticism is most apparent; and I have not been able to bridge it. The gap is like that between *langue* and *parole* in Saussure, or between grammar and the living language, or between a principle and its application. (In hermeneutics, as Hirsch reminds us, a difference was often discerned between subtlety of understanding and subtlety of explication—of articulating and applying one's understanding. Gadamer, however, thinks these are or can be fused.) On the whole, I favor moving "indeterminacy" from the area of grammatical, semiotic, or phenomenological reduction to that of humanistic criticism itself: that is, we take back from science what is ours; we do not allow ourselves to depend on the physical or human sciences for the model of a *mechanism* that fascinates by its anonymous, compulsive, impersonal character. (So, for example, on the strange foundation of unconscious process the most elaborate structures, including art, are built up.) Through interpretive criticism we ascertain the kind of relation we have to that mechanism, as writing and reading disclose it. Wordsworth's "dim and undetermined sense / Of unknown modes of being" is also what moved him to autobiography, and to define that which has no single, exclusively personal, locus. Yet the perspective disclosed may be, precisely, the absence of one and only one context from which to view the flux of time or the empirical world, of one and only one method that would destabilize all but itself, of one and only one language to rule understanding and prevent misunderstanding.

To put it another way: we read to understand, but to understand *what*? Is it the book, is it the object (in the world) revealed by the book, is it ourselves? Or some transcendental X? It is not difficult to insist that all these aspects must participate; and philosophical reflection from the side of phenomenology, as well as the critique of phenomenology by semiotics, hermeneutics, and linguistic analysis have distinguished between these aspects.[3] But the literary critic remains the "delegate" of the common as well as of the uncommon reader, and so cannot at each point rehearse distinctions that would displace reading as the enjoyable and liberal activity it is. Reading should always remain, on one level, an exemplary grappling of mind with text for the sake of immediate intellectual and moral benefits, such as "seeing" an idea, a sharper view of the relation between style and moral action, or between the comprehension (*Verstehen*) of literary sentences and intersubjective consensus (*Verständnis*). I will therefore risk bracketing various philosophical considerations in asserting the following.

We read, as we write, to be understood; yet what we gain is the undoing of a previous understanding. Indeterminacy, as a concept, resists formally the complicity with closure implied by the wish to be understood or the communication-compulsion as-

3. See, for example, Wolfgang Iser, *The Act of Reading*; Michael Riffaterre, *La production du texte*; Jacques Derrida, *Speech and Phenomenon*, trans. David B. Allison; and Ernst Tugendhat, "Phänomenologie und Sprachanalyse" in *Hermeneutik und Dialektik* 2, pp. 3–23. Tugendhat suggests that Husserl's "intentional act" is modeled on understanding names rather than sentences, with the result that the subject-object schematism is retained as primary instead of being subordinated to a hermeneutic and intersubjective perspective.

sociated with it. Criteria of correctness or correspondence (of *truth*) may be caught up in this complicity. Indeterminacy functions as a bar separating understanding and truth. Understanding is not disabled but is forced back on the conditions of its truth: for example, the legitimacy of its dependence on texts. If this seems too radical a perspective, there remains the puzzle that the reception of literary works is usually accompanied by an uneasiness about their reduction to meaning. Reduction *of* meaning, that is, may work against reduction *to* meaning. Reading itself becomes the project: we read to understand what is involved in reading as a form of life, rather than to resolve what is read into glossy ideas. As in collage or conceptual art, meanings (Rilke's "gedeutete Welt") are part of the medium of art, part of its matériel.

When I. A. Richards in *Principles of Literary Criticism* denies an "aesthetic state," and Hans-Georg Gadamer insists that "aesthetics must be subsumed by hermeneutics," they are reacting to a simplistic identification of the aesthetic with the beautiful, and of the beautiful (as in Yeats's case) with the peculiar *labor* of woman, the "heroic discipline of the mirror." The beautiful as *poesis* makes or makes up rather than destroys illusions. It meets the ravening, raging, uprooting character of thought as its contrary: aware of desire and self but accepting and even playing with appearances in a manner Nietzsche called Apollinian. "We have art so that we don't founder on the truth."

To make rhetoric reflective, to shift it from the sphere of raging thought to that of beauty and play, is also a way of describing Yeats's art. Yet, "How with this rage shall beauty hold a plea?" I want to append some remarks on rhetoric as the rage in question, and on indeterminacy as a modest concept that avoids the contrast—so easily lost in dialectical nuance—of meaning and beauty, or semantic and poetic truth.

The movement toward the "rhetorical question" characteristic of Yeats suggests in the second quatrain of "Leda and the Swan" that we can only formulate such questions after the event or stress the inevitable in the event. Yet the poem's final question has somewhat of a finer tone, for it obliges the reader to become active, even to risk something. The question now is like a balance-point, which one unbalances by taking it up. Though it remains "rhetorical" in form, a reader can, perhaps must, develop it. What was rhetorical is no longer clearly on the side of an inevitable, predetermined meaning, understood only *nachträglich, ex eventu*: after an event that seems to be the ground for the question. For what was rhetorical has moved through itself to the side of a more general meditative stance. We can *stand,* as it were, in that question, we can take our time and think of the relation of the human mind to what overthrows it. Is that relation one of complicity, or of gratuitous dignity (Pascal: the moral mind as a thinking reed that knows what crushes it), or is there some other way to credit, even to justify, knowingness?

The achievement of even this degree of indeterminacy turns rhetoric from a coefficient of power, which makes us victims also when we think we participate, to an imaginative or hermeneutic instrument of the pressured, time-haunted mind. Genuine rhetorical questions are therefore antirhetorical. Their "open-endedness, a refusal to speak the unspeakable, solve the unsolvable, resolve the unresolvable,"[4] discloses a freedom of thought that was in doubt.

Even a question that seems conventionally rhetorical, like Yeats's famous "And what rough beast, its hour come round at last, / Slouches toward Bethlehem to be born?" solicits the reader, appeals to his freedom, albeit in the context of apocalypse and *force majeure.* The reader can keep the question open or try to close it. Closing it, however, is not so easy. One can accept the figure to the point of identifying the "rough beast" as Anti-Christ, for example. One is unlikely, however, to give the figure so particular a reading that (1) an absolute identification of the beast is insisted on, despite the fact that the poet withholds its name, and (2) that the apocalyptic perspective is accepted, and the "hour come round at last" is said to be ours—an ending that can no longer be deferred by keeping the question a question. Should the reader claim he must credit the figure, and attribute to Yeats what Yeats, at least, believes (is it not the interpreter's task to follow or reconstruct an author's intention?) one must warn him

4. Barbara H. Smith, *Poetic Closure,* p. 250. For another discussion of the rhetorical question, see Paul de Man, *Allegories of Reading,* chap. 1.

that he may be attributing to Yeats what belongs to someone else, perhaps to the late and maddened Nietzsche.

To keep a poem in mind is to keep it there, not to resolve it into available meanings. This suspensive discourse is criticism, and it can be distinguished from the propaedeutics of scholarly interpretation as well as from the positivity of applied teacherly interpretation. The reader's "willing suspension of disbelief" is really a suspension of accommodating and allegorical meanings, the sort that would comfort a seduced yet disbelieving mind. What many consider "figurative" reading is but a way of avoiding the pressure of fiction on the mind, while a nonallegorical reading can insist on the plain presumption of the text. Thus, though I recognize the genre of "Leda and the Swan" as a *transposition d'art* or a vignette from Yeats's *légende des siècles,* I must refuse to let that divert me from questions about the authority of its author, the literalness of his claim, the mimetic texture of his vision. The seduction of understanding through a fiction should provoke something more active than bemusement or suspended disbelief: it should provoke me to break, however provisionally, the very frame of meaning I bring to the text. Perhaps "bracket" in Husserl's sense of the *epoche* would be better than "break" to describe this suspension of anticipatory ideas or theories (*Ideas,* pars. 30–33), for nothing is really broken, but rather freed for contemplation, analysis, and play.

The procedure seems peculiarly modern, though the *epoche* is a notion that goes back to the Sceptics, and Coleridge finely characterized Cartesian doubt (Husserl's starting point) as a "self-determined indetermination." It is interesting to think of the procedure, at least in the modern period, as a way of undoing a Classicism it still honors, or a way of depicting the attraction of a type of personality that maintains its demeanor despite a heightened or contradictory consciousness that threatens unity of being. "For the reflective individuality," Kierkegaard remarks, "every natural determination is a task,[5] and through and out of the dialectic of life emerges the clarified individuality as the per-

5. Cf. Hegel on the "beautiful soul" and the "blemish of determinateness," *Phenomenology,* pp. 632 ff. I quote from Kierkegaard's *The Concept of Irony* (1841), in the translation of Lee M. Capel.

sonality which at every moment triumphs and struggles still. Reflective individuality never attains the repose pervading beautiful individuality. . . . The harmonious unity of beautiful individuality is disturbed by irony. . . ." Yet irony itself, as in Socrates, can act as an *epoche* ("ataraxia") elevating itself beyond this disturbance, creating in effect a new Classicism.

This reconstituted Classicism which goes beyond the Neoclassicism of a previous era—though remaining indebted to it—is the equivalent in the art of the modern period of suspensive critical thought: *its* deconstruction of figures or forms of speech, of ideas with a crude yet actual power over how we think and act, of rhetoric as Yeats understood it. It is something that happens paradigmatically in the prose of a Gertrude Stein or a Robert Walser, in the way Picasso uses Mediterranean clichés, in the way Cubist and Modernist artists quote or abstract painterly motifs —the Nude, the Eiffel Tower, landscapes, any conventional subject or sign. The reduction of meaning in all these does not escape meaning; but what emerges, as also in Proust, are forms with elementary virtue, forms not "essential" but rather "essential-and-aesthetic," "essential surfaces." ("Make gay the hallucinations in surfaces," Wallace Stevens says.) As such, they cannot be given metaphysical grounding or more than fictive status. To attempt to ground them is, as Nietzsche knew, to founder ("zu Grunde gehen"). It leads to a Dionysian aesthetics, to the edge of a depersonalized and presumably transfigured state, that love-death haunting a post-Nietzschean, post-Wagnerian era.

Valéry saw what this "classical" reduction of meaning, or purified rhetoric, involved. His Narcissus is the very type of the artist-figure who desires to convert "aesthetic reflection" into reality, who wishes to incarnate it, found it in the empirically findable. "Que tu brilles enfin, terme pure de ma course!" That classic alexandrine resonates with a wealth of meanings: the line could be accommodated by the Narcissus myth and describe the haunting *imago*; the pun, hardly serious, on "terme" ("therme") and the nicer double-entendre of "terme pure" as "pure speech-term" and "pure end-term" evokes the poet's own quest for a purification of language. Yet all these readings are sustained by what is phenomenal without being an "image"; that is, derived from a source localized enough to be called an originating experience. If there is an "image," it is simply that of a bright point. Bright water, perhaps, on the horizon, like the Mediterranean Sea recollected:

> Ask yourself how a philosophical notion is born. As soon as I try to respond to this question, I am immediately led in spirit to the shore of a marvelously bright sea. There are reunited the sensory ingredients, the elements (or alimentary substances) of that state of soul in which the most abstract thought and the most comprehensive questions germinate: elements of light and breadth, of leisure and rhythm, of transparency and depth. . . . [Valéry, "Inspirations méditerranéennes"]

A return to the ocean or origin is a theme included in precluded form. It is a meaning we can posit only with a potential or reduced affect. This formal reduction of a reflection on origins is what gives the power of abstract art to the Narcissus fragment. Origin is not only refigured as end, that is, rhetorically reversed, but what image of origin might arise is here determined by, rather than determining, a verse-line that sustains itself, that has the fugacious stability of an extended point. The shining "term" is, in fact, like a vanishing point that predetermines formal space and allows a construction.[6]

Valéry's deconstructed point—indeed his entire style of writing—exemplifies and extends a precept in Verlaine's *Art Poétique*: "Fuis . . . la Pointe assassine." Boileau had already complained about the importation of the pointed style from Spain and Italy and its expansion to all occasions and genres. The point referred to by Verlaine is at once the assassin's poignard, the wounding witticism, and the epigrammatic *pointe* characterizing especially the sonnet. That form was being killed off by the conventional expectation that its ending should climax in a high point, an elevated or clenching closure. Valéry not only decenters this expectation, allowing each verse to produce its own *luisant,* but he frees "point" from any one representational idea: it becomes, as in geometry, the point-zero of constructivist thinking. Yeats also

6. Cf. my essay "Valéry's Fable of the Bee" in *The Fate of Reading*; also Anselm Haverkamp's important analysis of the concept of second immediacy in contemporary philosophies of art: "Valéry in zweiter Lektüre," *Poetik und Hermeneutik,* vol. 9 (1980).

draws back from "pointing" his sonnet and substitutes an open-ended question for a painterly and fixating idea. The "terme pure" remains indeterminate: the desired figure or face does not appear as a representation.

I am not sure why there has come to be less tolerance in Anglo-American circles for what Henry James, somewhat too jolly about it, called the "blest good stuff, sitting up, in its myriad forms, so touchingly responsive to new care of any sort whatever," which marked his rereading, and somehow inevitable rewriting, of the novels. (See his "Prefaces," especially that to *The Golden Bowl.*) Perhaps this relative nontolerance is due to James himself, to our having so much of him. No one has spoken more articulately of the commentary process, as it revises itself, of the "rate at which new readings, new conductors of sense interposed," and of the career of supersessive terms: "the history . . . of the growth of the immense array of terms, perceptional and expressional, that . . . in sentence, passage and page, simply looked over the heads of the standing terms."

James is a split and complicated case: on the one hand he believes (it is part of that strange jolliness, or of his capacity to "enjoy a sense of the absolute in . . . easy conditions") that a final, definitive revision will emerge, that there is a "flower" (if only a flower of speech) not absent from all bouquets.

> The term that superlatively, that finally "renders," is a flower that blooms by a beautiful law of its own (the fiftieth part of a second often so sufficing it) in the very heart of the gathered sheaf; it is *there* already, at any moment, almost before one can either miss or suspect it—so that in short we shall never guess, I think, the working secret of the revisionist for whom its colour and scent stir the air but as immediately to be assimilated." [Preface to *The Golden Bowl*]

On the other hand, James is tantalized, even outraged, by the image of revisionists who aren't such, who limit their responsibilities to the terms that come, who "lie down beside their work even as the lion beside the lamb." James, like Mallarmé, knows the terror or anguish that revision inspires, when the text becomes, once more, a garden of forking paths. What James calls "the process and the effect of representation—my irrepressible ideal," obliges him to quest for a final rendering, a determinate term, fugitive and superlative at the same time.

"Indeterminacy" is not a word to insist on. "Irony," if its history were kept in mind, would be preferable; when it was used by the New Critics it raised smaller fears. That may have been because they separated irony from a philosophical context that can be made to include, as in Kierkegaard's *The Concept of Irony,* the doubting of appearances, of phenomena, from Socrates on. This context includes the history of skepticism as well as of the overcoming of skepticism. Cleanth Brooks, among the New Critics, saw that irony had a similarity to paradox, that is, to statements or a type of statement that went against (*para*) established belief or received opinion (*doxa*); and he rescued it from being a simple and determinate figure of speech. It was presented as an open or tacit but always constant feature of works of art that a critic could formalize as a source of their value. Irony itself became, paradoxically, a value ascribed to art, and the analyses that showed this, particularly in *The Well-Wrought Urn,* were so tactful that one could not suspect them of being ironical. The urn lost its death-related character, and criticism gained a new and businesslike stability.

So irony's "practicality" was assured, and it became domesticated in literary studies. But its strange, featureless, even daimonic flexibility (able to assume any shape) was reduced to the status of serviceable Elf or Kobalt, the kind that helps poor shoemakers cobble shoes as long as no one tries to catch spirit in the act. The literary critic, indeed, was advised to be precisely that: a practical person who should not look beyond his last. Everything that was subversive or exalting, indeterminacy of meaning, or infinite negativity, or disruptive subjectivity, was embargoed. The embargo leaked, of course; also because literary-historical studies kept reintroducing the importance of irony as a larger theme, a more heroic and even pathetic—or counterpathetic—virtue, with religious and philosophical ramifications.

Kierkegaard distinguishes between doubt and irony on the basis that the doubting subject constantly seeks to penetrate an object that eludes him, while with irony the subject is always seeking to get free of an object that never acquires reality for him. "With doubt the subject is witness to a war of conquest in which every phenomenon is destroyed, because the essence always resides behind the phenomenon. But with irony the subject constantly retires from the field and proceeds to talk every phenomenon out of its reality in order to save himself, that is, in order to preserve himself in his negative independence of everything" ("For Orientation," in *The Concept of Irony*). Kierkegaard also distinguishes between the types of "nothingness" that ensue from doubt, irony, and mysticism. This scrupulous kind of reflection is left behind when the contemporary practical critic dismisses hermeneutic or philosophical thought, alleging that it empties literature of its human reality. As indeterminacy raises the specter of aestheticism a mock panic breaks out among the very people who are themselves emptying criticism by insisting on its purely grammatical or auxiliary function. The aesthetic flaw is really theirs, that of the "saints" who humbly mystify literature or art and turn away from all other knowledge.

Yet that there is a problem becomes obvious when scholars confront the issue of the Bible or sacred writing. What kind of *commitment* is it, to take the Bible as literature? Religious scholars may *doubt* the biblical text, but only in Kierkegaard's sense: its ultimate significance or reality-reference may elude them, but they continue to believe it is there. Adopting a literary approach, however, does not bring with it that necessary belief, nor a clear set of interpretive constraints, so that the text may indeed be nothing more than an object for study, or an object for a subject who pursues a self-satisfying but vain and virtuoso labor. The same consideration holds for secular literature as it raises ultimate issues. For here too it may be claimed that the critic, in his freedom, cannot go further than the Socrates of the *Apology* as Kierkegaard envisages him. The uncertainty of finding a correct explanation of death does not make Socrates uneasy; on the contrary, "this playing with life, this vertigo, inasmuch as death now appears as infinitely significant, now as utter nothingness, is just what pleases him."

It is therefore no accident that, in the present atmosphere, Leslie Brisman's *Milton's Poetry of Choice* should try to get beyond what Kierkegaard, also in *The Concept of Irony,* calls the

Socratic or syllogistic *aut-aut*. Brisman examines the "or . . . or" in Milton as a stylistic feature raising the problem of choice through textual but also spiritual *revision*. The problem is precisely that of going from the "or . . . or" taken conjunctively to the disjunctive Kierkegaardian realm of ethical decision, the "either/or." Brisman uses Kierkegaard explicitly, but the issue is not mediated by any single authority or tradition. Literary study conjures up at present a speculative and ethically unserious kind of inquiry—if ethical activity is associated with deliberation rather than speculation, with using the mind to make practical and binding choices. Yet it is useful to remember Alfred Kazin's remark: "The Marxists thought of literature as a military weapon in a planetary war, but ultimately treated it as a game. The Formalists gave their textual analyses the character of a game, but they were always playing for higher stakes than most people knew" (*On Native Grounds,* chap. 14).

Hegel considered Friedrich Schlegel a playboy philosopher because of his emphasis on irony in every realm of life; Kierkegaard considered Hegel's dialectic as not existential enough, and so comparably negative or prematurely universalizing in its effect on ethics. Kierkegaard valued the depth of Romantic irony and the seduction of "the aesthetic"—but he categorized the latter as an inadequate and ultimately unserious mode of dealing with either mortal anguish or immortal thoughts. The importance of Kierkegaard to philosophical thinkers in the twentieth century is related to his critique of Hegel's dialectic as an "aesthetic" maneuver, one that universalizes falsely, deprives existence of its "particularity" (a term that becomes important when aesthetics, as in Lukács, tries to overcome aestheticism), and so removes philosophy from the sphere of religious and social action. The relation of thought to *praxis* becomes, in one way or another, the crucial problem. The difference in traditions—empiricism in Richards and the British critics; Hegelianism or Marxism in Lukács, Adorno, Sartre, and Ortega; hermeneutics or Freud or Heidegger (or all of these) in Gadamer, Ricoeur, and certain American critics—does not affect this common aim of purging thought of aestheticism or similar evasions.

One need only open the first major books of Benjamin and

Adorno, respectively, to recognize this common aim. Benjamin's "Epistemo-Critical Prologue" to *The Origins of German Tragic Drama* (1927, though conceived ten years earlier) emphasizes the disparity between philosophy and doctrine, a disparity that can only be overcome through the very *form* of philosophy. "In its finished form philosophy will, it is true, assume the quality of doctrine, but it does not lie within the power of mere thought to confer such a form." Where, then, does that authoritative form come from? The fact that there must be representation, and that this representation is verbal ("the area of truth toward which language is directed"), leads Benjamin into an involved and fascinating series of Platonic, Kantian, Kabbalistic (name-mysticism) reflections. These include the formulation of a concept of *prose form* or *philosophical style,* which is clearly meant to save philosophy from the imputation of being on the side of poetry rather than truth—the charge that caused Plato to banish the poets from his Republic. Benjamin, turning Plato against Plato, defines philosophical style as "the art of interruption in contrast to the chain of deduction; the tenacity of the essay in contrast to the single gesture of the fragment; the repetition of themes in contrast to shallow universalism; the fulness of concentrated positivity in contrast to the negation of polemics." And he goes through Plato beyond Plato when he writes: "It is the task of the philosopher to restore, by representation, the primacy of the symbolic character of the word, in which the idea is given self-consciousness, and that is the opposite of all outwardly-directed communication. Since philosophy may not presume to speak in the tones of revelation, this can only be achieved by recalling in memory the primordial form of perception. Platonic anamnesis is, perhaps, not far removed from this kind of remembering; except that here it is not a question of the actualization of images in visual terms; but rather, in philosophical contemplation, the idea is released from the heart of reality as the word, reclaiming its name-giving rights. Ultimately, however, this is not the attitude of Plato but the attitude of Adam. . . ."

As for Adorno, his "Habilitationsschrift," published in 1933 as *Kierkegaard: The Construction of the Aesthetic,* begins so revealingly that I can dispense with further commentary:

> If one insists on understanding the writings of philosophers as poetry [*Dichtungen*] then one has missed out on their truth-content. The law of form in philosophy demands the interpretation of reality in agreement with the way concepts relate. Neither a proclaiming of the subjectivity of the thinker, nor the pure closure of a structure in itself, may decide its character as philosophy but only the following: whether reality has entered the concepts and identifies itself through them and substantiates them perspicuously.[7]

The importance of being earnest takes a somewhat different form today than in the 1920s and 1930s. But it still contains a perplexed meditation on the relation of philosophy and poetry, truth and method, ideas and representations. Nothing might seem nearer to the life we lead than the language we speak; and philosophical thinking has become primarily a thinking about language. But one feels trapped in language that is about language, or the sense that one cannot emerge from a verbal universe—not even into an Adamic essentialism of the Name. Nor has the spread of semiliteracy helped. Every statement, idiom, or idiolect has now its rights; and this situation of *surnomie,* where there are too many styles, terms, interpretations, leads to a low-grade *anomie* that is expressed in TV sitcom, its endless and insipid comedy of errors, or in the excessive theatricality of novels peopled by caricatures rather than characters, or in the witty and deliberate charlatanism of advertisements in a consumerist culture.

There is no presence; there is only representation and, worse, representations. The crisis focuses on that, not on language as such. It is a crisis of *evidentiality.* How do we save phenomena that cannot save themselves? Our mediating role is bound to be suspect, if truth is thought of as self-evidencing, as "the death of intention" (Benjamin). Yet we must think of it *also* as that. The

7. I can render Adorno's difficult German only approximately. The original runs: "Wann immer man die Schriften von Philosophen als Dichtungen zu begreifen trachtet, hat man ihren Wahrheitsgehalt verfehlt. Das Formgesetz der Philosophie fordert die Interpretation des Wirklichen im stimmigen Zusammenhang der Begriffe. Weder die Kundgabe der Subjektivität des Denkenden noch die pure Geschlossenheit des Gebildes in sich selber entscheiden über dessen Charakter als Philosophie, sondern erst: ob Wirkliches in die Begriffe einging, in ihnen sich ausweist und sie einsichtig begründet."

reflective person has to avoid being a mere reflex of others; a bundle of inherited intentions, a mediated rather than mediating will. The paradox is clear enough.

This is no new crisis; it is the old one; but a shift has indeed occurred. We ask not only what truth may be, in distinction from beauty or opinion or positive knowledge. We ask about the truth of evidence in a world where there are only representations; and about the tension between language and representation. What authority do texts enjoy? Why do we continue to rely on them? Are we investing them with the missing "ocular proof," or do they become documents of the resistance in us to the conversion of representation into presence?

The oldest detective story keeps being reenacted. On every side there is a self-incriminating lust for evidence. Hermeneutics is an art that grows out of perplexity, out of finding an enigma where we expected a kerygma. Evidence fails or is disabled, and unusual or ungovernable types of interpretation come into play. Science fiction too creates worlds in which the forces are unknown, and all appearances and testimonies risk being false.

No wonder some are scared witless by a mode of thinking that seems to offer no decidability, no resolution. Yet the perplexity that art arouses in careful readers and viewers is hardly licentious. It is the reality; it is only as strange as truth. It recalls the artificial nature or purely conventional status of formal arguments or proofs; the fact that human agreements remain conveniences with the force of law, metaphors with the force of institutions, opinions with the force of dogma. It recalls the prevalence of propaganda, both in open societies that depend on conversation, jawboning, advertising, bargaining, and in controlled societies that can become sinister and inquisitorial, adding to their torture chamber the subtlest brainwashing and conditioning devices without giving up the brazen and reiterated lie. Can any hermeneutics of indeterminacy, any irony however deeply practiced and nurtured by aesthetic experience, withstand either society while they are still distinguishable?

A Short History of Practical Criticism

What at present preoccupies scholars and students in the literary humanities is clear: the lack of interaction between their profession and the mainstream of society. Though this is a recurrent problem, I. A. Richards had thought to find a secure place for literary studies by denying the existence of a "phantom aesthetic state" and basing the critic's work on two pillars. "The two pillars upon which a theory of criticism must rest are an account of value and an account of communication" (*Principles of Literary Criticism,* 1924). Having established these principles, an eminently "practical criticism" became possible; the book *Practical Criticism* appeared some fifty years ago, in 1929; and the term, in its modesty and common sense, helped to assure the success of literary techniques of close reading.

Although in Empson's *Seven Types of Ambiguity* (1930) this effort at close and discriminating reading already showed a quasi-theological strain, and signaled trouble ahead for those who wished to "bound the infinite" of interpretive studies, certain developments of the 1930s led to an institutionalization of the "practical" approach to literature, which came to be known as the New Criticism. First, the political and economic unrest of that time made it important to protect the study of art from imperious demands of an ideological nature, emanating from politics, but also from positive philosophy and science; then, a move toward mass education, speeding up significantly after World War II, meant that teachers could not rely as much on the patience or privileged background of their students. Teachers had to educate as well as initiate; and new textbooks were developed to give students, more quickly than proved possible, a modest mastery of the cultural goods.

The expansion of literary studies within an academic framework meant that English took its place beside history and the "moral sciences" as a school to train the judgment. *Practical Criticism* was subtitled *A Study of Literary Judgment,* and literary judgment was deemed to be the best or most liberal preparation for other kinds of judgment in the practical world. This attitude was especially prevalent at Cambridge University, where F. R. Leavis's emphasis on the greatness of the native tradition, of vernacular literature, sought to replace the mystique still surrounding the Classics. A countermystique soon arose, with Leavis at its center: resisting the growing culture industry, the mindless media, the trend to uniformity, a new and militant clerisy tried to prevent the dulling of judgment and further corruption of society by modern techniques of management and rationalization.

In America a stronger process of democratization (among other factors) prevented a new mystique from being formed, although a few courses at Amherst, Columbia, Harvard, and Yale influenced deeply the minds of teachers who came into their own in the late 1950s and early 1960s. Sir Thomas Browne admired the Heathen who, deprived of Revelation, "sucked divinity" from nature; and so the American student was taught to extract meanings from literary texts independently of any higher or abstruse theory concerning language, art, and society. The student was, in fact, admonished to respect the mystery of those texts—even if that word was not used, but rather their "autonomy," "mode of existence," or "limits"—really the student's own limits. Literature was *not* politics, *not* religion, *not* philosophy, *not* science, *not* rhetoric, etc. These were real but extrinsic factors; instead an intrinsic approach to the mode of existence of the literary work of art had to be found (see René Wellek and Austin Warren, *Theory of Literature,* 1949). Yet no theorist of the time was able to define the differentiating "nothing."

That "nothing" has plagued us ever since. It acted as an unacknowledged theological restraint. The end of literary studies was not knowledge but rather a state of secular grace. That "nothing" also enforced the scientific notion that if literature was to be studied seriously it would have to be delimited as a department or field. Specialization, on the one hand, and a rigorous prohibition on the other (though couched as a principle of decorum), impeded the speculative contamination of art with anything else and led to an emptying out of the literary-critical enterprise. In the 1970s we find a growing awareness that "practical criticism" may have failed, both vis-à-vis society at large and, more peculiarly, within the academy.

We no longer see what is "practical" about practical criticism, except that as a reading technique it could help to stem a renewed tide of illiteracy. But as such it is already in competition with other, patently scientific techniques. A new "philosophy of composition," for example, is already subsuming Richards's "theory of criticism" and its two pillars of evaluation and communication. Leavis had relied on English as a native yet cultured language with its own long-nurtured and organic virtues: by a natural contagion the practiced reader of the great vernacular works would learn how to write and think a living English. But in America today English is increasingly subject to community standards, if not community control. And where it is most vital it escapes most standards, because new vernaculars are emerging, creole fashion. Practical criticism is relatively powerless in the face of these developments: it is a desperate search for reading and writing techniques that continue the study of grammar by other means. A gap opens up between advanced studies, which now seem quite impractical, and everyday classroom teaching, which is more elementary and disputatious than ever.

In this situation our self-doubt comes to the fore, even a tendency to self-blame. This alienation, this lack of effective interaction with society is, we think, our own fault: we have not done enough. Instead of deepening the idea of interpretation we turn against it. At best a new science, whether structuralism or semiology, is called upon to curb the adventurism or subjectivism of the reader; and it joins forces with those who denounce multiplying interpretations, seeing them as an economic need of the publishing professor rather than as an authentic literary and intellectual task. At worst, and spurred by retroactive idealization, the New Criticism is called upon as modest, practical, good enough; and set against the cerebration now going on, its philosophic pretensions, its conceptual armory and galloping jargon. Is not the new *theoretical* criticism destroying what might be saved of the *practical* side of our discipline?

To accept this line of thought is to inflict an additional wound on ourselves. We would be asking "the wild, living intellect" (Cardinal Newman) not merely to check itself but also to accept other social forces that continue unchecked. We would take it for granted that the other professions—law, business, science, social science—have so imperative or intimate a relation to the commonweal that they should continue to grow, or at least not hold themselves back. But if we have anything to blame it is not the life of the mind, or the striving of those in literary studies who are trying out new perspectives or saving the older ones—who are trying to understand philosophy (European or American) or thinking about exegetical traditions prior to science and as persistent as religion itself. If we must blame ourselves it should be for holding too narrow a conception of what is practical.

For we have not been able to persuade ourselves—and therefore whom can we persuade in society at large?—that what we are professing is as essential to society's well-being as law or business or the performing arts. Our best and most deserving publicist is Northrop Frye. His system is less a system than an influencing machine: an evangelical battery in an escalating mental war. But, in general, all our touted skill in rhetoric consumes itself in the polemic of critic with critic and school with school. That can be fun, and may sharpen some issues; yet now is also the time to examine the failure of practical criticism in terms of our narrowed conception of what is practical in the humanities and beyond them. Practical criticism never grew up.

I am so unused to this open kind of rhetoric that having written the above words I wish to cross them out. For I belong to the most liberal yet most reclusive of professions, one that has no real impact on society[1] except through undergraduate education. My rhetoric is devoted to thinking and writing about rhetoric. So are my interpretive skills. In short, the humanists find no way to graduate from their teaching function, which seems crafted to keep them in the academy. What strife or business there is does not engage a social group larger than school administrators or colleagues. Since the academy is, despite everything, a good place, one that protects the scholar's freedom to work on any topic that does not make him rich, we accept the trade-off that substitutes leisure for influence, and shape our lives accordingly.

Yet other academic disciplines open more effectively onto the world from which they also claim some protection. The political scientist, the social scientist, the social economist, the law professor, the scientist or medical expert are amphibious and live both within and beyond the academy. Entry and exit are via revolving doors. It is perfectly true that this leads to conflicts of interest and poses the problem of pure versus applied research. The isolation of the humanist may be a blessing in disguise. Yet there are signs at present that humanists, because of that isolation, have lost their currency, which is about all that was left after they had lost their authority. Unless we find some doors, revolving or not, that lead from the humanities into society, and unless some of our graduates go into other walks of life than teaching, or remain in touch with us even though they are in the nonacademic professions, the humanities are bound to become service departments to other divisions of the academy with more obvious and effective social outlets.

English, the largest enterprise in the humanities with the exception of history, is especially vulnerable to social discontent and administrative obtuseness. This is because English has a clear practical aspect which we have narrowed instead of expanded. For *English* is an umbrella word that connotes literacy; and the dif-

1. As Allen Tate remarked in "The Man of Letters in the Modern World" (1952), reprinted in *Collected Essays*: "Withdrawal has become the social convention of the literary man." But he justifies this withdrawal insofar as it rejects "the secularism of the swarm." I am in sympathy with those who see art and the academy as preserving individual judgment in a mass culture, but not with those who reject the experiment of universal education or the symbiosis of art and the environing culture.

ficulty of promoting literacy in the brave new world of mass education has finally reached the national consciousness. Why can't Johnny write? Why can't Sally read? What good is the B.A. or B.S. if the relation of writing skills to the student's intelligence is like the improvised strumming of a guitar? What are all those English professors doing?

The enormous courage implied by mass education is forgotten, and only the guilt of failure remains. The study of English bears the brunt of every change in educational policy as it relates to a perceived national purpose. After World War II the rage was all for the oral method of teaching languages, and "rhetoric"—as in the many rhetoric, communication, and speech courses then established—meant the ability to present onself effectively by the pronounced word. Every American was potentially his country's ambassador abroad; and within America too the hope was to have young people speak and enunciate articulately as a way of priming their eventual total literacy. It was, let us admit, a crash program: it did not underestimate, it simply ran scared of the problem of writing, and today we are left with the deficit of that older program, as well as with an accrued social mission.

The acquisition of literacy is not simply a "practical" matter that can be solved by the introduction of better techniques. There is no acquisition more motivated and sensitized by the social milieu. A curious accent or a peculiar idiom may stigmatize, *or* become a badge of militancy. "You taught me language," says Caliban to Prospero, "and my profit on it is, I know how to curse." The study of English, as of every language and literature, intertwines with the process of socialization; any disturbance in the one will lead to a disturbance in the other.[2]

Part of the disturbance, at present, is a growing illiteracy in

2. There is a glaring lack of competent sociological studies of literature. The Frankfurt School has made a difference, but John Gross's observation in *The Rise and Fall of the Man of Letters* that "if one thinks of the impact which Marxist ideas have had on modern English historical writing, it is odd that their influence on literary criticism should have been so negligible" remains valid. Since, as Alfred Kazin stated in *On Native Grounds*, "From Emerson and Thoreau to Mencken and [Van Wyck] Brooks, criticism had been the great American lay philosophy, the intellectual carryall . . . the secret intermediary between literature and society in America," a curious vacuum has been created, bounded by journalism on the one side and social science on the other.

the other professions. They seem to want to leave English to English departments. It is not possible, however, to specialize reading and writing by assigning them to the literary humanities. Moreover, if the latter were forced to confine their practice to teaching remedial courses in English and elementary courses in the foreign languages, the motivation that continuity and progress in a discipline bestow would be lost. As the teaching of science feeds on the higher reaches of the discipline, so it is with the study of literature. But the temptation of administrators today is to shift the resources of literature departments from advanced to basic courses: to make English wholly a service department remedying the growing or perceived illiteracy in the country and in the other professions. I agree that there is a job to be done, but let the professors of economics and history and politics and (why not) science pitch in. It is their plight too; it is they who often are not *practicing* English.

As I have said, English, when it gets beyond spelling and grammar, is not a technique but a cultural acquisition of great complexity: a literature as well as a basic literacy. Anyone who writes or produces a literate statement contributes to the way we think. Freud's *The Interpretation of Dreams* aims to found a science of mind; but whether or not it is successful in this aim it has become a book that is or should be read, and so is part of the literary humanities, subject to our methods of critique and interpretation. The Bible may be sacred, the word of God that has founded many religions, yet it too is part of the secular and even the unbelieving mind, subject to critical and interpretive thinking based on what we know of the literary humanities.

Of course, we too are at fault. Our own purity has confined us. The mysterious quiddity, the "je ne sais quoi" that separated our field of study from others into which language enters crucially, reduced us to being either negative theologians or pompously modest keepers of "the words of the tribe," their purity and correctness. We gave up one province after the other, especially to the social scientists; and then stood back to mock them, impotently, for writing influential books based (in our view) on a couple of clever and well-marketed ideas, formulations that might have served us for a witty digression or a sustained metaphor.

What can we expect from society once we have shrunk ourselves, like Blake's "Human Abstract"; once we have become hired grammarians or men and women whose main satisfaction is to correct (is that what was meant by judgment or evaluative criticism?) the way others write? Or who do not believe in advanced studies unless they produce *realia*: better editions of the text with better notes? I do not object to historical research; indeed, it needs at present more support than a short-sighted academic market is providing, a market that favors the latest or most enthusiastic form of packaging knowledge. I object to a state of affairs in which two of the largest departments in the academy, History and English, have barely any contact with each other; and where within literature departments the scholar who defines himself as a historian must labor away, resentful and lonely, though in hope of ultimate vindication.

When I say we have given up too much, I include history. History does not exist uninterpreted. Whether the scholar-critic conceives his task as clearing away the distortion of words in order to get to things themselves, or whether he conceives it as revealing the mediational or metahistorical element that cannot be cleared away—and in so doing challenges the positivistic striving for historical truth—style cannot be avoided, and makes every historical statement, and not only literary-historical statement, literary. Yet *history* is only one way of naming what we have given up. The humanities, as they divided into special fields, also gave up the study of law and (under somewhat different circumstances) religious texts. The study of letters fell back on "belles lettres" or "literature," as if that were more *natural* than these other *positive* disciplines. Yet can literary critics claim to know enough about interpretation without considering the relation of Vico to Roman law, or of the talmudic rabbis to the strictures of the Code? Or of Philo to the Septuagint? And if that seems too vast for our "practical" curriculum, how can we forget the general truth that for so long a time the interpretive activity developed with a view to or directed against documents considered binding?

I have argued that we have caused our own impotence by allowing the concept of practical criticism to reduce to its lowest social or utilitarian value. I have also suggested several reasons for this strange abdication from an already modest, if, in terms of an expanding student body, overburdened function. We have succumbed to our innate purity perplex; and we have been unable to formulate an effective defense of our profession. We have weakened ourselves intellectually and structurally. Only history, in the humanities, has been able to maintain some of its credibility in the national consciousness by making a compact with the social sciences. Or, when a medical, scientific, or business group tries to think about ethics, they invite a philosopher in, to salve their conscience and spice the proceedings. But the English professor holds no consultancies unless it be to inspect other English departments or advise the filming of a classic. Our graduates do not go into public walks of life and so cannot represent us there. They go back into the teaching profession.

Yet I am aware of a weakness in what I have argued—however correct my general perspective may be. For one's mood changes when the question is posed, What can be done? The economic realities seem overwhelming. To ask the literary humanities to take back their own, to reenter an abdicated sphere, is not specific enough and may be mind-bogglingly unrealistic.

For very few of the other professions now bother with us, and there is nothing to constrain them to do so. A vast superstructure supports their claim that they are useful and in the mainstream. More business leaders, lawyers, doctors, scientists—even actors, musicians, and directors—find gainful employment, despite anxieties that this too will end. But teachers, especially in the humanities, are not needed according to the gospel of the market. Nobody knows why that is so: why the profession that has more to do than any other with the life or death of literacy in this country is being economically depressed.

Is it our image? An image we ourselves have helped to project? Anti-intellectualism (including our own) affects all advanced teaching. Yet the other professions can often counter it by effective participation in public affairs. Those, however, who devote themselves fully to teaching and academic research are stuck with the adage that teaching is different from doing. The real school, runs the prejudice, is life itself.

If that is so, then why we have teachers at all becomes a mystery. To keep the kids off the streets, for a while? To have someone other than beleaguered parents struggle with such youthful energy, until the large children can take on life directly? To make some learning stick, so that, by a phenomenon of crystallization similar to falling in love, the young person's interest suddenly focuses? He is smitten by a lecture on the Third World or Egyptian mortuary treasures or Fission or the Magic of Numbers. He becomes absorbed in an issue of the *National Geographic* or an article in the *World Book*. From that time on—till he falls out of love—he is changed: his imagination has found a provisional home away from home, exotic, explorable, yet sage.

It is not different in Higher Education. Parents find it comforting to know where the kids are. And, presumably, they are learning something, though not doing anything in particular. Except for an occasional demonstration or protest march, they remain off the streets. The professor makes demands, but they are less harsh than ever: the students are bound to graduate, and then, having progressed beyond the demonic energy of adolescence, well prepared by their long moratorium, even eager for delayed responsibilities, they enter what is called Real Life.

Teachers, thus, are high-class servants of the family, even when paid by the state. Their own intellectual life, even their profession as such, is respected only insofar as it can make a tangible contribution to the persons they graduate. Besides, if they are too active in the mature business of the nation, they might be worse as teachers, they might teach their own politics or engage in advocacy. What holds for teachers holds more for those who teach them. Despite the number of students we teach, the modest remuneration, and a routine that can seriously hamper self-development, scholars in the humanities are seen as relatively unproductive. They are treated, I have suggested, as if they were advanced kindergartners; their activity cannot compete with lawyering, management, or the medical sciences. Even should another Dewey arise to show that art and those who open and broaden our access to it are essential to the well-being of society, to its quality of life, it is doubtful that the greater world would change its priorities. The first move must therefore come from the humanists themselves.

This move may seem like a self-betrayal, or at least a sacrifice. As the academy grows more complex internally, more in need of business management and governance, specialists are imported to do this task. But if the faculty itself could assume the task and pick up enough expertise—if the faculty, including the humanists, become the managers and provide what consultants or specialists may be necessary, then the image of the sheltered professor who is book-wise but not worldly-wise (Mr. Chips) will change, as real contact between the professional classes becomes the norm rather than the exception.

Also, to encourage contact between the professions, the concept of liberal education should be carried upward, into the graduate and professional schools. Medical students should be asked to take an advanced course in literary (or art) interpretation; so should students of law. Those in literature would do well to have a seminar with a clinical psychiatrist, or a professor of law dealing with legal interpretation. A single course may seem like a palliative. Very well: can we devise joint programs without jeopardizing the standing of the candidate? Is it so unthinkable to have a degree in English and in Law, Religious Studies, or Business? Could the universities, with the help of the foundations, establish continuing-education supplements in these fields? A literature student might then take a business or law degree either through a specially coordinated graduate school program or through a supplemental adult education program. Supporting these curricular activities but emphasizing the faculty as a group with its own intellectual life, small research centers encouraging faculty seminars should be established. These programs should be drawn up with the full knowledge and advice of the professional community outside the university.

As you carry liberal education up into graduate and professional schools, you would probably succeed, at the same time, in strengthening it at the undergraduate level, where it is faltering. For it is getting harder to promote a humanities discipline, English especially, as a preprofessional major. It does not seem to have the rigor found in math or biology or chemistry.[3] The reason

3. Even when there is a tough humanities major, preprofessional students will tend to shun it, as Lewis Thomas points out in a stinging attack on the premedical curriculum (see "Notes of a Biology-Watcher").

does not lie in the character of the major itself, but is the result of English being seriously weakened at the advanced level by our antipathy to theory and by having to absorb basic courses serving all majors. As interest in a graduate type of liberal education program grows, professors from the professional schools or other divisions might be expected to devise interesting undergraduate seminars, perhaps in conjunction with the humanities faculty. Moreover, the students graduating from such programs would prove to be better teachers within a liberal education curriculum, or would enter their professions with an extended appreciation of it. What I am suggesting is already happening in haphazard and wasteful fashion, as when the Ph.D. in history or English, who fails to get a job, enters law school or tries for an M.B.A.[4]

Who will bear the cost of this, in a period of fiscal retrenchment? A great deal of money is presently being channeled into interdisciplinary or cross-disciplinary programs at the research level; a great deal of money too goes into experimental undergraduate programs that die after a few years. What tends to be left out is precisely the area that needs help: graduate programs in the humanities. Not in order to keep or support more students —everyone agrees that curtailment is necessary, and is in fact taking place—but in order to put graduate and professional education on a broader base, and to allow the humanities to play a full rather than a service role in the university and in national affairs.

For practical criticism to grow up, the discipline of literary studies must rejoin the humanities. It must become what it hoped

4. At a time when a leading firm feels obliged to deny a report that it has offered $60,000 for an M.B.A. on first appointment, insisting that the sum in question has not reached $40,000 (see "Letters" in *Business Week*, 29 January 1979), we may safely suggest that it would not be more expensive for the universities to have some of their own professors gain the requisite business expertise. The average salary of professors in top institutions (around $35,000) is clearly less than what some first-year M.B.A.s are earning. Moreover, the present fiscal disarray of many colleges and universities run primarily (or exclusively) by nonhumanist administrators and boards offers no prima facie justification for the prejudice that favors their management capability. The humanities, because more general in character and more discriminating and even suspicious of words (they lead the student to decode hidden or surreptitious meanings, or to look beyond the literal meaning by a historical and methodical reflection) should actually facilitate the transfer of skilled intelligence from one area to another, and produce people with the ability to think about both educational and fiscal development.

it would be: the training, in the fullest sense, of personal judgment, by passing the student through the fires of interpretation and exposing him not only to literature narrowly conceived but also to important texts in philosophy, history, religion, anthropology, and so forth. If we give special attention to fiction and poetry, it is because they are insufficiently examined elsewhere, and not because they are privileged. In exchange we must hope that other departments of knowledge will augment their interest in fiction and poetry, and in interpretive methods developed by us.

This becomes even more important as the future of reading grows more uncertain. Competing media, mixed media, a proliferation of documents, and the usual doubt concerning the value of refined interpretation in the face of catastrophe and political demand make practical criticism appear an academic phenomenon wrongly usurping the whole of literary inquiry. For practical criticism is more of a pedagogical and propaedeutic than mature activity: the mind of the novice is sharpened by way of a direct inspection of the materials, but also acculturated by recalling significant books on which other books have built, or can build. Perhaps this is the right time to return to the original vision that inspired what is now the stubborn basement of literary study in the university.

My argument has been that practical criticism is no longer practical, that it is outflanked, on the one side, by composition theory, and on the other by interpretation theory. Its own theory is limited to a claim that it is an empirical science and that literature is an intensive rather than perverted form of thinking in language. The concept of organic form that it has occasionally espoused is not tenable except as a metaphor of limitation: human consciousness, as it tends toward endless elaboration, endless revision, is attracted to the idea of self-limiting structures, secular or natural ("organic") equivalents to the check imposed on knowledge by religious faith. The general tendency of practical criticism has been to fudge on the role of theory in scientific endeavors and even to occlude it in the literary domain.

However, for Richards, its modern founder, practical criticism was not an end but a means: an empirical provocation for a theory that remained absent. It "is the oddest thing about language," he remarks, ". . . that so few people have ever sat down to reflect systematically about meaning." And: "One would expect that our libraries would be full of works on the theory of interpretation, the diagnosis of linguistic situations, systematic ambiguity and the functions of complex symbols." In point of fact, "there is no other human activity for which theory bears so small a proportion to practice. Even the theory of football has been more thoroughly inquired into" (*Practical Criticism,* "Summary," para. 18). Reading those words fifty years later, it must strike us as ironic that for so much Anglo-American criticism (and despite the interest in Peirce) what Richards saw as a provocation to theory merely confirmed the prejudice against it, and that the initiative passed so completely to Europe that practice there bears too small a proportion to theory.

The resistance to theory in Anglo-American criticism goes together with a resistance to imported ideas, from non-English countries or from other fields of inquiry, the social sciences, in particular. Here and there an exception is made to the code-revealing or convention-clarifying aspects of semiotic and linguistic thought. There are some good reasons underlying the resistance to theory: here I wish to signal only the bad ones.[5] Too many consider philosophical questions impractical—obfuscating, not life-related. This is a misunderstanding of understanding. We live with a false conception of the rift between theory and practice; so the rift keeps growing and is consolidated in discourse. Because of that it is impossible to find in English a work of philosophical criticism as profound as Karl Jaspers' book on Schelling (1955). Sartre's interpretations of Genet and Flaubert may be more controversial, but they also contain a powerful synthesis of philosophical, social, and literary perspectives.

Even when we engage theory, we often do so to delimit it. We claim, for example, that the only function of hermeneutics is to aid close reading in its quest for correct or verifiable meaning. Theory has no standing in itself. Yet the emphasis on correctness

5. For some good reasons, see R. P. Blackmur's critique of I. A. Richards in "A Critic's Job of Work" (1935), which remains the most concise and balanced, and which includes the following judgments: "It is possible that he ought not to be called a literary critic at all. . . . The apparatus is so vast, so labyrinthine, so inclusive—and the amount of actual literary criticism is so small that it seems almost a by-product instead of the central target."

in interpretation, and the elaboration of proofs, is as close to theology as to science.

Practical criticism is just *one* form of exegesis, when the whole history of interpretation is considered. It is so attractive because it *is* exegesis, but also because it is accommodated to what students can manage, given the complexity of art. Accommodation is no simple matter, however. It has a conceptual affinity to the theological doctrine of condescension. Philosophical criticism in the European tradition (Sartre, Heidegger, Ortega, Lukács, Derrida) is far less accommodating. It breaks down, correlatively, the distinction between *Dichter* and *Denker,* between creative and discursive modes of thought. To the practical critic of the Anglo-American persuasion, philosophical criticism is a self-inflated rival of philosophy on the one hand, and of creative writing on the other.

The conflict of practical with philosophical criticism is a real war, which has lasted for more than fifty years and has intensified in the last decade. Practical criticism is constrained by a *neoclassical* decorum, permitting only that "order of discourse" which is conversational, and which excludes heavily laden terms imported from overspecialized or ideological sources.

The danger in this undergraduate or undeveloped form of practical criticism is that it may foreclose the interpretive activity, not only vis-à-vis literary texts but also vis-à-vis the possibility of understanding literary history. Most of us are indeed less comfortable with theory texts, and don't like to think of them as literary. But theory texts are part of the world of texts, not apart from it. We can consign them, of course, to a discrete series, that is, exclude them by a criterion of genre. Yet their existence, and in considerable numbers at present, makes such an exclusion doubtful in terms of the history of criticism and its relation to a history of literature.

If literary theory is becoming a genre, what is it a genre of? Any such calculus would soon be Polonian. It is better to take the standpoint that criticism informed or motivated by theory is part of literary criticism (rather than of philosophy or an unknown science) and that literary criticism is within literature, not outside it. "Literariness" may be an ingredient in any form of writing. Surely the minimal assumption for studying either literary or literary-theoretical texts is that they are part of the process of understanding, of hermeneutic revision, and this process is endless.

All histories of literature deal with texts that are central, authoritative, or whose authority is in dispute. They can evade, but only by subsuming, such legitimating concepts as authority, unity, universality, priority, propriety—which also belong to the history of criticism. Tradition, moreover, is just another word for the *secular canon*: and how that canon is constituted or revises itself has been the subject of fruitful speculation, from T. S. Eliot and E. R. Curtius through Roland Barthes, Harold Bloom, and Frank Kermode.

I myself am inclined to argue that every literary theory is based on the experience of a limited canon or generalizes strongly from a particular text-milieu. To take the metaphysical poets as one's base or touchstone, and to extend their "poetics" toward modern poetry and then all poetry, will produce a very different result from working from Cervantes toward Pynchon, or from Hölderlin toward Heidegger. I remain skeptical, therefore, about the possibility of a truly comprehensive literary theory or literary history. A Theory of English Literature may be more within reach than a Theory of Literature—even a Theory of Western Literature, if we extricate historically the operative dichotomy of East and West, the important idea of *Westering* (and its affinity to the *translatio studii*), and ideological fixations on the East as the source of sunburst, creative vigor and . . . disenchantment (see Edward Said's *Orientalism* for the darker side of that magical geography). We are not beyond the spell of Orienda or some other Fata Morgana. "The West is preparing to add its fables to those of the East," said Thoreau. At some point, no doubt, the East appears as just another mask or avatar for the *arche*; and archetypal theory emerges. But the place of emergence remains historical.

The concept of representation, in its link to the rise of the vernacular and national literatures in the West, would provide another starting point. Yet what is clearest today, and has been since Nietzsche, is the drive of the interpretive mind to revise or reverse, to unmask itself as well as its object, to penetrate so deeply that everything human is alien to it, and even language appears arbitrary or self-authorized. This drive, this revisionary desire (perhaps for an *unmediated vision*), is not unfrightening, and it leads us to ponder the link between philosophical criticism and the strange, overextended thought of poets, mystics, and even systematic thinkers, as they map their infinity.

The tradition of practical criticism, so narrow at present, has limited our awareness of the relation of literature to the practical life, which includes law, religion, economics, and the process of institutionalization itself. If the question is raised of art's effectiveness, or the critic's—who examines the arts to see what light they may throw on conduct or what "criticism of life" they propose—then we must integrate these matters into our thought without abandoning our special knowledge of the importance of symbols and inscriptions to the life of the mind.

Those symbols and inscriptions should have the last word. The plea I have made is not just for programs of study that would encourage entrepreneurial activities and assure the humanist a bigger slice of the pie. I certainly wish to see a closer bonding between the different professions in the university, so that what is defined as "practical" is not left to a small, segregated group. But this does not mean giving up the special province of the humanities; on the contrary, it means defining it more clearly. While humanists can contribute as much as others to the running of a university and to the formulation of public policy, they do bring their own set of qualities to every task. They will not easily sacrifice anything to anything else: they take their time, and ponder —often elaborately—whether a new step does not entail an exclusion rather than an advantageous change or transformation. So the inspiring teacher in the humanities will always be pointing to something neglected by the dominant point of view, or something blunted by familiarity, or despised by fashion and social pressure. He is incurably a redeemer—not in the highflying sense but in the spirit-embedding sense. His active life is spent in uncovering and preserving traces of the contemplative life—those symbols and inscriptions—buried in layers of change. Like Wordsworth's poet, the humanist recalls forgotten voices, arguments, artifacts, "things silently gone out of mind and things violently destroyed." He *reinscribes* us, to use a current expression; and the expression is good, because life in culture is a palimpsest that can only be deciphered by a species of "thick description." It is a mistake to think of the humanist as spiritualizing anything: on the contrary, he materializes us, he makes us aware of the material culture (including texts) in which everyone has always lived. Only the passage of time spiritualizes, that is, volatilizes and deracinates; we are in transition; our life remains a feast of mortuary riddles and jokes that must be answered. In the shape of that answer everyone participates who takes time to think about time.

Select Bibliography

The bibliography contains full documentation for all book-length studies and some of the articles mentioned in the text or the notes. Works of poetry and fiction have not been included.

Abrams, Meyer H. *Natural Supernaturalism: Tradition and Revolution in Romantic Literature.* New York: W. W. Norton, 1971.

Adorno, Theodor W. *Kierkegaard: Konstruktion des Ästhetischen.* Tübingen: Mohr, 1933.

———. *Negative Dialectic.* Translated by E. B. Ashton. New York: Seabury Press, 1973. First published in German in 1966.

———. *Über Walter Benjamin.* Frankfurt am Main: Suhrkamp Verlag, 1970.

Anders, Günther. *Die Antiquiertheit des Menschen: Über die Seele im Zeitalter der Zweiten Industriellen Revolution.* Munich: Beck, 1956.

Arnold, Matthew. *The Complete Prose Works of Matthew Arnold.* Edited by R. H. Super. Ann Arbor: University of Michigan Press, 1960–77. "The Function of Criticism at the Present Time" and "The Literary Influence of Academies" are printed in vol. 3; "The Study of Poetry," in vol. 9.

Auerbach, Erich. *Literary Language and Its Public in Late Latin Antiquity and in the Middle Ages.* Translated by Ralph Manheim. New York: Pantheon, 1965. First published in German in 1958.

———. *Mimesis: The Representation of Reality in Western Literature.* Translated by Willard R. Trask. Princeton: Princeton University Press, 1953. First published in German in 1946.

Bakhtin, Mikhail. *Rabelais and His World.* Translated by Helene Iswolsky. Cambridge, Mass.: MIT Press, 1968. Written in 1940; first published in Russian in 1965.

Barfield, Owen. *Poetic Diction: A Study in Meaning.* 2d ed. London: Faber & Faber, 1952. First published in 1928.

———. *Saving the Appearances: A Study in Idolatry.* London: Faber & Faber, 1957.

Barthes, Roland. *A Lover's Discourse.* Translated by Richard Howard. New York: Hill and Wang, 1978. Originally published in French as *Fragments d'un discours amoureux.* Paris: Seuil, 1977.

———. "Proust et les noms." In *To Honor Roman Jakobson: Essays on the Occasion of His Seventieth Birthday.* 3 vols. The Hague: Mouton, 1967. I: 150–58.

Behler, Ernst. *Klassische Ironie, Romantische Ironie, Tragische Ironie: Zum Ursprung dieser Begriffe.* Darmstadt: Wissenschaftliche Buchgesellschaft, 1972.

Benjamin, Walter. *Gesammelte Schriften.* Edited by Rolf Tiedemann and Hermann Schweppenhäuser. Frankfurt am Main: Suhrkamp Verlag, 1972–77.

———. *Illuminations.* Edited and with an Introduction by Hannah Arendt. Translated by Harry Zohn. New York: Schocken, 1969.

———. *The Origin of German Tragic Drama.* Translated by John Osborne. London: NLB, 1977. Originally published in German in 1927.

———. *Reflections: Essays, Aphorisms, Autobiographical Writings.* Edited and with an Introduction by Peter Demetz. Translated by Edmund Jephcott. New York: Harcourt, Brace, Jovanovich, 1978.

———. *Schriften.* Edited by T. W. Adorno and Gretel Adorno. 2 vols. Frankfurt am Main: Suhrkamp Verlag, 1955.

Bialik, C. N. *Essays.* Berlin: Jüdischer Verlag, 1925.

Blackall, Eric. *The Emergence of German as a Literary Language, 1700–1775.* Cambridge: Cambridge University Press, 1959.

Blackmur, Richard P. "A Critic's Job of Work." In *Language as Gesture.* New York: Harcourt Brace, 1952.

———. *A Primer of Ignorance.* Edited by Joseph Frank. New York: Harcourt Brace, 1967.

Blanchot, Maurice. *Le pas au-delà.* Paris: Gallimard, 1973.

Bloom, Harold. *The Anxiety of Influence: A Theory of Poetry.* New York: Oxford University Press, 1973.

———. *Blake's Apocalypse: A Study in Poetic Argument.* Garden City, NY: Doubleday, 1963.

———. *Kabbalah and Criticism*. New York: Seabury Press, 1975.
———. *A Map of Misreading*. New York: Oxford University Press, 1975.
———. *Shelley's Mythmaking*. New Haven: Yale University Press, 1959.
———. *The Visionary Company: A Reading of English Romantic Poetry*. 2d ed. Ithaca: Cornell University Press, 1971. First published in 1961.
———. *Yeats*. New York: Oxford University Press, 1970.
Booth, Stephen. *An Essay on Shakespeare's Sonnets*. New Haven: Yale University Press, 1969.
Booth, Wayne C. *Modern Dogma and the Rhetoric of Assent*. Chicago: University of Chicago Press, 1974.
Bourne, Randolph. *History of a Literary Radical and Other Essays*. Edited by Van Wyck Brooks. New York: B. W. Huebsch, 1920.
———. *The Radical Will: Selected Writings, 1911–1918*. Edited by Olaf Hansen. Preface by Christopher Lasch. New York: Urizen, 1977.
Brisman, Leslie. *Milton's Poetry of Choice and Its Romantic Heirs*. Ithaca: Cornell University Press, 1973.
Brooks, Cleanth. *The Well-Wrought Urn: Studies in the Structure of Poetry*. New York: Harcourt Brace & World, 1947.
Brooks, Van Wyck. *America's Coming-of-Age*. New York: B. W. Huebsch, 1915.
———. *Letters and Leadership*. New York: B. W. Huebsch, 1918.
———. *Opinions of Oliver Allston*. New York: E. P. Dutton, 1941.
Brown, Norman O. *Closing Time*. New York: Random House, 1973.
———. *Life Against Death: The Psychoanalytic Meaning of History*. Middletown, CT: Wesleyan University Press, 1959.
———. *Love's Body*. New York: Random House, 1966.
Buber, Martin. *I and Thou*. 2d ed. Translated by Ronald G. Smith. New York: Scribner's, 1958. Originally published in German in 1923.
Burke, Kenneth. *A Grammar of Motives*. Englewood Cliffs, NJ: Prentice-Hall, 1945.
———. *The Philosophy of Literary Form*. 3d ed. Berkeley: University of California Press, 1973. First published in 1941.
———. *The Rhetoric of Religion: Studies in Logology*. Boston: Beacon Press, 1961.
Carlyle, Thomas. *The French Revolution*. 2 vols. London: J. Fraser, 1837.
———. *Past and Present*. London: Chapman and Hall, 1843. A good modern text is that edited by Richard D. Altick. New York: New York University Press, 1977.
———. *Sartor Resartus: The Life and Opinions of Herr Teufelsdröckh*.

London: J. Fraser, 1834. The standard modern text is edited by C. F. Harrold. New York: Odyssey Press, 1937.

Cavell, Stanley. *The Claim of Reason: Wittgenstein, Skepticism, Morality, and Tragedy.* New York: Oxford University Press, 1979.

———. *The Senses of Walden.* New York: Viking Press, 1972.

Curtius, E. R. *European Literature and the Latin Middle Ages.* Translated by Willard R. Trask. Princeton: Princeton University Press, 1953. First published in German in 1948.

Davie, Donald. *Purity of Diction in English Verse.* New York: Oxford University Press, 1953.

De Man, Hendrik. *Der Kampf um die Arbeitsfreude.* Jena: E. Diederichs, 1927.

De Man, Paul. *Allegories of Reading: Figural Language in Rousseau, Nietzsche, Rilke, and Proust.* New Haven: Yale University Press, 1979.

———. *Blindness and Insight: Essays in the Rhetoric of Contemporary Criticism.* New York: Oxford University Press, 1971.

———. "Shelley Disfigured." In *Deconstruction and Criticism.* New York: Seabury Press, 1979.

De Sélincourt, Basil. *The English Secret and Other Essays.* London: Oxford University Press, 1923.

Derrida, Jacques. *De la grammatologie.* Paris: Minuit, 1967. *Of Grammatology.* Translated by Gayatri Spivak. Baltimore: Johns Hopkins University Press, 1976.

———. *La dissémination.* Paris: Editions du Seuil, 1972.

———. *L'écriture et la différence.* Paris: Editions du Seuil, 1967. *Writing and Difference.* Translated by Alan Bass. Chicago: University of Chicago Press, 1978.

———. *Glas.* Paris: Galilée, 1974.

———. *Marges de la philosophie.* Paris: Minuit, 1972.

Douglas, Mary. *Purity and Danger: An Analysis of Concepts of Pollution and Taboo.* London: Routledge & Kegan Paul, 1966.

Eliot, T. S. "From Poe to Valéry" (1948). Now in *To Criticize the Critic and Other Writings.* New York: Farrar, Straus & Giroux, 1965.

———. "The Frontiers of Criticism" (1956). In *On Poetry and Poets.* New York: Farrar, Straus & Giroux, 1957.

———. "The Function of Criticism" (1923). Now in *Selected Essays.* New York: Harcourt, Brace & World, 1950.

———. *The Sacred Wood.* London: Methuen & Co., 1920. Includes "Tradition and the Individual Talent" (1919).

———. *The Use of Poetry and the Use of Criticism.* Cambridge, Mass.: Harvard University Press, 1933.

Ellmann, Richard, ed. *The Artist as Critic: Critical Writings of Oscar Wilde.* New York: Random House, 1969.

——— and Feidelson, Charles, eds. *The Modern Tradition: Backgrounds of Modern Literature.* New York: Oxford University Press, 1965.

Emerson, Ralph Waldo. *The Complete Works of Ralph Waldo Emerson.* Edited by Edward Waldo Emerson. 12 vols. Boston: Houghton and Mifflin, 1903–04.

———. *Journals and Miscellaneous Notebooks.* Edited by William H. Gilman and others. 14 vols. Cambridge, Mass.: Harvard University Press, 1960–78.

———. *The Letters of Ralph Waldo Emerson.* Edited by Ralph L. Rusk. 6 vols. New York: Columbia University Press, 1939.

Empson, William. *Seven Types of Ambiguity.* 2d ed. London: Chatto and Windus, 1947. First published 1930.

Feidelson, Charles. *Symbolism and American Literature.* Chicago: University of Chicago Press, 1953.

Ferenczi, Sándor. *Thalassa: A Theory of Genitality.* Translated by Henry A. Bunker. New York: W. W. Norton, 1968. Originally published in German as *Versuch einer Genitaltheorie.* Leipzig: Internationaler Psychoanalytischer Verlag, 1924.

Ferguson, Frances. *Wordsworth: Language as Counter-Spirit.* New Haven: Yale University Press, 1977.

Fish, Stanley E. *Self-Consuming Artifacts: The Experience of Seventeenth-Century Literature.* Berkeley: University of California Press, 1972.

Fletcher, Angus. *Allegory: The Theory of a Symbolic Mode.* Ithaca: Cornell University Press, 1964.

Foucault, Michel. *L'ordre du discours.* Paris: Gallimard, 1971.

Freud, Sigmund. *The Standard Edition of the Complete Psychological Works of Sigmund Freud.* Under the General Editorship of James Strachey. 24 vols. London: Hogarth Press, 1953–74.

———. *Beyond the Pleasure Principle* (1920). Translated by James Strachey. *Standard Edition,* vol. 18, pp. 3–64.

———. *The Interpretation of Dreams* (1900). Translated by James Strachey. *Standard Edition,* vols. 4 and 5.

———. *Totem and Taboo* (1913). Translated by James Strachey. *Standard Edition.* vol. 13, pp. 1–161.

———. *The Uncanny* (1919). Translated by Alix Strachey. *Standard Edition,* vol. 17, pp. 219–52.

Frye, Northrop. *Anatomy of Criticism: Four Essays.* Princeton: Princeton University Press, 1957.

———. *Fearful Symmetry: A Study of William Blake.* Princeton: Princeton University Press, 1947.

———. *The Modern Century.* Toronto and New York: Oxford University Press, 1967.

———. *The Secular Scripture: A Study of the Structure of Romance.* Cambridge, Mass.: Harvard University Press, 1976.

Gadamer, Hans-Georg. *Truth and Method.* Translation edited by Garret Barden and John Cummings. New York: Seabury Press, 1975. First published in German in 1960.

Geertz, Clifford. "Found in Translation: On the Social History of the Moral Imagination." *Georgia Review* 31 (1977): 788–810.

Genet, Jean. *Journal du voleur.* 2d ed. Paris: Gallimard, 1949. First published in a limited edition, probably 1948. Translated as *The Thief's Journal* by Bernard Frechtman. With a Foreword by Jean-Paul Sartre. New York: Grove Press, 1964.

———. *Oeuvres complètes.* 4 vols. Paris: Gallimard, 1951–68. The essay on Rembrandt, "Ce qui est resté d'un Rembrandt déchiré . . . ," is included in vol. 4.

Greene, Thomas M. "Petrarch and the Humanist Hermeneutic." In *Italian Literature.* Edited by G. Rimanelli and K. J. Atchity. New Haven: Yale University Press, 1976.

Gross, John. *The Rise and Fall of the Man of Letters.* London: Weidenfeld and Nicolson, 1969.

Halpern, Joseph. *Critical Fictions: The Literary Criticism of Jean-Paul Sartre.* New Haven: Yale University Press, 1976.

Hartman, Geoffrey H. *Beyond Formalism: Literary Essays 1958–1970.* New Haven: Yale University Press, 1970.

———. *The Fate of Reading and Other Essays.* Chicago: University of Chicago Press, 1975.

———. *The Unmediated Vision: An Interpretation of Wordsworth, Hopkins, Rilke, and Valéry.* New Haven: Yale University Press, 1954.

Hegel, G. W. F. *Hegels Theologische Jugendschriften.* Edited by Herman Nohl. Tübingen: Mohr, 1907. Translated as *Early Theological Writings* by T. M. Knox and Richard Kroner. Chicago: The University of Chicago Press, 1948.

———. *Phenomenology of Spirit.* Translated by A. V. Miller. With analyses of the text and a Foreword by J. N. Findlay. Oxford: Clarendon Press, 1977.

———. *Sämtliche Werke. Jubiläumsausgabe.* Edited by Hermann Glockner. Stuttgart: Frommann, 1927–30. The *Phänomenologie des Geistes* is vol. 2 of this edition.

———. *Vorlesungen über die Aesthetik. Sämtliche Werke,* vols. 12–14.

Heidegger, Martin. *Briefe über den 'Humanismus'* (1947). In *Wegmarken.* Frankfurt am Main: Klostermann Verlag, 1967. *Letter on Humanism.* In *Basic Writings.* Edited by David F. Krell. Translated by F. A. Capuzzi and J. G. Gray. New York: Harper and Row, 1977.

———. *Einführung in die Metaphysik.* Tübingen: Niemeyer, 1953. *An Introduction to Metaphysics.* Translated by Ralph Manheim. New Haven: Yale University Press, 1974. First published 1935.

———. *Erläuterungen zu Hölderlins Dichtung.* 2d ed. Frankfurt am Main: Klostermann Verlag, 1951. First published in 1944. *Elucidations of Hölderlin's Poetry.* Translated by Keith Hoeller. University, Ala.: University of Alabama Press, 1978.

———. *Sein und Zeit.* 7th ed. Tübingen: Niemeyer, 1953. First published in 1927. *Being and Time.* Translated by John Macquarrie and Edward Robinson. New York: Harper and Row, 1962.

———. "Der Ursprung des Kunstwerks" (1936). In *Holzwege.* Frankfurt am Main: Klostermann, 1950. Translated by Albert Hofstadter as "The Origin of the Work of Art." In *Poetry, Language, Thought.* New York: Harper and Row, 1971.

Hirsch, E. D. *Validity in Interpretation.* New Haven: Yale University Press, 1967.

Holland, Norman. *The Dynamics of Literary Response.* New York: Oxford University Press, 1968.

———. *5 Readers Reading.* New Haven: Yale University Press, 1975.

Horkheimer, Max. *Critical Theory: Selected Essays.* Translated by Matthew J. O'Connell and others. New York: Herder & Herder, 1972. First published in German in 1968.

Howe, Irving. *The Decline of the New.* New York: Harcourt Brace & World, 1970.

Huizinga, Johan. *Homo Ludens: A Study of the Play Element in Culture.* Translated by R. F. C. Hull. Boston: Beacon Press, 1950. First published in Dutch in 1938.

Husserl, Edmund. *Ideen zu einer Reinen Phänomenologie und Phänomenologischen Philosophie.* Halle: Max Niemeyer, 1913. *Ideas: General Introduction to Pure Phenomenology.* Translated by W. R. Boyce Gibson. London and New York: Macmillan, 1931.

Iser, Wolfgang. *The Act of Reading: A Theory of Aesthetic Response.* Baltimore: Johns Hopkins University Press, 1979. First published in German in 1976.

James, David G. *Scepticism and Poetry: An Essay on the Poetic Imagination.* London: Allen & Unwin, 1937.

James, Henry. Preface to *The Golden Bowl*. In *The Art of the Novel: Critical Prefaces*. Introduction by Richard P. Blackmur. New York: Scribner's, 1935. These Prefaces were written by James for the New York Edition of the Novels. New York: Scribner's, 1907–09.

James, William. *The Principles of Psychology*. 2 vols. New York: H. Holt and Co., 1890.

Jameson, Fredric. *Marxism and Form: Twentieth-Century Dialectical Theories of Literature*. Princeton: Princeton University Press, 1971.

Jaspers, Karl. *Schelling: Grösse und Verhängnis*. Munich: R. Piper, 1955.

Jauss, Hans-Robert. *Kleine Apologie der Ästhetischen Erfahrung*. Konstanz: Universitätverlag, 1972.

Jay, Martin. *The Dialectical Imagination: A History of the Frankfurt School and the Institute of Social Research, 1923–1950*. Boston: Little, Brown and Co., 1973.

Jünger, Ernst. *Der Arbeiter: Herrschaft und Gestalt*. Hamburg: Hanseatische Verlagsanstalt, 1932.

———. *Über die Linie*. Frankfurt am Main: Klostermann, 1950.

Kant, Immanuel. *Was ist Aufklärung?* (1784). In *Aufsätze zur Geschichte und Philosophie*. Edited by Jürgen Zehbe. Göttingen: Vandenhoeck & Ruprecht, 1967. *What Is Enlightenment?* In *The Philosophy of Kant: Immanuel Kant's Moral and Political Writings*. Edited and translated by Carl J. Friedrich. New York: Modern Library, 1949.

Kazin, Alfred. *On Native Grounds: An Interpretation of Modern American Prose Literature*. New York: Harcourt Brace, 1942.

Kermode, Frank. *The Sense of an Ending: Studies in the Theory of Fiction*. New York: Oxford University Press, 1967.

Keyserling, Hermann. *Europe*. Translated by Maurice Samuel. London: J. Cape, 1929. A translation of *Das Spektrum Europas*. Stuttgart: Deutsche Verlag, 1928.

Kierkegaard, Søren. *The Concept of Irony*. Translated by Lee M. Capel. Bloomington: Indiana University Press, 1968. First published in Danish in 1841.

Krieger, Murray. *Theory of Criticism: A Tradition and Its System*. Baltimore: Johns Hopkins University Press, 1976.

———. *A Window to Criticism: Shakespeare's Sonnets and Modern Poetics*. Princeton: Princeton University Press, 1964.

Lacan, Jacques. *Écrits*. 2 vols. Paris: Seuil, Collection "Points," 1970–71. First published in 1966. Several of these essays have been translated by Alan Sheridan. In *Écrits: A Selection*. New York: Norton, 1977.

Lausberg, Heinrich. *Elemente der Literarischen Rhetorik.* 2d Edition. Munich: Max Hueber Verlag, 1963.

Lawrence, D. H. *Studies in Classic American Literature.* New York: T. Seltzer, 1923.

Leavis, F. R. *The Common Pursuit.* London: Chatto and Windus, 1952.

———. "The Complex Fate." Introduction to Marius Bewley's *The Complex Fate: Hawthorne, Henry James, and Some Other American Writers.* London: Chatto and Windus, 1952. Reprinted in Leavis's *Anna Karenina and Other Essays.* New York: Simon & Schuster, 1967.

———. "Literary Criticism and Philosophy." An exchange with René Wellek. In *The Importance of Scrutiny.* Edited by Eric Bentley. New York: New York University Press, 1964. Leavis's half of the exchange is also reprinted in *The Common Pursuit.*

Lévi-Strauss, Claude. *The Savage Mind.* Chicago: University of Chicago Press, 1966. First published in French in 1962.

Lewisohn, Ludwig, ed. *A Modern Book of Criticism.* New York: Boni and Liveright, 1919.

———. *Up Stream: An American Chronicle.* New York: Boni and Liveright, 1922.

Lukács, George. *History and Class Consciousness: A Study in Marxist Dialectics.* Translated by Rodney Livingstone. Cambridge, Mass.: MIT Press, 1971. A translation of the revised German edition. Berlin: Herman Luchterhand Verlag, 1968. First published in German in 1923.

———. *Soul and Form.* Translated by Anna Bostock. Cambridge, Mass.: MIT Press, 1974. First published in German in 1911.

Macdonald, Dwight, ed. *Parodies: An Anthology from Chaucer to Beerbohm—and After.* New York: Random House, 1960.

McLuhan, Marshall. *The Gutenberg Galaxy: The Making of Typographic Man.* Toronto: University of Toronto Press, 1962.

Marcuse, Herbert. *Eros and Civilization.* Boston: Beacon Press, 1955.

———. *Reason and Revolution: Hegel and the Rise of Social Theory.* 2d ed. New York: Humanities Press, 1954. First published in 1941.

Miller, J. Hillis. "Ariadne's Web: Repetition and the Narrative Line." *Critical Inquiry* 3 (1976): 57–77.

———. "The Critic as Host." In *Deconstruction and Criticism.* New York: Seabury Press, 1979.

Murdoch, Iris. *Sartre: Romantic Rationalist.* New Haven: Yale University Press, 1953.

Nietzsche, Friedrich. *Beyond Good and Evil: Prelude to a Philosophy of the Future* (1886). Translated by Walter Kaufmann. New York: Vintage Books, 1966.

———. *The Birth of Tragedy* (1872). Translated by Walter Kaufmann. New York: Vintage Books, 1966.

———. *Ecce Homo* (written 1888, but first published 1908). Translated by Walter Kaufmann. New York: Vintage Books, 1968. Published with *On the Genealogy of Morals* (1887).

———. *Gesammelte Werke, Musarionausgabe.* 23 vols. Edited by R. Oehler, M. Oehler and F. C. Würzbach. Munich: Musarion Verlag, 1920–29.

———. *The Use and Abuse of History* (1874). Translated by Adrian Collins. Indianapolis: Liberal Arts Press, 1949.

———. *Thus Spoke Zarathustra: A Book for All and None* (written 1883–85; first complete edition 1892). Translated by Walter Kaufmann. New York: Vintage Books, 1966.

Norden, Eduard. *Agnostos Theos: Untersuchungen zur Formengeschichte religiöser Rede.* Leipzig and Berlin: B. G. Teubner, 1912.

———. *Die Geburt des Kindes: Geschichte einer Religiösen Idee.* Leipzig and Berlin: B. G. Teubner, 1924.

Ogden, C. K. *Debabelization.* London: Kegan Paul, Trench, Trubner and Co., 1931.

——— and Richards, I. A. *The Meaning of Meaning.* London: Kegan Paul, Trench, Trubner and Co., 1923.

Ong, Walter J. *The Barbarian Within.* New York: Macmillan, 1962.

———. *The Presence of the Word: Some Prolegomena for Cultural and Religious History.* New Haven: Yale University Press, 1967.

Ortega y Gasset, José. "In Search of Goethe from Within." In *The Dehumanization of Art and Other Writings on Art and Culture.* Translated by Willard R. Trask. Garden City, NY: Doubleday, 1956.

Pater, Walter. *Appreciations.* London: Macmillan, 1889.

———. *Miscellaneous Studies.* London and New York: Macmillan, 1895.

———. *Plato and Platonism.* London and New York: Macmillan, 1893.

———. *Studies in the History of the Renaissance.* London: Macmillan, 1873. The second edition of 1877 was retitled *The Renaissance: Studies in Art and Poetry* and omitted the "Conclusion."

Poirier, Richard. *A World Elsewhere: The Place of Style in American Literature.* New York: Oxford University Press, 1966.

Polanyi, Michael. *Personal Knowledge: Towards a Post-Critical Philosophy.* Chicago: University of Chicago Press, 1958.

Pottle, Frederick. "The Case of Shelley." *PMLA* 67 (1952): 589–608. Published in revised form in *English Romantic Poets: Modern Essays in Criticism.* Edited by M. H. Abrams. New York: Oxford University Press, 1960.

———. *The Idiom of Poetry*. Ithaca: Cornell University Press, 1941.
Poulet, Georges. "Phenomenology of Reading." *New Literary History* 1 (1969): 53–68.
Ransom, John Crowe, et al. *I'll Take My Stand: Resolve and the Agrarian Tradition*. New York: Harper and Brothers, 1930. Reprinted with an Introduction by Louis D. Rubens, Jr. Baton Rouge: Louisiana State University Press, 1962.
———. *The New Criticism*. Norfolk, CT: New Directions, 1941.
———. *The World's Body*. New York: Charles Scribner's Sons, 1938. Second, revised edition published by Louisiana State University Press. Baton Rouge, 1968.
Richards, I. A. *Coleridge on Imagination*. New York: Harcourt Brace and Co., 1935.
———. *The Philosophy of Rhetoric*. London and New York: Oxford University Press, 1936.
———. *Practical Criticism: A Study of Literary Judgement*. London: Kegan Paul, Trench, Trubner, 1929.
———. *Principles of Literary Criticism*. London: Kegan Paul, Trench, Trubner, 1924.
Ricoeur, Paul. *Freud and Philosophy: An Essay on Interpretation*. Translated by Denis Savage. New Haven and London: Yale University Press, 1970. First published in French, 1965.
———. *The Symbolism of Evil*. Translated by Emerson Buchanan. Boston: Beacon Press, 1969. First published in French in 1960.
Riffaterre, Michael. *La production du texte*. Paris: Seuil, 1979.
Ruskin, John. *The Queen of the Air: Being a Study of the Greek Myths of Cloud and Storm*. London: Smith, Elder & Co., 1869.
———. *Sesame and Lilies*. London: Smith, Elder & Co., 1865.
Santayana, George. *Some Turns of Thought in Modern Philosophy*. New York: Charles Scribner's Sons, 1933.
Sartre, Jean-Paul. *Being and Nothingness: An Essay on Phenomenological Ontology*. Translated by Hazel E. Barnes. New York: Philosophical Library, 1953. First published in French in 1943.
———. *Saint Genet: Actor and Martyr*. Translated by Bernard Frechtman. New York: George Braziller, 1963. First published in French in 1952.
———. *Situations I*. Paris: Gallimard, 1947.
———. *What Is Literature?* Translated by Bernard Frechtman. New York: Philosophical Library, 1949. First published in French in 1948.
Schlegel, Friedrich. *Athenaeum*. Eine Zeitschrift von A. W. Schlegel und F. Schlegel. Berlin: Bey F. Vieweg, 1798–1800.

———. *Dialogue on Poetry and Literary Aphorisms*. Translated by Ernst Behler and Roman Strue. University Park: Pennsylvania State University Press, 1968.

Scholem, Gershom. *Walter Benjamin: Die Geschichte einer Freundschaft*. Frankfurt am Main: Suhrkamp Verlag, 1975.

Shattuck, Roger. *The Banquet Years: The Origins of the Avant Garde in France*. New York: Harcourt Brace & World, 1958.

Smalley, Beryl. *The Study of the Bible in the Middle Ages*. Oxford: B. Blackwell, 1941.

Smith, Barbara Herrnstein. *Poetic Closure: A Study of How Poems End*. Chicago: University of Chicago Press, 1968.

Spitzer, Leo. *Essays in Historical Semantics*. New York: S. F. Vanni, 1948.

Steiner, George. *After Babel: Aspects of Language and Translation*. New York: Oxford University Press, 1975.

———. *On Difficulty and Other Essays*. New York: Oxford University Press, 1978.

Szondi, Peter. "Schleiermachers Hermeneutik Heute." In *Sprache im Technischen Zeitalter* (1976), pp. 95–111. Also in *Poétique* 1 (1970): 141–55.

Tate, Allen. *Collected Essays*. Denver: A. Swallow, 1959.

Tennyson, G. B. *Sartor Called Resartus: The Genesis, Structure, and Style of Thomas Carlyle's First Major Work*. Princeton: Princeton University Press, 1965.

Thomas, Lewis. "Notes of a Biology-Watcher." *The New England Journal of Medicine*, 25 May 1978. Reprinted in *The Snail and the Medusa*. New York: Viking Press, 1979.

Todorov, Tzvetan. *The Poetics of Prose*. Translated by Richard Howard. Ithaca: Cornell University Press, 1977. First published in French in 1971.

Trilling, Lionel. *Beyond Culture: Essays on Literature and Learning*. New York: Viking Press, 1965.

Tugendhat, Ernst. "Phänomenologie und Sprachanalyse." In *Hermeneutik und Dialektik* 2. Edited by R. Bübner et al. Tübingen: Mohr, 1970, pp. 3–23.

Valdés, M. J., and Miller, O. J., eds. *Interpretation of Narrative*. Toronto: University of Toronto Press, 1978.

Valéry, Paul. "Introduction to the Method of Leonardo da Vinci." In *Leonardo, Poe, Mallarmé*. Translated by Malcolm Cowley and James R. Lawler. Princeton: Princeton University Press, 1972. First published in French in 1895, marginalia added 1929–30.

———. *Oeuvres de Paul Valéry,* 2 vols. Edited by Jean Hytier. Paris: Bibliothèque de la Pléiade, Gallimard, 1957–60.

———. "Poetry and Abstract Thought." In *The Art of Poetry.* Translated by Denise Folliot. Princeton: Princeton University Press, 1958. First published in French in 1939.

Vico, Giambattista. *The New Science.* Translated from the Third Edition (1744) by Thomas Goddard Bergin and Max Harold Fisch. Ithaca: Cornell University Press, 1948. First published in Italian in 1725.

Warren, Robert Penn. *Selected Essays.* New York: Random House, 1951.

Watson, George. *The Literary Critics: A Study of English Descriptive Criticism.* Harmondsworth: Penguin Books, 1962.

Weinrich, Harald, ed. *Positionen der Negativität.* Munich: W. Fink, 1975.

Weiskel, Thomas. *The Romantic Sublime: Studies in the Structure and Psychology of Transcendence.* Baltimore: Johns Hopkins University Press, 1976.

Wellek, René. *A History of Modern Criticism, 1750–1950.* 4 vols. to date. New Haven: Yale University Press, 1955–.

———. *Kant in England, 1793–1838.* Princeton: Princeton University Press, 1931.

——— and Warren, Austin. *Theory of Literature,* 3d ed. New York: Harcourt, Brace and World, 1963. First edition, 1949.

Whitaker, Thomas. *Swan and Shadow: Yeats's Dialogue with History.* Chapel Hill: University of North Carolina Press, 1964.

Wilde, Oscar. *Intentions.* London: James R. Osgood, McIlvaine & Co., 1891. Includes "The Critic as Artist" and "Pen, Pencil and Poison."

Williamson, George. *The Senecan Amble: Prose Form from Bacon to Collier.* Chicago: University of Chicago Press, 1951.

Wilson, Edmund. *Axel's Castle: A Study in the Imaginative Literature of 1870–1930.* New York: Charles Scribner's Sons, 1931.

———. *To the Finland Station: A Study in the Writing and Acting of History.* New York: Harcourt, Brace and Co., 1940.

Wimsatt, W. K. *Hateful Contraries: Studies in Literature and Criticism.* Lexington: University of Kentucky Press, 1965.

Winnicott, D. W. *Playing and Reality.* New York: Basic Books, 1971.

Wittgenstein, Ludwig. *Philosophical Investigations.* 3d English Edition. Translated by G. E. M. Anscombe. New York: Macmillan, 1968. First published in English in 1953.

———. "Remarks on Frazer's 'Golden Bough.'" Translated by A. C. Miles and R. Rhees. *The Human World* 3 (1971): 18–41.

Index